Investigating *Charmed*

INVESTIGATING CULT TV

Series Editor: Stacey Abbott

The **Investigating Cult TV** series is a fresh forum for discussion and debate about the changing nature of cult television. It sets out to reconsider cult television and its intricate networks of fandom by inviting authors to rethink how cult TV is conceived, produced, programmed and consumed. It will also challenge traditional distinctions between cult and quality television.

Offering an accessible path through the intricacies and pleasures of cult TV, the books in this series will interest scholars, students and fans alike. They will include close studies of individual contemporary television shows. They will also reconsider genres at the heart of cult programming, such as science fiction, horror and fantasy, as well as genres like teen TV, animation and reality TV when these have strong claims to cult status. Books will also examine themes or trends that are key to the past, present and future of cult television.

The first books in **Investigating Cult TV** series:

Investigating **Farscape** by Jes Battis
Investigating **Alias** edited by Stacey Abbott and Simon Brown
Investigating **Charmed** edited by Karin Beeler and Stan Beeler

Ideas and submissions for **Investigating Cult TV** to
s.abbott@roehampton.ac.uk
p.brewster@blueyonder.co.uk

INVESTIGATING CHARMED

The Magic Power of TV

Edited by Karin Beeler
and Stan Beeler

I.B. TAURIS

LONDON · NEW YORK

Published in 2007 by I.B.Tauris & Co Ltd
6 Salem Road, London W2 4BU
175 Fifth Avenue, New York NY 10010
www.ibtauris.com

In the United States of America and Canada
distributed by Palgrave Macmillan, a division of St Martin's Press
175 Fifth Avenue, New York NY 10010

ISBN 978 1 84511 480 0

A full CIP record for this book is available from the British Library
A full CIP record is available from the Library of Congress

Library of Congress Catalog Card Number: available

Typeset by JCS Publishing Services, www.jcs-publishing.co.uk
Printed and bound in the Czech Republic
FINIDR, s.r.o.

Contents

PART THREE: VISUAL POWER, PLACE AND GENRE

Acknowledgements

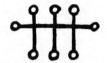

We would like to thank all of the people who have contributed to the making of this book: Philippa Brewster at I.B.Tauris for her enthusiastic support of the project, and for guiding us through the publication process; our publishers, I.B.Tauris for producing this edition and for promoting television studies and popular culture. We also extend our thanks to Stacey Abbott, the editor of the I.B.Tauris Investigating Cult TV series, and wish to show our appreciation to our contributors for their enjoyable essays. Lisa Kincaid provided some wonderful *Charmed*-appropriate drawings as well. Finally, we recognize the important role of *Charmed* fans in ensuring the international success of the show and in helping it achieve cult status.

To Amelia, our Charmed One

Notes on Contributors

Karin Beeler is an Associate Professor in English and Chair of Anthropology at the University of Northern British Columbia. Her current research interests include fantastic literature, television and film. She has published *Tattoos, Desire and Violence: Marks of Resistance in Literature, Film and Television* (McFarland, 2006) and articles in a variety of areas including Canadian literature and comparative literature studies. Her most recent project is a book-length study of women with visionary powers in television and film.

Stan Beeler is Chair of English at the University of Northern British Columbia. His areas of interest include film and television studies, popular culture and comparative literature. His publications include *The Invisible College: A Study of the Three Original Rosicrucian Texts*, *Reading Stargate SG-1* co-edited with Lisa Dickson (I.B.Tauris, 2006) and *Dance, Drugs and Escape: The Club Scene in Literature, Film and Television Since the Late 1980s* (McFarland, 2007).

Valerie Carroll is a graduate in American Studies from Saint Louis University and is currently Instructor of Women's Studies at Kansas State University. Her teaching and research interests are women and popular culture and American narratives of community. She is currently working on her book, *(Re)Presenting and Representing on Girl Power TV: Resistance and Domination on Charmed, Dark Angel, and Buffy the Vampire Slayer* (in progress).

Randall Clark is an Assistant Professor of Communication and Media studies at Clayton State University in Atlanta, Georgia. He is the author of *At a Theater or Drive-In Near You: The History, Politics and Culture of the American Exploitation Film* (Routledge, 1995). He has conducted research on American popular culture, particularly television, with publications and presentations on *Perry Mason, Combat, Wiseguy, Gilligan's Island, My Favorite Martian* and *The Man from U.N.C.L.E.*

James R. Knecht is a PhD candidate in screen studies and critical theory at Oklahoma State University. His research interests include masculinity in film and television, horror films and teen television. He serves as Associate Editor for *Film & History*, as Television Area Chair for the Southwest/Texas Popular Culture Association/American Culture Association Conference, and as webmaster for *Iron Horse Literary Review*. He also works for the Oklahoma State University athletic department tutoring in English and composition.

Susan Latta is an Assistant Professor in the Department of English at Indiana State University, where she teaches classes in English language and professional writing. In addition to these areas, her research interests include rhetoric and composition, cultural studies and women's studies. She has published articles in *English Journal*, *Teaching English in the Two Year College*, *English Leadership Quarterly* and *Post/Identity* as well as three book chapters and many regional and national conference presentations.

Suzann Martin is a student at the University of Northern British Columbia. Her interests include film and television, especially foreign films, fantasy and science fiction television and Japanese animation.

Michaela D.E. Meyer is an Assistant Professor of Communication Studies at Christopher Newport University. She received her PhD in Communication Studies and a Certificate in Women's Studies from Ohio University. Her contributed chapter was part of her capstone project for the completion of the Women's Studies program. Meyer's publications interrogate the representation of women on television, including essays on *Lost*, *Smallville*, *Charmed*, *Law & Order* and *Dawson's Creek*.

Catriona Miller graduated with a PhD from the University of Stirling and is now a Lecturer at Glasgow Caledonian University, where her research interests include media policy, postmodernism, Jungian film/ TV studies and the archetypal dimensions of horror, science fiction and fantasy. She recently published 'Apocalypse Now, Or Then?' in *British Science Fiction Television: A Hitchhiker's Guide* (editors John Cook and Peter Wright, I.B.Tauris, 2005).

Stephanie Morgan is a student at the University of Northern British Columbia. She is interested in participatory culture, especially in relation to fan communities in television, film, and Japanese animation.

Alison Peirse is researching an AHRC-funded PhD on Classic Horror Film at Lancaster University. She has recently lectured in film studies at Lancaster University and Leeds Metropolitan University. Her other research interests include the destruction of the male body in werewolf films and she has presented papers on *Werewolf of London* (1935) and

Dog Soldiers (2002). She is also interested in the reworking of horror film aesthetics in contemporary television series including *Charmed* and *Supernatural*.

Peter Rans is Director of Cooperative Education and an Adjunct Professor in the English Department at the University of Northern British Columbia in Canada. He holds a PhD in English Literature from Dalhousie University, and earlier degrees in Literature and History from Sheffield University and University of East Anglia. His literary interests include postmodernism, the Gothic novel, fantasy and myth. He was the co-script writer and narrator of the short film *Yggdrasll* screened at the Atlantic Film Festival in Halifax in September 2006.

Markus Reisenleitner teaches in the Division of Humanities at York University, Canada and is also affiliated with the Department of Cultural Studies at Lingnan University in Hong Kong. His recent research has focused on urban imaginaries and theories of space and the environment. Publications include a monograph on images of the Middle Ages in nineteenth-century popular literature, an introduction to cultural studies and several edited volumes on cross-cultural constructions of Central Europe and North America.

Caroline Ruddell is Lecturer in Film and Television at St Mary's College, University of Surrey. Her research and teaching interests include the representation of identity and subjectivity in film and television, film theory, fantasy, gender studies and South-East Asian media. She has written on *Buffy the Vampire Slayer* and is on the editorial board for *Watcher Junior: The Undergraduate Journal of Buffy Studies*.

Sabine Schmidt studied German, Romance languages and literature, and modern history at the Universities of Mannheim and Lyon. She works as a lecturer and translator in Germany. Her main interests lie in the literature of the nineteenth century, gender studies and media analysis. Her publications are centred on the works of Adalbert Stifter, Jean Paul, August Lafontaine, Theodor Fontane, Sir Galahad (aka Bertha Eckstein-Diener, Helen Diner) and recently the role of the other in *Stargate: SG-1*.

Susan J. Wolfe is Professor of English and Professor and Chair of Languages, Linguistics, and Philosophy at the University of South Dakota. She has published essays on English syntax, historical linguistics, feminist aesthetics, literature and popular culture, and is co-editor of *The Coming Out Stories* (Persephone Press, 1980), *The Original Coming Out Stories* (Crossing Press, 1989), *Lesbian Culture: An Anthology* (Crossing Press, 1993) and *Sexual Practice/Textual Theory: Lesbian Cultural Criticism* (Blackwell, 1993).

Charmed *Cast List*

Charmed Ones

Prudence 'Prue' Halliwell	Shannen Doherty
Piper Halliwell	Holly Marie Combs
Phoebe Halliwell	Alyssa Milano
Paige Matthews	Rose McGowan

Male Characters

Andy Trudeau	Ted King
Darryl Morris	Dorian Gregory
Leo Wyatt	Brian Krause
Dan Gordon	Greg Vaughan
Cole Turner	Julian McMahon
Chris Halliwell (Adult)	Drew Fuller
Victor Bennett	Tony Denison in Season One
	James Read in Seasons Three–Eight
Samuel Wilder	Scott Jaeck
Wyatt Halliwell (Adult)	Wes Ramsey

Female Characters

Billie Jenkins	Kaley Cuoco
Grams (Penny) Halliwell	Jennifer Rhodes
Mom (Patty) Halliwell	Finola Hughes
Elise Rothman	Rebecca Balding

Introduction

KARIN BEELER AND STAN BEELER

IN 1998 THE series *Charmed*, which was produced by Aaron Spelling for Paramount, first aired on the Warner Brothers (WB) network. Since its inception, the show has garnered a worldwide audience and an almost fanatical following on the internet. Although cancelled after eight seasons, strategically timed DVD releases and network syndication in the US market have moved the series to cult status and a continuing market share. *Charmed* was created by Constance M. Burge, a multi-talented writer/producer who has worked on a host of popular woman-centred television series, including *Ally McBeal*, (1997) and *Judging Amy* (1999).

During the course of its production *Charmed* demonstrated a remarkable staying power and a dedicated international following of fans despite budget cuts and cast changes. *Charmed* soldiered on for five seasons even after the departure of its most famous actor, Shannen Doherty, at the end of Season Three. It is clear that, despite the relatively narrow focus of its original target market, *Charmed* is a series with wide appeal and, what is perhaps even more important in the ephemeral world of fantasy and science fiction television, stamina. The continued popularity of the series is evidenced not only by consistent middle-of-the-pack television ratings – even in syndication – but also by an impressive number of *Charmed* websites, discussion groups, blogs, fanfic and licensed *Charmed* novels, including one by Constance M. Burge, the series' creator.

Charmed is the story of three sisters who discover that they are powerful witches and take up the crusade against the demonic population of their home city of San Francisco. This is an interesting variation from the rather clichéd use of Salem, Massachusetts as an important historical site for witches. The city of San Francisco provides *Charmed* with an upbeat, contemporary flavour through the liberal use of establishing shots as a way of framing storylines and characters. The series underwent numerous transformations over the years but still maintained the central presence of its leading female characters. *Charmed* focuses upon the empowerment of young women in a paradoxically sexy yet decidedly third-wave feminist framework that challenges some of the assumptions of earlier forms of feminism or what it means to be a 'powerful' woman. Third-wave feminism does not necessarily recognize a contradiction between sexually attractive, fashion-conscious women, individualism and traditional feminist ideals such as equality, collectivist movements and empowerment in the workforce.[1]

In *Charmed* the initial group of three sisters consists of Piper (Holly Marie Combs), Prudence (Shannen Doherty) and Phoebe Halliwell (Alyssa Milano) who form 'the power of three' in the first few seasons; at the end of Season Three, Prue dies and is replaced by a new half-sister called Paige (Rose McGowan). Their powers are represented as a combination of inherited abilities and research-based spell casting. Important components of the series premise are the matrilineal source of the sisters' powers as well as the concept of feminine solidarity, with the matrilineal connection stretching back to Melinda Warren, a witch in seventeenth-century Salem, Massachusetts. The Halliwell sisters have inherited not only their powers from the female side of their family, they have also acquired the Book of Shadows – a compendium of spells and explanations of supernatural materials compiled by these female ancestors, including their mother.

Charmed lasted eight seasons because of its appeal to a clearly defined target market – primarily young women – raised in the traditions of feminism but strongly attracted by the movement sometimes termed 'girl power' by the press or third-wave feminism and postfeminism by academics. Third-wave feminism emerged in the late 1980s as a new generation's response to some of the ideas of second-wave feminism, and *Investigating Charmed: The Magic Power of TV* considers the impact of *Charmed* as a series produced in the era of third-wave feminism or postfeminism. *Charmed* first aired in 1998, in a decade that saw the emergence of other series with powerful female, 'kick-ass' heroes: *Buffy the Vampire Slayer*, *Xena*, *Dark Angel* and *Witchblade*. Scholars have often used the terms third-wave feminism and postfeminism interchangeably, and readers will note that in this collection some contributors opt for the former term, while others choose the latter. Critics such as Rebecca Walker, Rory Dicker and Alison Piepmeier make a distinction between third-wave feminism as a movement that is explicitly supportive of feminist principles, and postfeminism as a term synonymous with 'beyond feminism'. While acknowledging the complexity of these critical debates surrounding feminism(s), we believe that an extended theoretical discussion of these terms falls outside the scope of this collection.

The contributions in *Investigating Charmed* consider various facets of the long-running series, including its incorporation of many elements that make it such an engaging work of 'fantasy' television or telefantasy: wicca, witchcraft, myth, fairy tale, narrative patterns, ritual, special visual effects, Gothic architecture, horror and comedy. Each one of these chapters inevitably addresses the roles of *Charmed*'s central female characters, also known as the 'Charmed Ones'. The three major divisions in *Investigating Charmed* are Part One: 'Witchcraft, Wicca, Magic and Community', Part Two: 'Feminist Power', and Part Three: 'Visual Power, Place and Genre'. Part One focuses on the magical and spiritual aspects of the series. The first chapter in Part One, Michaela Meyer's '"Something Wicca This Way Comes": Audience Interpretation of a Marginalized Religious Philosophy on *Charmed*', discusses the portrayal of the Wiccan faith in the series through close readings of the *Charmed* narrative and through an analysis of survey data from *Charmed* fans. Meyer explains that Wicca and witchcraft are not synonymous and indicates how *Charmed*, unlike other popular series, follows many of the philosophical premises of the Wiccan faith, including the Theory of Levels, the Theory of Polarities and a belief in reincarnation. Susan Latta's 'Reclaiming Women's Language for Power and Agency: The Charmed Ones as Magical Rhetors' cautions against viewing *Charmed* as 'an instruction manual for Wicca' but demonstrates how the show provides an alternative mythology for women by depicting women who use the magical power of words or language. The 'interconnection of empowered individuals and collective action' as depicted in *Charmed* serves as a kind of third-wave feminist rhetoric. The magical bond of the collective or the group of three sisters is explored further in Caroline Ruddell's 'The Power of Three: Strength in Numbers and "Wordy" Witchcraft'. The significance of 'three' in the series, the ritual of the spoken word in spells and the power of the magical text in the Book of Shadows emphasize the postfeminist quality of *Charmed*; like other popular shows of the same period, *Charmed* acknowledges the role of friends who assist the main character(s).

Ritual and family receive further consideration in Sabine Schmidt's '"We Are Witches, Dear. We Can Do Anything": Dynamics of Ritual, Familial Tradition and Female Identity in *Charmed*' and in

Valerie Carroll's 'The Power of Three as *Communitas*: Moments of Subversion on *Charmed*'. Schmidt analyzes *Charmed* in the context of ritual theory, and addresses various facets of ritual: the use of certain material objects, the incorporation of a specialized language and the importance of gestures. Schmidt argues that the Charmed Ones use a combination of innate ability and knowledge in order to perform their magic. The presence of family members such as the sisters' immediate family (Penelope and Grams) or a witch ancestor like Melinda Warrick reinforce the importance of family tradition and ritualistic behaviour. Valerie Carroll provides a new way of examining the role of community in *Charmed* through the term *communitas*, 'a defensive social group made up of the marginalized'. Examining the sister witches in the context of *communitas* allows one to recognize moments of subversion in the series despite the influence of the power of patriarchy in the sisters' lives.

Part Two of *Investigating Charmed* explores the diversity of the question of feminist possibilities in *Charmed*. In '"I Just Want to Be Normal Again": Power and Gender in *Charmed*', Catriona Miller continues to discuss *Charmed* as a potentially contradictory text. Citing Foucault's statements on power, comments by a second-wave feminist like Mary Daly and postfeminist critics, Miller identifies the existence of various competing discourses in the series: feminist discourse(s), patriarchal discourse and consumer discourse.

Randall Clark alludes to a different kind of competition in the TV series through a discussion of the death of the eldest sister Prudence at the end of Season Three, and through the introduction of Paige, a new long-lost sister. In 'The Power of Two – Plus One', Clark notes the challenges faced by the sisters in a male-dominated society. He emphasizes differences between Prue and Paige, concluding that Paige is a more powerful character than Prue and that the inclusion of Paige allows the other sisters to become stronger. Clark not only considers the television series, but also addresses representations of the characters in the novelization of the series.

In '*Charm*ing the Elders: Girl Power for Second-Wave Feminists', Susan Wolfe offers her own 'reading' of *Charmed* based on her generational affiliation with second-wave feminism. As a lesbian feminist Wolfe tries to account for her fascination with the show despite its heterosexual content, de-emphasis on political concerns and audience base of younger women. While the Charmed Ones appear to be feminine and fashion-conscious third-wave feminists who counter the second-wave feminists' interest in social and political change, they embrace some of the goals reminiscent of an earlier generation: a belief in the community of women, the expression of feminist spirituality and the power of matrilineal connections. Wolfe concludes that though she is a second-wave feminist, there is much to be said for 'a series that reflects the ordinary lives of young women ... who are also karate-kicking, fireball-throwing female heroes'. The discussion of second- and third-wave feminism is pursued further in Karin Beeler's chapter 'Old Myths, New Powers: Images of Second-Wave and Third-Wave Feminism in *Charmed*'. The series makes frequent use of fairy tales or myths, and includes representations of ancient and modern feminine forces, which roughly correspond to second- and third-wave feminist ideas. The 'old' order is usually portrayed through images such as the crone and the sea hag, and the new order consists of the Charmed Ones. Yet the complexity of the second-wave/third-wave interaction may also be embedded within the 'younger' generation of the Charmed Ones, thus demonstrating how the sites of second-wave/third-wave power/debate may become associated with the internal struggle of a single character. Alison Peirse's 'Postfeminism Without Limits? *Charmed*, Horror and Sartorial Style' provides an interesting conclusion to Part Two by combining a discussion of postfeminism and its limitation by patriarchal values in *Charmed* with a study of horror film aesthetics. Peirse argues that the excessive femininity associated with postfeminism as represented by Phoebe and Paige develops into an image of the monstrous feminine body.

Part Three, the final section of the collection, includes a number of contributions that not only recognize the central figures of the Charmed Ones in the series, but also consider the importance of a variety of visual, structural, architectural and genre-based effects as techniques that solidify feminine bonds and the realm of the domestic sphere. Stan Beeler's 'There is Nothing New in the Underworld: Narrative Recurrence and Visual Leitmotivs in *Charmed*' uses musical metaphors to examine the patterns of plot and visual recurrence in the series. He compares the iterative nature of the series to the structure of Baroque music.

In 'It Really Isn't All Black and White: Colour Coding, Postfeminism and *Charmed*', James Knecht highlights the strength and intelligence of the lead characters, demonstrating how 'special-effect-generated magic' has allowed the postfeminist series to explore gender roles and role reversals. These visual effects include colourful outfits and numerous magical effects that are also colour coded. The gendered and urban dimensions of visual spaces are explored in Markus Reisenleitner's 'There's No Place Like *Charmed*: Domesticity, the Uncanny, and the Utopian Potential of the City'. According to Reisenleitner, *Charmed*'s depiction of San Francisco's 'urban imaginary' acts as a backdrop for the transformation of 'male-coded spaces of modern urbanity' into representations of female agency. The final chapter in the collection, '(Un)Real Humour: The Roles of Comedy and Fantasy in the First Season of *Charmed*', by Peter Rans analyses the influence of the collision of two important genres in *Charmed*: fantasy and comedy. Rans considers the different forms of comedy in 'the dialogue, in the character creation and in the visual gags that are the heart of the series'.

Since this book is also intended to serve as a useful source of information on the series as a whole, we have included a list of cast members and an episode guide covering all eight seasons of *Charmed*; the episode guide is an important resource for viewers who want a quick overview of the show's development over the years. Unlike other popular series, *Charmed* did not develop a spin-off; however, its longevity, together with a plethora of non-television franchise products – book series, *Charmed* Dolls, pseudo-magical paraphernalia – indicate that the series is worthy of serious discussion as an influential cultural phenomenon. This collection of papers reflects the diverse responses to the series in academic circles and in popular culture; *Charmed* has an existing academic presence and has appeared as a subject in such disparate venues as conferences on television, popular representations of witchcraft, the Gothic, fantasy, young adult literature/culture, 'girl power' and feminism. *Investigating Charmed* is a unique collection that should appeal to academics and other fans of the series around the world, while fostering a continuing interest in the representation of women in popular culture and telefantasy.

PART ONE

Witchcraft, Wicca, Magic and Community

'Something Wicca This Way Comes'

Audience Interpretation of a Marginalized Religious Philosophy on Charmed

MICHAELA D.E. MEYER

ITCHES ARE IN. From popular movies such as *The Craft* and *Practical Magic*, to recording artists like Godsmack and Kittie, to television series like *Sabrina, Buffy the Vampire Slayer* and *Felicity*, depictions of witchcraft in mainstream American culture are increasing. *Charmed* is a unique case of witches in popular culture because series creator Constance Burge often alluded to her intention to use Wicca as the primary philosophical grounding for the series.[1] The term Wicca is not synonymous with witchcraft. Wicca is a particular subsection of witchcraft, in the way that Catholicism or Protestantism are subsections of Christianity. Individuals who practice under the umbrella of witchcraft are encouraged to follow a path that most closely matches their own personal conceptualizations of morality and ethics.[2] Wicca is one of these paths, and centres on reverence for the Goddess and the God as manifested in nature.[3] Wiccan practitioners are predominantly women, given the religion's inclusion of the Goddess; however, both sexes are allowed to practise. Thus, the use of Wicca, as opposed to the general witchcraft used in *The Craft* or *Sabrina*, distinguishes *Charmed* from other popular culture depictions of witches.

The question then becomes, how does *Charmed* portray the Wiccan faith, and how is that message interpreted by audiences? To answer this question, I will first provide a textual analysis of the *Charmed* narrative. Textual criticism, or close readings of media narratives, is commonly associated with rhetorical studies, and aims to 'interpret the intentional dynamics of a text'.[4] In this case, the writers chose to adhere to a Wiccan philosophical frame, particularly during the first three seasons of *Charmed* under Burge's creative control. To answer the second part of the question, I offer survey data from *Charmed* fans. These fans responded to a set of questions about the series and its representation of Wicca over a six-month period (January to June 2001) on *Charmed* internet message boards and discussion groups.[5] Through a combination of these two methods, I find that fans observed the series, drawing parallels between the experience of Wicca and other more familiar concepts such as Christianity, family and feminism. Thus, the series is able to create a discursive space from which non-Wiccan audience members can appreciate an alternative religious paradigm.

Wiccan Philosophy on Charmed

Although no official text explains the entire religious philosophy of the Wiccan faith, some general categories of belief exist. Wiccan rationale rests on two main theories: the Theory of Levels and the Theory of Polarity.[6] The Theory of Levels is used to define the structure of the universe, while the Theory of Polarity defines the activity of the universe. Wiccans see structure and activity as inseparable, and therefore paradoxical. A way to understand these two concepts is to think in terms of Western and Eastern religious philosophy:

> Eastern religions tend to focus on the first part of the paradox, holding the view that in reality all things are one and that separation and individuality are illusions. Western religions stress individuality and tend to see the world as composed of fixed and separate things. The Western view tends to encourage individual effort and involvement with the world; the Eastern view encourages withdrawal, contemplation, and compassion.[7]

The Wiccan philosophy holds that each facet is equally valid and embraces the idea of paradoxical belief. Also central to the Wiccan faith is a belief in reincarnation; Wicca teaches that reincarnation is the way that an individual's soul is perfected throughout time, and that one lifetime is not sufficient to attain the goals of the spiritual plane.[8] Thus, a narrative must demonstrate an understanding of the concept of levels and the concept of polarity, as well as display a belief in reincarnation for it to educate the audience accurately on the Wiccan belief system. *Charmed* depicts all three ideas as central to the sisters' lives, and thus orients the audience to a Wiccan philosophical perspective.

The Theory of Levels asserts that different structural realities exist on spiritual and physical planes, and that each level has its own unique laws and dynamics. The physical, astral, spiritual and mental planes are examples of generally accepted levels.[9] *Charmed* adheres to the

Theory of Levels because the characters recognize that these levels exist and that they will not always understand the structure of their world. Prue, for example, gains the power to astral project, allowing her to transport between the astral and physical planes.[10] Phoebe recognizes that there are 'eleven planes of existence'.[11] Leo tries to explain the structure of the spiritual plane he belongs to by saying, 'There are different levels up there, a hierarchy'.[12] These other planes of existence appear consistently in *Charmed*. For example, the Demon of Illusion exists on a separate plane where the sisters' powers do not work. The Demon explains this by saying, 'This is the world of illusion, and you girls are reality. Your powers, unlike mine, cannot cross between the two'.[13]

The sisters realize that they will not always understand the laws within different planes but that they must try to follow them. For example, Prue warns both her sisters, 'Just because we're witches doesn't mean we're above the laws of nature – or the Wiccan ones.'[14] Phoebe echoes Prue's concern when faced with the potential marriage of Leo and Piper: 'These are the rules that we live by now. I'm just not so sure we should be helping Piper break them.'[15] They do not always understand why they are thrust into the positions they are, but are constantly reminded that everything happens for a reason and that everything happens in its own time. Therefore, *Charmed* narratively depicts the Theory of Levels by recognizing the existence of levels and the different laws within those levels.

The Theory of Polarity maintains that activity within any plane occurs by the interaction of pairs and complementary opposites.[16] For example, the interaction of white and black can produce varying shades of grey – but grey would not exist without the interaction of the two opposites. Other common dualities are male/female, positive/negative and good/evil. Interaction relies on the strength of each part of the duality, and the manifestation of any activity in an individual's reality is a result of the interplay between the two opposites, promoting balance as an important spiritual concept.[17] *Charmed* represents the Theory of Polarity throughout its narrative. For example, the sisters' powers are turned evil when Prue is forced to marry a warlock. Reflecting on the situation, Prue observes,

Prue: They didn't just plant evil inside of me or us for that matter. There had to be something there for them to turn to begin with.

Leo: That doesn't make you evil, Prue – you have to choose to be evil voluntarily.

> *Prue:*   All I'm saying is that if evil weren't enticing why would there
> be any? I mean, to pretend that we're never attracted to it is like
> pretending that it doesn't exist.[18]

In Season Two, Piper's doctor accidentally injects himself with the sisters' blood and gains their powers. He proceeds to kill drug dealers and other criminals, harvesting their organs for patients in need.[19] His struggle between the two polarities costs him his life, demonstrating that good and evil intentions can exist simultaneously. In another episode, after Phoebe travels to a previous life, Prue explains that, 'It's just as natural to be bad as it is to be good. That's how we know what good is, it's how we're able to make the choice to be good.'[20] Thus, the never-ending struggle between good and evil in the series represents one of the key polarities recognized in the Wiccan tradition.

Another polarity that frequently occurs in *Charmed* is the idea of wrestling with an 'inner demon'. In Season One, Prue meets Brendan, a half-demon who is called to join his brothers to become the evil Charmed Ones. Instead, he chooses to enter the priesthood, which is the only way to lose his demonic powers.[21] Brendan's nature as a half-demon reinforces the idea that good and evil coexist, and that one can choose to be good. A similar theme reemerges when the half-demon Cole appears in Season Three with a similar story. The rooting of polarities in characters allows the audience a chance to identify with those characters, and in essence allows the audience to identify with the Wiccan worldview.

Finally, the show also incorporates a belief in reincarnation. Reincarnation in a Wiccan sense is the belief that the soul is a fragment of the Divine and will eventually return to the Divine after it experiences all things in life.[22] Not all Wiccans believe in literal reincarnation, but most view the world as a cycle of birth, death and rebirth.[23] This concept also appears frequently in *Charmed*. Most obviously, the relationship between Leo and Piper is framed as 'soulmates' within the text – their souls are destined to be together as part of their spiritual transgression. In the episode 'Pardon My Past' (2.14), the issue of past lives is specifically addressed when Leo explains that past lives are 'how our souls evolve, how we grow as individuals from one life to the next'. Phoebe goes into a past life to understand how her individual actions in the past affect her present day powers. During this journey, she sees her sisters and Leo, and when she returns to the present day, Leo explains that these images were not actually her sisters but rather the past lives of her sisters: 'We all tend to travel in the same circles of family, friends, even enemies throughout our various lives. That's why our souls . . . recognize each other, so we can keep finding each other. That's what soulmates means.' In addition to the discussion of soulmates, representations of ghosts, reincarnations of spirits and the recognition of life as continuous rather than ending at death occur frequently. The sisters are often visited by their deceased grandmother and mother, further demonstrating to the audience that one's soul does not disappear after death. Therefore, in a textual sense, *Charmed* is clearly rooted in a Wiccan philosophy of life incorporating the Theory of Levels, the Theory of Polarities and a belief in reincarnation.

How Do Audiences Interpret Wicca in Charmed?

Wiccan critics and fans alike have commended *Charmed* for its relatively accurate portrayal of the Wiccan religion and its treatment of magic, in particular that magic has consequences and is not to be used for personal gain. In fact, audience respondents who identified themselves as Wiccan emphasized that their interest in the series began because of the series' use of Wicca as a basis. They did, however, observe that the show does not portray everything about Wicca accurately. For example, Sean observed that he was, 'disappointed that they felt they needed to tie Wicca into Christianity à la demons and angels (Whitelighters) but most shows about Witchcraft that are not glitzy in some way are pretty boring'. Mystique RisingSun agreed, explaining how the show juxtaposes Wicca and Christianity: 'Demons are found in Christianity, not in Witchcraft. They've given demons names of Gods and Goddesses, GOOD Gods and Goddesses, no less. But, it IS television. Without the added effects and such, doing a show on Wicca, or even Witchcraft in general, would be pretty boring.'

Both of these audience members emphasize that Wicca exists in the series, but that elements of Christianity more familiar to the audience are also present. In addition, they speak of 'glitz' and 'added effects' – an important element of the science fiction genre of *Charmed*. Thus, although they are interested in the religious aspects of the series, these philosophical underpinnings are not their only rationale for watching the show. Renea sums it up:

> Sure, there are a lot of Wiccans out there that are complaining about how *Charmed* is so fake, but I think that if it was too realistic the general public wouldn't like it. I mean if *7th Heaven* was all about preaching and God says this and God says that no one would watch it. It's the same with *Charmed*. *Charmed* shows real aspects of Wicca that the general Christian and such audience can relate to.

In a sense, Renea summarizes an underlying need to recognize the political economy of a series. The fusing of Wicca and Christianity is viewed as an economic necessity for the series – in order for the programming to reach a wider audience, the inclusion of more commonly understood symbols is essential.

Audience members who identified as non-Wiccan indicated that this fusing is, at least on some levels, successful. Non-Wiccan audience members reported that the show gave them a positive impression of the religion. For example, Al B. noted, 'It doesn't seem like there's an abundant amount of Wiccan elements discussed. What it does show seems positive toward the Wiccan image.' Similarly, Smurf replied that through her interaction with Wiccan fans online, as a non-Wiccan she believed 'they did enough research to get enough of the information right to please the audience, and we can all relate to them'. This respondent connects Wicca to the characters on *Charmed*, observing that we can 'relate to them'. Another respondent, Wordmage, said, 'I believe that Wicca is basically good, and that the show is correct in its portrayal of witches as people who feel and love and hurt just like anyone else.' Thus, the show's connection between Wiccan and non-Wiccan elements, whether symbols of Christianity or just basic human emotion, is what allows non-Wiccan audience members to identify with the text; in this way, the series successfully opens the audience to positive impressions of the Wiccan religion. As The Charmed One explained, '*Charmed* puts me in the position of being a bit of witch while watching the show.' By finding a place where one can be 'a bit of a witch', even if one does not adhere to Wiccan teaching or philosophy, audiences come to understand the Wiccan faith.

The juxtaposition of Christian and Wiccan elements presents an interesting rhetorical fusion. Kenneth Burke's notion of 'equipment for living' is relevant here, in that through structural variations in the narrative, audience members can confront their lived situations.[24] Audiences find usefulness in *Charmed* because it allows them to perform the part of 'witch', either by reinforcing deeply held religious beliefs (as for audience members who identify as Wiccan) or by allowing an ideological connection to these non-dominant beliefs without sacrificing the dominant order (as for audience members who do not identify as Wiccan). By doing so, *Charmed* creates a new perspective that fuses meaning from the combination and blend of textual fragments.[25] In other words, the audience is given the opportunity to deconstruct their previous stereotypes of witches (old hags on brooms) and reconstruct a more humanistic view of witches (stylish young women trying to make it on their own).

In addition to embedding Christian imagery in the narrative, *Charmed* also draws heavily on the concept of family. Respondents emphasized the bond between the sisters as a key reason for connecting to the narrative. For example, Psyche said,

> Whenever I watch Charmed I am so very much connected to the three sisters. I feel that I am a part of them, a part of their family. And I believe that is what the creators of this series wanted to accomplish – to make the audience feel like they are part of the show and not just a viewer from the outside.

Psyche draws a connection between the sense of family and her interest in the show, and furthermore claims that this family narrative was intended by the series' creators. Similarly, Cyberspace Warlock claims, 'the show makes the audience think about what's the best thing to be done. In effect, the show teaches the audience to extract reason for everything'. In other words, the narrative frequently stresses the three separate subject positions of the sisters and invites the audience to identify with a particular sister's viewpoint. The sisters continually debate about what course of action to take, advocating that no one particular voice is correct, but rather that the multiplicity of voices is to be cherished. Queen Jubes reinforces this by noting:

> Heroines as strong, powerful, and courageous as the Charmed Ones can often be extremely unrealistic, sometimes even completely so, and with no emotion tied in. . . . we are gifted with their struggles to save the day and/or rescue the innocent(s), their denial of problems/ tragedies/pains, the fact that even heroines still lose some battles, the loss of loved ones, the loss of loved ones that could have been saved, and even the unwillingness to save the day.

Queen Jubes' comment that audiences are 'gifted' indicates that part of the viewing pleasure for the audience is being able to identify with the struggle of each sister.

Critical Implications of Wicca on *Charmed*

Through a brief analysis of the textual focus on Wicca, and discussion by fans about these representations, some critical implications emerge related to media literacy. First, the fan data reveals that *Charmed* serves an educative function for the audience. Bradley Courtenay, Sharan Merriam and Lisa Baumgartner claim that academics know very little about how mainstream individuals gain access to and learn the norms, values, beliefs and practices of marginalized, unacknowledged, or socially stigmatized groups such as Wicca.[26] Although Wicca is recognized as a legal religion in the United States, Wiccans do not proselytize, seek to convert others, or practise openly in most cases; thus, it is often difficult to find practising Wiccans, and even more difficult to find publicly functioning groups or covens.[27] Thus, the information available to individuals about Wicca is often limited to what they can glean from mediated messages – books, the internet, film and television.

Ethnographic work has discovered that mediated images of stigmatized discourse often serve as the primary means through which audiences understand the stigmatized subject.[28] Thus, the mediated representation presented in *Charmed* may, in some cases, be the only access audiences have to the Wiccan faith or philosophy. The series allows the oppressed voice (Wicca) visibility without excluding non-Wiccan audience members. In fact, Smurf, a self-identified non-Wiccan, commented, '*Charmed* has further interested me in the culture of Wicca, probably because I am [the] type of person that wants to know if it is true, therefore I end up looking up more about Wicca, and get deeper and deeper into it.' Similarly, Ryan took this to another level, commenting, 'I memorize their spells but that doesn't make me a witch, does it? I just like the show and somehow I feel more CONNECTED when I know the spells right in mind.' Obviously, these fans were educated enough by the series to seek out additional information about Wicca – learning about the religion, performing spells, getting 'deeper and deeper into it'. Given the responses from fans, *Charmed* is actually raising social awareness about Wicca on one level.

Whether intended by the creators to serve an educative function or not, *Charmed*'s appeal to both audience segments certainly influenced its ability to sustain eight seasons of television programming. In fact, one of the most prominent themes of the series emphasized the bond between the sisters, and thus presents individual action and social context as an important polarity in women's lives. Much like the Wiccan Theory of Polarity, the representation of the three sisters on *Charmed* offers a plurality of voices, or in many cases, three unique perspectives.[29] In other words, each sister is entitled to her opinion on magical issues, but the Power of Three ultimately prevails – they must act together interpersonally to accomplish their goals. Audience members emphasized feeling connected to the sisters, particularly to their plurality of voices. Thus, the interpersonal relationships between the sisters became the primary vehicle through which many of the show's problems were resolved. As these interactions may be the *only* exposure that some audience members have to any particular Wiccan concept, audiences may use the interpersonal context of the show as a way to define, mediate and change their own understanding of how the self acts in a social context and ultimately how the audience understands the Wiccan faith.[30]

Although the show is potentially serving this educative function through interpersonal channels, Wiccan audience members did express concern about the show's seclusion of the sisters. Even though the show as a whole is positive in its portrayal of the Wiccan faith, its mandate that the sisters' powers cannot be shared with the non-magical world furthers the mystery surrounding Wiccan practice. In fact, because the sisters cannot use their powers in situations where mortals may view them, their magic becomes a secret to be protected rather than a tool of empowerment. As Jen W. put it,

> The sisters are forbidden to let 'mortals' know that they are witches and have powers. That is the only part of the show that bugs me. As a witch, I am guarded about who I share that information with, but if we truly want to break down the barriers and prejudices, we need to get it out there that Wicca is not a 'dark secret'.

As a result of their 'dark secret', the sisters are consistently shown as struggling to balance their magical and non-magical lives. Storylines are frequently tied back to the sisters' home, the Halliwell Manor, because the Book of Shadows cannot be removed from the manor, though on countless occasions demons tried to steal it. Furthermore, demons attack the Charmed Ones more often at their home than in their 'normal' lives. As scholars have noted, the rooting of women's power in the home has been representative of their influence within private spheres.[31] These 'super powerful' witches are in a sense confined to their home, guarding their secret from those around them. This continues to play out throughout the series, when each of the sisters is forced to give up her 'normal' career in light of her 'magical' powers.

Conclusion

Charmed presents an interesting case study of the representation of a marginalized religion in contemporary media. As our mediated landscape continues to expand, scholars are concerned with whether or not audiences are actually processing and interpreting messages they see on television and connecting these to their everyday lives. In other words, our culture's focus on media literacy continues to expand.

Theorist Joshua Meyrowitz makes a strong case that there are multiple media literacies, in that media literacy should be conceptualized as a number of literacies because audiences are expected to perform a range of analyses in order to be considered literate.[32] It is simply not enough that the audience process the blatant content of a television series – they must also dissect these representations on a deeper level. Stuart Hall observes that audiences frequently engage in negotiated readings of popular texts, meaning that audiences devise alternative readings of rhetorical messages that are contrary to the author's original aim.[33] Thus, although the creators of *Charmed* may not have fully intended their narrative to encourage audience members to learn more about the Wiccan faith, in some instances audience members reported that this did occur. Also, the fusing of Christian and Wiccan imagery puts audiences in a position to interpret these hybridized images, thus positioning them to become literate consumers of fictional media.

Reclaiming Women's Language for Power and Agency

The Charmed Ones as Magical Rhetors

SUSAN LATTA

IN THE SPRING of 2006, when the US television networks WB and UPN announced they would merge to create a new network, the CW, media coverage of the upcoming season hardly noted that the new network's autumn line-up would not include the programme *Charmed*. Premiering in 1998, *Charmed* chronicled the adventures of three sisters, Prue, Piper and Phoebe (and, after Prue's death, long-lost sister Paige), who learned, after the death of their grandmother, that not only had they inherited supernatural powers from their mother's family, a line of hereditary witches dating back to colonial America, but also that they were, in fact, the Charmed Ones, a fabled trio of sisters who, together, the legend told, would join their individual powers to battle evil and to herald a new generation of witchcraft on earth. The programme, which had struggled in its last few years on air, had never been a darling to network executives;[1] nevertheless, its fan base helped it to survive for eight years on the WB network, riding the wave of earlier girl-power programmes such as *Buffy the Vampire Slayer*.

While other girl-power fantasies focused on the heroine's power as expressed in her physical prowess, *Charmed* was unique in that its supernatural elements were grounded, albeit loosely, in the popularity of earth religions and goddess spirituality. The practice of Wicca, as both a family tradition and a set of specific spiritual beliefs and rituals, is at the core of the show. The symbol of the witch – used for generations as a derogatory term to stigmatize and sometimes brutalize women who transgressed social norms – was reclaimed and presented as a positive image. The Halliwell sisters, the Charmed Ones, are witches who use the powers they have inherited, as well as more mundane powers they learn on their own, to solve mysteries, protect innocents and fight the forces of darkness that seek to claim the world for their own devious purposes.

While *Charmed* certainly is not an instruction manual for Wicca, and, like most media images of women, sends mixed messages about women's roles[2] and power,[3] the programme does provide a unique view of a process of revisionist mythmaking inherent in both the feminist and women's spirituality movements. The myth of the Charmed Ones provides viewers with an alternative interpretation of the role of strong women in society, one in which women can discover and reclaim a heritage of powerful women that has, until recently, been obscured. The presentation of this tradition of witches, and the secrets of their craft as revealed in the Halliwell family's Book of Shadows, provides an alternative mythology of women empowered by words, women who can, quite literally, change the world through both the power of their actions and the power of their language.

Science fiction and fantasy provide important forums for marginalized groups to create worlds in which they are included and central, possessing means of power denied them in the real world. Feminist writers and critics have used elements of myths and legends as the basis for their revising of women's roles and power. As Starhawk notes, 'the strongest mythogenic force at work today . . . is feminism'.[4] Speaking of women poets, Alicia Ostriker notes that:

> Whenever a poet employs a figure or story previously accepted and defined by a culture, the poet is using a myth, and the potential is always present that the use will be revisionist, that is, the figure or tale will be appropriated for altered ends . . . ultimately making cultural change possible.[5]

For, example, this process of revisionist mythmaking in science fiction has been illustrated by Osherow's discussion of the reclamation of the demon Lilith in science fiction as a positive character[6] and in fantasy, most famously, by Marion Zimmer Bradley's retelling of the Arthurian legends in *The Mists of Avalon*.[7]

Charmed engages with this revisionist process on several levels, most obviously with the symbol of the witch, long used to silence 'wise women' who posed a threat to the patriarchal order. Cast as evil, particularly from the Christian tradition (as the family minister tells Piper in the first episode, the Bible instructs Christians 'Thou shalt not suffer a witch to live'[8]), the Halliwell sisters contest this portrayal on several levels. First, the sisters are not entering into a pact with the devil or any demonic forces; the reason for their power is to fight against those same forces. In the series' premier, Piper, after her conversation with the not-so-helpful minister, is understandably very concerned with the possibility that inheriting her powers has made her evil and is greatly relieved when she finds that she can, indeed, walk into a church without being struck dead by the hand of God. In addition, both Prue and Piper wear crosses, and the family celebrates Christmas as well the Wiccan sabbats. The message is that modern witches are not evil enemies of Christians, that they respect and tolerate others' beliefs. In addition, the sisters do not actively seek their power for personal gain; they inherit this power that is theirs by birthright through their inheritance in the matriarchal line of Halliwell witches. As Phoebe states in the episode 'I've Got You Under My Skin' (1.2), 'witchcraft is a chick thing', passed on from the mother to daughters.

A second, more explicit example of the revision of the image of the witch occurs in the episode 'All Halliwell's Eve' (3.4). On Halloween, the sisters are pulled back through time to 1670 Virginia. Cole/Belthazor (still in his half-human, half-demonic form) has been sent into the past by the Triad rulers of the Underworld to eliminate the Halliwell line by seizing Melinda Warren, the original matriarch of the family, from her mother at birth. Whining about the derogatory images of witches on Halloween decorations, Phoebe is less than thrilled at the holiday, but, much to her own and her sisters' surprise, later embraces those stereotypes to save Melinda and her mother, Charlotte, from the witch hunters who are trying to kill them. Trapped in the past without their hereditary powers, the sisters must learn the craft from Ava, the coven leader. 'Magic is all around you', Ava instructs them and shows how the very images Phoebe previously disdained, such as the conical hat and the broom, are actually sources of women's power. The implication, when Phoebe takes to the broom and flies into the night to frighten the witch hunters, is that Phoebe's flight was the impetus for the iconic image of the witch flying across the moon, and that the power and nobility inherent in Phoebe's flight have been distorted by the men who viewed it, and patriarchal society since, into a grotesque of women's wisdom. We are subtly reminded of that distortion, and of its original power, when at the end of the episode the camera lingers on a jack-o-lantern that Phoebe sets on the bar at the Halloween party at Piper's club, P3, proudly carved with a witch in flight on her broom.

This overt revision of the image of the witch is more subtly continued in the mythology of the tradition of the Halliwell witches. The establishment of a family of strong, powerful women, deeply connected to their line and to the wisdom of that line as passed on in the family's Book of Shadows, contests the image of women as powerless objects acted upon but who cannot act, who are silenced and cannot speak or write their truth and, consequently, cannot make any meaningful changes to society. As such, the mythology of the Halliwell witches also provides an antidote to the silencing and obscuring of women of words.

A key element of the Charmed Ones' myth is the importance of the connection of language and power in magical practice. Over the last forty years, scholars in linguistics and literary theory have examined the ways that language practices have excluded women and have worked to reify women's oppression. In addition to postulating that language itself excludes women and prevents their agency in the world, literary and rhetorical scholars have attempted to reclaim women's texts and theorize specific practices of writing production. Gilbert and Gubar, in their analysis of Victorian women writers, argue that one reason that women were not more prominent as literary authors was that they were socialized to see themselves as object rather than agent. Instead of acting in the world, women used their creativity to shape a persona appropriate to the role to which society assigned them. Women's creative energy, thwarted by societal limitations and expectations, resulted in what Gilbert and Gubar call the anxiety of authorship, 'an anxiety built from the complex and often barely conscious fears of authority which seems to the female artist to be by definition inappropriate for her sex.'[9] Therefore, an important part of women finding their voices and agency is discovering a tradition of women's language and women's writing in which they as novice writers can situate themselves; strong women using language powerfully, not just for individual development and expression but as a way of making an impact in the world.

In his history of the relationship between rhetoric, magic and the imagination, Covino points out that these three terms, usually seen as separate, in reality have had a strong connection throughout Western history. It is this connection, he argues, that makes magical rhetoric (or rhetorical magic) just such a possible transformative force in society. Magic, he notes, falls into disfavour when scientific, logical and mechanistic views are emphasized. Citing various scientific efforts to debunk magic, the supernatural and the occult through the centuries, Covino asserts that the basis of this fear of magic is the fear that some force other than those sanctioned by official apparatuses (governments, academia etc.) can change or redefine reality.[10] de Romilly points out that, since Classical times, both magic and rhetoric have become redefined as deceptive and irrational.[11] Consider, for example, contemporary uses of these terms, where rhetoric can be used to paint an opponent's arguments as empty or when a belief in magic automatically designates one as superstitious. Irrationality and deception are the enemies of scientific, logical, rational thought, so those who can be painted as irrational or deceiving are automatically discredited, their legitimacy and power denied. The magus speaks in an 'occult' language, a language outside language forms officially sanctioned and approved, and thus is a threat to the established order.[12] The iconic image of the magician is of the intermediary between the realm of the imagined and the real world, the figure that acts to manifest from the imaginary into the actual. What a coup, then, to recreate the image of the magician as one of disempowering others, of a trickster using his abilities for power over others, bending the gullible and the ignorant to his will, and using, as Covino puts it, arresting magic, magic that binds and constrains others against their will.[13] This notion of coercive magic is offensive to Wiccan practitioners, who consider carefully 'wise choices' in the use of magic, consistent with their belief that all is interconnected through the divine immanent in all creation.[14] As Curott notes, 'Because magic works by the principle of interconnectedness, in doing spellwork what we do to another we do to ourselves.'[15]

It is easy to see, then, how the powers that be would be doubly interested in corrupting the image of the female magician – the witch – along the same lines. However, whereas the arresting magician is accepted as being an agent of language, albeit an 'evil rhetor',[16] women traditionally have been socialized to believe that they cannot speak. As Glenn notes, since 'rhetoric always inscribes the relation of language and power in a particular moment (including who may speak, who may listen or who will agree to listen, and what can be said), canonical rhetorical history has represented the experience of males, powerful males, with no provision of allowance for females.'[17] As mentioned above, the same lack has been true in the literary canon; hence the importance, in both fields, of reclaiming the tradition of women authors. By denying women the act of linguistic agency, society denies them the possibility of acting in the public sphere as agents of change. By rediscovering women who did speak and write, we rediscover powerful women whose contributions were hidden and have been forgotten by later generations.

Reclaiming the image of the witch is particularly important, for not only is she an image of a powerful wise woman, but she is also an image of a woman rhetor as well. Magic, as practitioners explain, is working with the energy of the universe,[18] and Covino argues that rhetoric is an analogous practice because 'it is the interaction of different kinds of energy'.[19] Citing the work of Kennedy, Covino describes this interaction: 'Rhetoric is the *natural* practice of both animals and humans acting under the aegis of a common communicative urgency,

. . . the invocation of invisible powers within a sympathetic universe of widely shared signifiers; that is, magic.'[20]

The witch, then, is not only a feminist icon because she can kick demon ass (although, as depicted on *Charmed*, the vanquishing of evil is certainly presented as a moment to savour). The witch is also an important icon because she represents the ability to use language to transform reality in ways that do not necessarily have to be arresting but rather in magical language acts that can be generative as well. Transformation may be best initiated by those who have been excluded and marginalized from a particular culture, those who have little to lose by transgressing societal norms. Witches, who 'haunt the hedges' of society, are ideally positioned to create radical change.[21] This generative magic is 'the practice of disrupting and recreating articulate power: a (re)sorcery of spells for generating multiple perspectives'.[22] The Charmed Ones' use of language in spellcraft illustrates another strand, then, of a revision of the myth by establishing a women's tradition of language use that empowers rather than disempowers women and positions them as agents intervening in the world.

The Book of Shadows, the 'canonical' text for the Charmed Ones, is a collectively written book to which all Halliwell witches have contributed, beginning on the first page with the invocation to grant the Charmed Ones their powers. It is important to note here that a Book of Shadows is unique to a solitary or a coven; that is, there is no one authoritative book to which all witches subscribe. Starhawk notes that the power of the word in a Book of Shadows is not be understood as 'The Word' as in Christian theology, but rather as 'the power of symbolic action that unlocks the starlit awareness of [the unconscious mind]'.[23] In *Charmed*, the Book of Shadows consists of a pastiche of texts, descriptions of demons and warlocks, recipes for potions, spells and invocations, cobbled together as the need arises by the Halliwell witches. While Starhawk notes that the Book of Shadows has traditionally functioned as just such a 'recipe book', she points out that the book is now more of 'a personal journal',[24] and Curott has entitled her memoir of discovering Wicca *The Book of Shadows*. Author Silver RavenWolf describes the Book of Shadows as a 'spiritual testimony', a text 'whose words are important and assist in chronicling personal or group growth through the information contained'.[25] For the Halliwell witches, the Book of Shadows represents the collective wisdom of the women in the family, wisdom that has been lost not only to the sisters but also to society at large. Sanders emphasizes how important it is in feminism for all generations to share their stories but notes that for young women these stories provide a reminder that 'their rebellion has a precedent'.[26] One criticism of third-wave feminism has been that younger feminists have forgotten the struggles waged by their mothers and grandmothers as they encountered sexism and discrimination in their respective generations. For third-wave feminists, an understanding that their struggles are not new but share common themes with women of earlier generations can provide not only a sense that they are not alone but also a sense of solidarity, that they are acting as yet another generation of women who are determined to participate in and transform society.

As such a collection of stories from generations of women, the Book of Shadows represents an important spiritual journey for the sisters as they rediscover the power of their matriarchal lineage. In the aforementioned Halloween episode, Ava, the coven leader, is astonished that the most powerful witches of all time can be so ignorant of basic wisdom; Phoebe emphasizes 'we can get it [wisdom] back if you teach us.' Women's wisdom is not forever lost but can be recovered and passed on to future generations through the book, remembering and re-establishing a tradition of foremothers upon which future women can rely. 'Knowledge and reverence', as the sisters learn in colonial Virginia, is the key; at the end, Phoebe vows to reclaim this heritage – 'So much knowledge, so much power that we lost, but we will get it back.' The importance of the Book of Shadows' function is emphasized by the fact that when the sisters come into their powers, both of the matriarchs in their family, their mother and Grams, have died; the book is their only source of knowledge, their only connection to the past and the only explanation they have of how their power works. Such a separation represents just one instance of a 'chilling of matrilineal relations', as Howie and Tauchert put it, as a primary way in which patriarchy severs ties among women.[27]

The Book of Shadows consists of spells already written, spells the sisters write, and spells that can be written by Halliwell ancestors post-mortem when the need arises to communicate. Unlike canonical religious texts of other traditions, the Book of Shadows, then, is a dynamic rather than static text, constantly changing to meet the exigent needs of the Halliwell lineage as its future is written (and rewritten) by the sisters and family members from past, present and future. Just as 'energy is constantly in motion. It cannot be stopped',[28] women's written tradition is analogously fluid. Athough, at first, the sisters approach the book as an encyclopedia or a 'recipe book', they learn from their ancestors that spells can be composed, that the act of using language to invoke an action is one that they too can use and adapt for particular situations. Thus, the use of language is also by its nature a rhetorical act, situated in a particular moment of time. The spell intervenes in the energy of the situation to shape and alter it; the spell-caster is a powerful agent of change – even if she is not cognizant of that power at the time of its utterance. For example, when in 'That '70s Episode' (1.17) the sisters read a spell to send them back in time to prevent the warlock Nicholas from killing them and stealing their powers, they are sent back to their childhood, to the time when both their mother and grandmother were still alive. Before sending the sisters back to confront the warlock, Grams tells the sisters she will compose a specific vanquishing spell against Nicholas. Astonished, Phoebe admits that she did not realize that they could compose spells – up to this point the sisters had been relying on the Book of Shadows as a compendium of previously discovered knowledge. Grams replies 'We are witches, dear. We can do anything!' To their amazement (and relief), when the sisters return to their time, the Book of Shadows now includes a page entitled the 'Nicholas Must Die Spell'. By learning the history of those spells in the Book of Shadows, and by learning that spells are dynamic language acts emerging from the necessity of the moment, the sisters also begin to realize the power they wield to shape reality through the words that they use.

Interestingly, the authors of the Book of Shadows can guide the sisters in their reading of the text. Because of its patchwork composition, the Book of Shadows seems to have no index or table of contents; obviously, finding the relevant information on a particular demon, spell or potion can take considerable time, time not necessarily available when attacking demons are blowing up the Halliwell Manor. Throughout the series, during such difficult moments, the Book of Shadows spontaneously opens to the relevant page (often interpreted as Grams flipping through the pages to guide them to the necessary passage). Also, on one occasion, the book actually created a dialogue with one of the sisters. In the episode 'From Fear to Eternity' (1.13), Prue discovers that the information concerning the Demon of Fear they are confronting is written in Patty's, their mother's, handwriting. Since Prue is having difficulty understanding the information Patty sent her in a dream about the demon, Patty gives additional information about how to vanquish the demon in the book. Later, after Prue overcomes her fear of admitting her feelings, Patty writes on the page of the book as Prue is reading it, 'Thanks for letting them [your sisters] into your heart'. The act of communication, then, is not one-way: the process of reading and interpreting the Book of Shadows is not necessarily the work of a lone reader, but is an interactive process between writer and reader, one that can reach across time (and the afterlife) to have a direct and immediate effect on the reader's life.

While each sister has an inherited power (freezing time, premonitions or moving objects), and develops over the course of the programme other, mundane, powers (such as Phoebe's martial arts training or Paige's degree in social work), each also has the ability, through spellcraft, to speak action into being. Ava explains that a woman's 'walk of wisdom' leads to power, and power frightens the fearful and the ignorant. Prue makes the connection to women's power and the denigration of the symbol of the witch or 'wise woman' at Halloween: if witches are made to look silly – depicted as the hag on the broomstick – it is a deliberate attempt of a (patriarchal) society, threatened by women's power, to frighten women away from embracing their power. Through their experience with the coven in colonial Virginia, the sisters learn that the stereotype of a witch is not a truth but an identity constructed by patriarchy to disempower them. When we realize that these stereotypes are not eternal truths naturalized to seem like common sense, but rather constructed roles, these roles can be deconstructed, revised or discarded, By changing the signification system (language), change can be initiated by individuals within that system.[29] Recognizing that reality is socially constructed, and thus can be 'changed collectively', is an important aspect of Wiccan justice and ethics.[30] Accepting that one constructs one's identity through language, and that one has the ability to use language to enact change in the world, is also a strong step towards personal empowerment.

The most powerful spells, however, require the Power of Three, a consensus of the Charmed Ones, speaking the spell together and standing in unity against a foe. Each witch can recite or create a spell, but an individual's power may not be sufficient to empower the spell to manifest. For example, when trying to send the adult Charmed Ones back to the 1990s, Grams, portrayed throughout the series as an extremely powerful witch, does not have sufficient power to send the sisters back, even with Patty's help. Only when the sisters – working together in agreement – pronounce the spell does it manifest and transport them forward in time. This act is repeated throughout the series, from using the Power of Three to vanquish the Source of All Evil to the Avatars' need to gain the sisters' consent to cooperate in their attempt to establish Utopia. This connection of the power of the word with collective action and individual power is an important one: no one person, no matter how powerful, can necessarily make a significant change by herself, yet neither can a collective, working together yet unempowered, effect significant change. The interconnection of both empowered individuals and collective action provides an important model for social action: no matter how talented individuals may be, for profound change to happen we must come together, in consensus, to use the power of our words to create change.

Renegar and Sowards, in their exploration of what a theory of rhetoric for third-wave feminists might look like, stress the importance of language in social change. They argue that we must recognize 'the potential transformative power of new language [which] highlights the rhetorical nature of the process of social change'.[31] An examination, then, of how language can cross individual boundaries and encompass diversity is necessary in order to 'suggest avenues by which feminists can participate in the transformation of the existing social order'.[32] Thus, rather than being 'evil rhetors', the sisters are magical rhetors, able to imagine the change they desire in the world and, together, use the magic of language to call that change into being.

The Power of Three

Strength in Numbers and 'Wordy' Witchcraft

Caroline Ruddell

☿

I︫N MUCH OF mainstream cinema a 'lone', often male, hero frequents the screen, but in many examples of 'postfeminist' television shows, such as *Charmed*, the protagonists are accompanied by friends and colleagues who assist them in their adventures. In *Buffy the Vampire Slayer* Buffy has the 'Scooby Gang', in *Xena: Warrior Princess* Xena has Gabrielle, and in *Charmed* Piper, Phoebe and Prue/Paige have each other, as well as assistance from characters like Leo. Part of the focus of this chapter will be the fact that the protagonists of the show are three sisters (rather than one central character); it shall be argued here that their strength and power is continually aligned with sisterhood and their status as a three. Within the premise of a show based on the supernatural, their power is also indicated through magic. The sisters rely not only on each other to defeat their foes (as well as dealing with 'normal' everyday concerns), significantly they also rely heavily on the written word in the form of the Book of Shadows, and their spells are performed as speech acts.[1]

Core to the story arcs of *Charmed* is the fact that 'three' is more powerful than 'one', 'two' or any other number; the show is built on the premise that three Halliwell sister witches must be in existence to draw upon the 'Power of Three' (often through the spoken word in spell format), to enhance their magical power. So important is this to the structure of the show that when one sister dies another must be discovered to replace her. At the close of Season Three the eldest sister Prue dies, and Season Four opens with Piper and Phoebe lacking the Power of Three and therefore feeling not only grief-stricken but also very vulnerable. It is only with the arrival of Paige (their long-lost half-sister) that the Power of Three is reinstated once more, allowing the sisters to continue in the vein of vanquishing demons and saving their 'innocents'. This is only possible if three sister witches exist (and if they are able to perform their magic through the spoken and written word in the form of spells). In an industrial context, television shows such as these are maximizing their audience share by appealing to a wide range of viewers through the inclusion of a variety of characters. The sister witches in *Charmed* are likely to appeal to a range of viewers through their different personalities, as well as their changing identities in relation to magic. What is often most apparent about long-running television series, such as *Charmed*, is the opportunity to develop character and character inter-relations over a substantial length of time, which is specifically related to viewer pleasure.

Through several seasons *Charmed* charts the story of the three sisters as they discover their witch powers and learn to navigate the tricky business of concealing their witch identities from the world while battling the many demonic forces that attack in every episode. Their victories against demonic forces are often directly due to successful spells that the sisters write or find in the Book of Shadows, and then perform (to be explored shortly). The three sisters are placed firmly within the bracket of the 'good', while the many demons they face are depicted as downright evil; magic in the show is therefore based on a Manichaean model where good and evil coexist. Tanya Krzywinska argues that a television show such as *Buffy the Vampire Slayer* blurs the line a little between good and evil, and as such magic can often be seen as relativistic;[2] *Charmed*, however, sticks more rigidly to a good/evil divide.[3] The show also makes much of the difficulties the sisters face when dealing with family life, often in the form of sibling rivalry as well as the affection they clearly feel for each other. The show focuses on the personal lives of these women in terms of careers, relationships and family issues; magic in the show is therefore often directly entwined with the sisters' personalities, emotions and actions in relation to current issues in their life.

For example, in the fifth episode of the first season, 'Dream Sorcerer' (1.5), Piper and Phoebe cast a spell to attract a lover of the opposite sex. Both sisters are feeling lonely and in need of some attention, which is the reasoning behind the performance of the spell (a spoken ritual, performed as speech acts, where the women outline their preferences in men). As often seems to be the case in mainstream television witchcraft, the spell goes awry, or is too strong, and the women receive more attention than they bargained for, to the end that they become afraid of all the attention that they are receiving.[4] Arguably, the moral of the episode is to be careful what you wish for, as Piper and Phoebe pay for casting a 'personal gain' spell to attract the opposite sex, yet the episode also allows magic to comment on the two sisters' state of mind in relation to their romantic lives. By bringing the opposite of the sisters' true feelings about their sex life to fruition, the episode humorously uses magic to make a statement about their emotional state and in turn allows for development of character through literalizing their feelings through magic. Magic becomes therefore a medium of expression within the show, as it is often in *Buffy the Vampire Slayer*.

Within this same episode an unwanted admirer, the 'dream sorceror', stalks Prue; he threatens to kill Prue in her dreams because she shows no interest in him romantically or sexually in the 'real'. Prue is indifferent to a new love interest as she is struggling with her on/off relationship with police officer Andy, with whom she labours to hide her status as witch. The episode allows viewers insight into the characters' state of mind as well as their psychological make-up; Piper and Phoebe are lonely, while Prue struggles with maintaining a difficult relationship and is afraid of being hurt. What is also apparent is Piper's love of romance, domesticity and home cooking, made clear in her spell and therefore choice of man, while Phoebe has a 'wilder' taste in men and Prue's status as the oldest of the three leaves her with more 'grown-up' issues to deal with. These aspects of character are all made evident in the magic used in this episode; Piper and Phoebe's spell is treated with humour while Prue's liaison with the dream sorcerer is depicted as dangerous and potentially fatal.

Similarly in 'From Fear to Eternity' (1.13), a few episodes later, the demon Barbas targets only single witches by bringing their fears to life. The episode hints at the sisters' troubled personal lives; in early seasons they often worry that being witches will doom them to a single life forever, and partners (even Leo, who is fully aware of their identities) often problematize the mix. In this same episode it becomes apparent that Prue avoids saying 'I love you' to her sisters, which they find evasive and guarded. The episode brings out family and personal issues between the sisters and it is through defeating the demon (and her fears) that Prue learns to express her feelings for her sisters. It is also noteworthy that Prue's biggest fear is drowning (which Barbas attempts to do to her through magic) just as their mother did, which links magic to Prue's deep-seated feelings about the death of her mother. Magic and spells continue to be used to comment on the characters' psychological state throughout the series, but what is also striking about the sisters' use of magic is its continual alignment to text and the spoken word, upheld throughout the show (discussed later). Magic is not simply a means to an end in the show but is connected to family, identity and modes of expression; family and ancestry play a large role in shaping the sisters' actions (their mother and grandmother often return from the grave to help them in various situations) and most obvious is the bond between the characters as sisters. Perhaps most apparent in the sisters' use of magic is the fact that three is more powerful than one or two, and this is expressly linked to their blood relations as sisters; this is a thread that runs throughout the show.

The importance of 'three' is made apparent in the very first (aired) episode of the first season, 'Something Wicca This Way Comes' (1.1), where Phoebe returns from New York to stay with Piper and Prue after their grandmother (Grams) has died. The sisters do not know they are witches, as Grams had previously 'hidden' their powers until she felt the sisters were ready to accept them and the responsibility that comes with them. As the sisters continually fought when Grams was alive so they do again upon Phoebe's return; particularly tense is the relationship between the somewhat unruly Phoebe and the rather uptight and responsible Prue.

Despite this tension, Phoebe finds the Book of Shadows[5] (a name that is linked with Gerald Gardner[6] and Wiccan culture in general) in the attic and says the first incantation she finds, which inadvertently lifts Grams' spell and allows the sisters to embrace their newfound powers:

Phoebe: The Book of Shadows.
          Hear now the words of the witches,
          The secrets we hid in the night.
          The oldest of gods are invoked here.
          Great work of magic is sought.
          In this night and in this hour,
          I call upon the ancient power.
          Bring your powers to we sisters three.
          We want the power.
          Give us the power.

Phoebe says the spell as a spoken ritual over the Book of Shadows without intent or will and yet the spell 'works' to allow the sisters to become witches. Ironically, magic brings the sisters closer together, and this is depicted in the visual through a photograph in the house that morphs (through special effects) to show the sisters standing much more closely together than they were in the original photograph. The show makes it apparent in the very first episode that without close sisterhood the three would have little or no power as witches. This is evident throughout the show; for example, the division that Cole[7] causes between Phoebe and her two sisters eventually renders them without the Power of Three when Phoebe chooses Cole over them. This episode also introduces early on the fact that power for the three witches is most often illustrated through the spoken word. At the end of this first episode the witches vanquish their first warlock by chanting 'the power of three will set us free', which further enforces the idea that 'three' is integral to their magic, as well as the spoken and written word; this emblematic incantation is one that the witches use several times in the show.

The concept of 'three' is also exemplified in the narrative of the Season Five episode 'The Day the Magic Died' (5.15), which leaves the world with no magic, good or bad. In this instance the sisters have to rely on each other (without magic) to help themselves and the world. Key to the episode is the fact that life is much more difficult for the sisters without magic, but what is also apparent is that they have strength through their sisterhood as well as their usual powers; their close family ties as sisters inform their power through witchcraft. In this episode Paige and Phoebe attend a summit meeting with demons in an attempt to form a temporary truce so that they can all restore magic to the world (good and bad). As they are suspicious of the demons they prepare various protective weapons such as aerosol cans filled with a range of potions. Viewers are generally used to seeing the witches ably dispatch demons with a flick of Piper's hand or with a spoken spell, but the making of these weapons seems heavy handed, difficult and time consuming. The two sisters (they are without Piper) do escape despite a more difficult battle than usual; their safety is much more endangered in this instance and not just because they have lost their powers, but also because Piper is absent. The sisters win out, however, and Phoebe and Paige manage to get back to the manor (which is how they usually refer to their home) in time to protect Piper and to be there for the birth of her baby. The episode enforces the sisters' strength as a team because even without magic the Power of Three is still strong; at the close of the episode Paige and Phoebe deliver Piper's baby with no help from magic.

In a rather different sense 'three' is also integral to the episode 'Which Prue is it Anyway?' (1.16), where Prue transmutes into three 'Prues' in order to protect herself and her sisters from the demon Luther. The three Prues are literal embodiments of different aspects of Prue's personality: one is the 'real' Prue while the other two are enhancements of her character allowing her to perform much more strongly in the face of evil. Ultimate power in the show is continually linked with the concept of 'three' to the extent that the sisters discourage each other from moving out; they are stronger still when residing in the family house (the manor). For example, despite protest from her sisters, Piper announces she would like to move out in 'Pre-Witched' (3.17) as she has a new life with Leo. However, in the end Piper is uncomfortable leaving the manor and decides to stay. At the close of the episode the

Book of Shadows closes by itself and the symbol (denoting three) glows, which suggests that their magic (symbolized by the book) is stronger when they reside together. This same symbol moves apart when the sisters experience problems and issues between them in this episode; the separated symbol of three, rather than as a 'whole', illustrates the problems they are experiencing as sisters, which in turn leads to problems with their magic.

At several points in the show one of the sisters thinks of leaving, or actually does leave, but it seems that the family history in the house and strong sibling links draw the sisters back to the household and generally keeps them there. Several episodes refer to the sisters' family line and ancestry, such as 'All Halliwell's Eve' (3.4) where the sisters travel back in time in order to protect a coven from witch hunters, only to discover that a baby they save is one of their own ancestors. The sisters' own mother and grandmother are referred to constantly and they even appear at times in ghost form, for example to attend Piper and Leo's wedding. Through referring to the family line of witches the show reminds viewers how powerful the three are in relation to their previous family members, who, while not necessarily operating as individuals, were unable to draw on the Power of Three as the sisters are. The show also draws on authors such as Anne Rice, whose novel *The Witching Hour* (and sequels) depicts an extensive family of witches; such families are present too in films such as *The Witches of Eastwick* (George Miller, 1987, USA) and *Practical Magic* (Griffin Dunne, 1998, USA). In these examples, witches of the present are therefore often able to 'borrow' power from their ancestors, or at least frighten their enemies with the knowledge that they come from a long line of experienced witches. Perhaps most poignantly, the visual presence of the sisters' ancestors (in ghost form or in the many pictures on the walls in the manor) also suggests that power in the show is far from being linked with one person; Piper, Phoebe and Prue/Paige are all powerful in unique ways with their different magical powers, but they are always at their strongest when they use magic together.

While strength (and safety) is clearly indicated through sisterly 'togetherness' in *Charmed*, it is the use of witchcraft that gives the sisters their supernatural power and bolsters their status as both 'different' and 'special'. While in other similar television shows (and film) 'kick-ass' lead female characters dominate the screen (such as Buffy, Xena, or Max in *Dark Angel* and Zoë in *Firefly*), in *Charmed* the sisters' power is articulated largely through witchcraft (which is inseparable from their sisterhood), and is expressed through speech, language and text. I have argued elsewhere that in *Buffy the Vampire Slayer* Willow's magical power (and split identity) is expressly indicated through magical speech and text;[8] here I suggest that in *Charmed* the sisters' expression of power is demonstrated in a very similar way, even though they have learned to defend themselves physically along the way. In postfeminist texts that centre on the supernatural, female power is not only associated with the body, it is also aligned with speech, text and language; in this sense the television witches can have their cake and eat it too as they are physically strong as well as being smart with the written word.

All the sisters possess physical fighting abilities; in earlier seasons Phoebe led the way by learning kickboxing and she continues to use these skills in the sisters' fight against demonic forces. Gradually Prue and Piper also learned some of these skills and utilized them in fights; Paige similarly shows some skill at fighting, although perhaps less so than Piper and Phoebe; she does, after all, have the option of orbing away from danger if necessary. The sisters seem increasingly to use physical violence against demons, yet they cannot vanquish them in this way. The episode 'Bite Me' (4.18), for example, opens with Piper under attack from a Harpy demon; she beats the demon back with some impressive fighting skills, allowing Paige to orb in with Phoebe. They cannot vanquish the demon, however, until they all say a spell together (which presumably one of the sisters had prepared beforehand) and this successfully eliminates the Harpy demon; violence buys the sisters time, but it is only through their magical power, the spoken words of a spell, a potion or Piper's power of vanquishing, that demons can be defeated. Physical strength in the show is not core to destroying enemies (as it is with many male-protagonist-based action films, for example); it is a combination of strengths (physical and otherwise) that allows the sisters to continue to defeat their enemies.

In early episodes, Phoebe's interest in acquiring physical fighting ability seemed to be due to her magic (the power of premonitions) not being an 'active' power; Piper's power of freezing demons and Prue's ability to move things with her mind often left Phoebe feeling a little useless in the actual vanquishing of demons. This roused her initial interest in learning how to defend herself and win a physical fight; however, it also urged her to start researching magic and demons using the Book of Shadows (which in the show is used in the traditional Wiccan sense as it is a personal spell book for the family; the sisters therefore add to the book as they write new spells). In earlier episodes Phoebe was often more prepared in terms of how to vanquish demons than Prue or Piper, although they quickly caught up, particularly Prue.

Phoebe's interest in 'text' also results in her being the first of the sisters to begin writing her own spells, and in the Season Two episode 'Chick Flick' (2.18) Phoebe makes a spell up on the spot:

Prue: Pheebs, we need a spell.
Phoebe: Okay, but we know nothing about this guy. I can't just whip one up.
Prue: Oh, he's making a break for it.
Phoebe: Um, 'evil that has travelled near, I call on you to disappear, elementals hear my call, remove this creature from these walls.'

While this first spell does not have the effect that Phoebe desires, it still gives the impression that she is more confident in spell writing and more familiar with the Book of Shadows and its content; she becomes increasingly adept at making up spells quickly. Phoebe also starts to wear glasses in Season Two, which, in a rather stereotypical manner, outlines her character as more 'bookish' than her two sisters; this also acts as a forerunner to her later job/image as professional columnist/ writer, where she is often seen in glasses bent over a laptop computer. In Seasons Four and Five it appears that Paige takes on the role of researcher; as Phoebe's job of an advice columnist takes up much of her time, Paige is often the sister reading up on the latest demon attack. Paige also leaves her job as a social worker to concentrate full time on being a witch. Paige therefore spends much of her time researching magic, and later becomes aligned with the magic school in the show, further enforcing her academic status.

Paige, as the 'new' youngest sister, shifts easily into the role of researcher when she becomes a Charmed One, and expresses much interest in spell writing, in the Book of Shadows and in ways of vanquishing demons. Paige writes her first spell in the Season Four episode 'Lost and Bound' (4.12) in the form of a haiku, which the sisters perform together:

Piper, Phoebe, Paige: 'The brittle winter gives way to flowers of spring, Ludlow is vanquished.'
Phoebe: What the hell was that?
Paige: It was a haiku. I couldn't do the rhyming thing.

As Paige notes, the spell does not rhyme as is usual of the other sisters' spells; however, it still works and Phoebe expresses her surprise at this. Paige's spell indicates that while the sisters' magic works as a trio, the individualism of each sister comes through in aspects of their magic, such as their spell writing. Just as Paige takes on some of Phoebe's earlier specialities, so Piper takes on the role of eldest sister and much of Prue's former responsibility for her younger siblings. Her power becomes more active, and along with the ability to freeze, she acquires the ability to blow things up and vanquish demons with a swift movement of her hands.

Piper also has a talent for potion making, and she is often seen in the kitchen of the manor bent over a bubbling cauldron or saucepan surrounded by various multi-coloured liquids. In early seasons, potion making linked Piper's magic with her passion for cooking and her desire to own a restaurant. She is often seen in the kitchen cooking up potions either alone or with her sisters, as for example in the beginning of 'Sleuthing With the Enemy' (3.8), where the sisters are in the kitchen surrounded by pots, pans and potion ingredients, or in the Season Six episode 'Love's a Witch' (6.5), where Piper is seen glancing at the Book of Shadows (as if it were a recipe book) and then over several bubbling saucepans surrounded by ingredients on the kitchen table. The scene is lit warmly and in the cosy kitchen Piper looks every part the mother/housewife at home, except she is making a potion rather than a family dinner. The link between potion making and cooking in the show is evident in the ritual of adding correct ingredients and following a recipe, and this in turn is linked to the kitchen and domestic life in the home; Piper can be seen in terms of domesticity as her identity within the sisterhood is often that of homemaker, particularly when she becomes a wife and mother. Piper is also the least enthusiastic of the three about being a witch and on many occasions wishes for a 'normal' life, particularly once she has children.

Potion making remains a constant throughout the show; it is a vital aspect of the sisters' power, and is continually linked with spell making and the sisters' status as 'three'. Potions enforce the sisters' spoken spells and they often make potions together as a trio (either in the kitchen or the attic). Potions seem to provide an extension of power, particularly when combined with spells, and the sisters often brandish potions as weapons, throwing them violently at enemies. For example, with the potion they make to vanquish Cole they each throw a small vial of liquid at him in turn; the potion throwing works as a narrative strategy in that they throw the potions one by one. As Phoebe is the last to throw hers, the show builds tension through a close-up on her face as she pauses. Because of her love affair with Cole this scene builds drama through clear indecision on Phoebe's part as to whether she should vanquish Cole. In a less dramatic episode, 'House Call' (5.13), all three sisters prepare a potion to summon a witch doctor as their house has been taken over by the residue of all the evil demons they have vanquished there. Phoebe says a spell, followed by Paige throwing in the last ingredient:

> *Phoebe:*   Uh, get the snakeskin ready, and after I read the spell, then
>   you [to Paige] throw it in.
>   Free us from the ties that bind,
>   Of evil magic intertwined,
>   We call upon The One who cures,
>   He who's to The Dark inured.
> *Paige:*   Ready?
> *Witch Doctor:*   How may I be of service?

In this instance, the combination of the Power of Three, a potion and a spoken spell results in the appearance of the witch doctor. While potions provide a large part of the sisters' power, it is the use of text and the spoken word (through spoken and written spells and the Book of Shadows), and the combination of these magical elements, that provides the sisters with their most active fighting power on a long-term basis.

The sisters' power is linked most strongly in the first instance to the Book of Shadows and secondly to their emotions. The Book of Shadows provides the sisters with their power in the first episode and it continues to provide a source of information, spells and potion recipes for the witches. Leo (the sisters' guide and Whitelighter[9]) suggests that the book is in fact an extension of themselves. This is evident in the book's continual growth through each Halliwell generation (as more is added). The book is so important to the Halliwells that, unless tampered with, it cannot leave the house and it protects itself from evil by not allowing anyone who is not 'good' to touch it (as for example at the beginning of 'The Power of Three Blondes' (6.4), where three evil sisters attempt to steal the book but it moves itself away each time they try to take it). In the Season Two episode 'Witch Trial' (2.1) the demon Abraxas does manage to steal the book through the use of dark magic. He reads it backwards, which removes the text from the book and undoes the good magical work done by the sisters. In order to reverse this and restore their book the sisters have to recall a spell from memory and speak it aloud to vanquish Abraxas, which they do effectively: 'Hear now the words of the witches, the secrets we hid in the night, the oldest of gods are invoked here, the great work of magic is sought . . . In this night, and in this hour we call upon the ancient power.' The episode brings to light the importance of the book (as well as text and the spoken word) to their magic, as without it they would lose all their powers. This text is integral to their performance of magic as spoken words or speech acts. The book therefore provides a basis for performative speech/magic acts.

Furthermore, the recollection of the spell in 'Witch Trial' seems to have a Gardnerian influence, as well as more general aspects of Wiccan practice (as does much of the show, perhaps most notably with the name of the Book of Shadows, but other examples include the use of crystals, casting the circle and pentagrams). In his *The Meaning of Witchcraft* Gardner discusses the idea of words 'speaking themselves', and he suggests that memory must not hinder this process. He writes:

> I prefer to think that doing the imitative act, making the model of the thing, etc., are simply useful means of focusing the mind. This is reinforced and driven into the unconscious mind by a repetition of words (the Spell). This need not be in the form of a rhyme at all, but rhythm or alliteration are an aid to memory; that is, you cannot drive a thing into your unconscious and fix your mind pinpointed on your object if you have to stop and think what the next word is, and the act of reading distracts your attention, however slightly. In fact, you want something which almost says itself.[10]

In a similar line of thought, Kevin Saunders (a Wiccan writer and practitioner) suggests '[s]peech is used in ritual to help strengthen the visualisation and thus the power of one's will'.[11] Both these Wiccan writers (or magical practitioners) suggest the importance of the spoken word in ritual, and *Charmed* makes use of Wiccan-based concepts such as this throughout the show.

For Saunders, and in much Wiccan practice, the power of will can be strengthened through the spoken word. Will or intent in the show – in a magical sense – is intriguing; the sisters seem to need to have faith in themselves and their magic for it to be successful, and as a result if they experience emotional problems, or a lack of will, their magic suffers (as discussed below). Will is not always necessary for a spell to work, however. For example in 'Animal Pragmatism' (2.13) three of Phoebe's university friends use a recording of Phoebe's voice saying a spell to turn animals into men (they cannot do this themselves as they have no power):

Andrea: Okay, let's do this. Say it with me.
Andrea, Tessa, Brooke: From strike of twelve count twenty-four, that's how long the spell is for, turn these gifts into a mate, and then my lonely heart abate.
Tessa: Okay, that was fun. Can I go now?
Andrea: Wait, didn't Phoebe say some of the words were wrong?
Brooke: Why don't you call her?
Andrea: I don't have to. The power of technology.
Phoebe's voice: No dates required. From strike of twelve count twenty-four, that's how long the spell is for, if to abate my lonely heart, enchant these gifts I thee impart.

Phoebe has no intent in this instance as her friends simply recorded her as they were discussing witchcraft, while she did not believe it to be a serious conversation. Unlike other forms of will-based magic, the spell does work however: animals are turned into three naked men as the correct words are spoken by a powerful witch, despite the fact she is not even there.

Often in the show the sisters must vanquish a demon by saying a spell together. In terms of the visual appeal of the show, the use of spells spoken by the three indicates clearly that their power is strongest when they are three and it allows for supernatural elements to come into play as often spells are followed by special effects where the demon vanishes into thin air. For example, in the final vanquishing of Cole (albeit a rare instance when a potion without a spell is enough to despatch him), an image of his skull is superimposed with the image of his face in agony before he disappears into a ball of fire. More often demons visually disintegrate or disappear in a fireball after a spell, potion or a combination of both has vanquished them. The show suggests that words have power, and particular words will have certain effects if spoken by the right person in the right order; the show therefore makes use of a pre-Structuralist model of language where words have power and can mean very different things for different beings.[12] Similarly, the show also draws on superstitions around words, or the idea that words may have power, as discussed by J.G. Frazer in relation to certain cultures and the power of ancestors' names.[13]

Just as text and the spoken word are integral to the sisters' magic, so are their emotions and relationship with each other. Leo tells the sisters many times that their powers are linked to their emotions. In 'Primrose Empath' (3.6) Prue is tricked by Cole into taking on the attributes of an Empath, who can feel others' emotions; she is not meant to have this power and it almost drives her insane but it also allows her to get in touch with other peoples' feelings. Within the episode Prue comments that her power is linked to her emotions generally but the episode highlights that emotion, magic and indeed family are closely intertwined throughout the show.

Similarly, in 'Exit Strategy' (3.20) Phoebe states that Piper's emotions are linked to her magic as she starts blowing things up instead of freezing them, which is her usual power. Piper's stress in trying to organize 'normal' aspects of life such as getting a passport (so that she and Leo may go on a honeymoon) while Leo is constantly called to the Elders causes her stress levels to rise, and her power of freezing transforms into a more violent power. Such a transformation is exemplary of the show's conflation of magic with emotion. Piper has to learn over time to control her newfound power and it eventually becomes an asset to the three. Phoebe and Paige's magic is also linked to their emotional states in further episodes. In 'The Eyes Have It' (5.6) Phoebe's stress at being overworked as a newspaper columnist causes her to lose her power of premonition; it is only on gaining a more balanced lifestyle that she regains it. In 'A Paige from the Past' (4.10) Paige's trauma at losing her adoptive parents in a car accident is revisited in the episode and it becomes apparent that the younger Paige, who was also in the car, orbs out during the accident without realizing it; her power was achieved through this traumatic event, which links her magic to her emotion from an early stage. Power for the three is therefore linked to their emotional state, as well as magical text through the Book of Shadows and their many spoken spells.

Charmed is a show that allows for three protagonists to have equal weighting in terms of screentime and storylines. As noted earlier, this is an industrial strategy that opens up more possibilities for viewer identification. *Charmed* is also one of a number of shows that centralizes the concept of female power and this is indicated largely through the supernatural power of witchcraft, which ultimately relies on the written word and spoken spells for its greatest effectiveness. As a trinity the witches are extremely powerful, and while this is indicated through their sisterhood, use of potions, and various other devices, the text of the Book of Shadows and the spoken word in spell form continue to provide their most constant power. By allowing their emotions to fuel their magic the sisters manage to defeat most of the evil that comes their way, which is arguably related to them trusting their emotion and instinct, notions that are often traditionally linked to the concept of the feminine.

The show does provide a positive model for female viewers in that the characters are powerful and are more than capable of vanquishing their enemies; between the three sisters they also manage to have successful careers as well as family life, and on top of that they manage to maintain their witch identities. However, the show also places the sisters' power within the framework of a traditional gender view where femininity is continually aligned with the home and – in particular – family values, which are most apparent in their close sisterhood. Central to the show is that without being 'three' the Charmed Ones cannot exist and their magic could never have materialized, and indeed the Book of Shadows is expressly linked to the sisters as a group of three and is indicated as such through the symbol of the triquetra. As a three they can defeat all manner of evil, and it is always as a trio that they gather the most strength; three, it seems, certainly is the magic number.

'We Are Witches, Dear. We Can Do Anything'

Dynamics of Ritual, Familial Tradition and Female Identity in Charmed

SABINE SCHMIDT

ITUALS AND RITUALISTIC behaviour always have been and still are an integral part of human life and human societies, in tribal communities as well as in modern, post-industrialized societies. Like myths, their function and form is subject to historical and social change. They can serve to worship gods and other deities, to ward off evil, to influence the forces of nature. As rites of passage they can indicate and sanction the development of the individual and his or her standing in their society, for instance in the form of the Holy Communion, the confirmation or the bar mitzvah. They also can emphasize the symbolic portent of marriages or funerals, graduations, inaugurations, sports events – to name but a few.

In the past, rituals have been seen as instruments of social control, with the focus on religious rituals and ethnological field studies of so-called 'primitive societies' emphasizing the static and conservative nature of the ritual act. In contrast, modern research projects study ritual as a dynamic process and ask questions about the presence of ritual in our everyday life, for instance in phenomena like online religion, fan communities, or the use of rituals as a political tool. They ask about the origin and the disappearance of rituals, about their flexibility in a society subjected to change and about their function. As a result of the inter-, even multi-disciplinary approach in 'ritual studies', a wide range of definitions exist. Every act that follows a preordained order can become a ritual, depending on the intent of the people doing or observing the act, the presence of certain material objects, or the use of specialised language and gestures.[1] What do ritual and modern ritual theory, one might be tempted to ask, have to do with the TV show *Charmed* and its protagonists?

Prue, Piper, Phoebe and (later) Paige use potions, spells and incantations to defeat the warlocks, demons and other 'forces of evil' threatening them and the innocents in their care. This raises the question how the Charmed Ones use these ritualistic elements – and how they grow individually and collectively as the Power of Three by doing so.

One might also consider the origins of most of the rituals they use; in other words, to ask about the Book of Shadows, their family's legacy and their subsequent acceptance or rejection of their inheritance. The Charmed Ones' fight for the 'greater good' of humanity – the goal of most modern uses of rituals or ritualizations – thus takes place in the tension-filled area between tradition and innovation, between adherence to protocol and rebellion, between status quo and change.

The following subsections will first show how a typical ritual in *Charmed* works, by analysing the introductory scene of the show's pilot and then by examining the Halliwells' use of ritual. I will investigate the possible connection between the way ritualized elements are used and the self-awareness and self-assurance of the Charmed Ones as women and witches. This chapter will examine how the dynamic use of rituals, a demanding familial tradition, potentially disruptive elements in the form of 'good' or 'evil' supernatural creatures, individual preferences and social expectations – especially in areas concerning personal, sexual and professional fulfilment – form a potentially explosive mixture of dichotomies.

'She Was a Solitary Practioner'
– Or the Witch as She Should Be

> Auger de gomay. Auger de gomay.
> Ancient One of the Earth so deep,
> Master of Moon and Sun,
> I shield you in my Wiccan way,
> Here in my circle round,
> Asking you, protect this space,
> And offer your sun force down.

The first episode of the show *Charmed*, 'Something Wicca This Way Comes' (1.1), shows a young woman, later identified as Serena Fredricks, feeding her cat, kneeling in front of an altar and chanting the above words after lighting several candles with the tip of her index finger.

This eighty-three-second sequence thus contains all the elements of a ritual, in this case a religious ritual. It introduces the main themes of the show: witchcraft and the use of ritual, the existence of supernatural powers and the threat from warlocks, demons and others. It also provides the viewing public with a matrix of how witches 'normally' worship and practise, as well as presenting the inherent dangers of this practice.

Serena's altar is set up on a low round table covered with a dark-blue cloth. It is decorated with dried plants, a bowl of herbs, a small knife, something resembling a straw puppet and three red, three white and three dark-green candles. These mostly ordinary items are taken out of their natural context and put into a devotional setting that endows them with a symbolic portent and value about which one can but speculate – due to the lack of further information and the fact that Serena is killed before she can bring the ritual to its end. Together with the silver chalice she deposits in the centre of the altar table, these objects stand for the 'material plane' necessary for every ritual.[2]

The young woman consecrates the room by lighting the candles and thus and only then does she validate the symbolic arrangement on the table (the 'material plane') as an altar. Her devotional posture and formal gestures, together with other ritualized movements, form the so-called 'kinetic plane' and thus are constitutive of the creation of a sacral area as an indispensable requirement for the 'verbal plane' of the ritual. This verbal plane is the prayer itself, which starts with the invocation of a higher power, a mysterious – or at least not easily identifiable – entity: 'Auger de gomay'.[3]

Serena shows her respect to the 'Master of Moon and Sun' but her prayer is not just a supplication to an omnipotent being. She not only asks for protection, she also offers it, and in a way proves her ability to 'shield' the addressee of the prayer in her 'Wiccan way' by showing her mastery over the fire; she proves her worthiness. Serena's relationship with this being or entity or god is supposed to be of mutual benefit, and as such transcends the confines of worship and enters the realm of a protective ritual. It does not put her on an equal footing with the divine but is a testament of her self-confidence and a fundamental statement on the reciprocal nature of her religious beliefs.[4]

The young woman's calm demeanour and the fluidity of her movements leave no doubt that these private devotions are an integral part of her (daily) routine, as natural as feeding her cat. The fact that her altar is not relegated to behind the doors of a closet or put in a corner of the bedroom like a Catholic prayer chair from the past, but is instead situated in the middle of her living room corroborates this interpretation. It furthermore indicates that there is no break between the practice of her religion and her normal daily life.

In the end, however, neither her half-spoken protection spell, nor her seemingly unambiguous practice of her 'Wiccan ways', nor her poised self-confidence can save her from the power-hungry warlock who kills her to gain her powers. The fact that Serena is murdered by someone she knew well, Piper's fiancé Jeremy, furthermore hints at the recurrent problems inherent in the combination of magical abilities and responsibilities with the pursuit of personal happiness as a 'normal' woman.

Serena's efficient use of the 'material', the 'kinetic' and the 'verbal plane' of a ritual leaves no doubt that she follows a well thought-out and well-practised legacy. The Halliwell sisters, in contrast, seem to improvise a great deal throughout the show, at least during the early seasons. Later their improvisations are based on knowledge and experience rather than luck.

The Charmed Ones, however, always rely heavily on the fact that they were born witches. They have innate 'supernatural' abilities: Prue and Paige move objects with their minds, Piper can freeze time, and Phoebe sees the future; these are powers that will grow to astonishing proportions over time.[5] In fact, despite meeting the founder of their line, Melinda Warren, early in Season One ('The Witch is Back', 1.9), they only gain an appreciation for the traditions of witchcraft and magic, as well as the wisdom lost over the centuries, in the Season Three episode 'All Halliwell's Eve' (3.4).

'The Witch's Journey is a Walk of Wisdom Collected Over the Years'

At the beginning of the show the sisters almost completely depend upon the Book of Shadows and its recipes. However, a humorous reference to a mistake in 'Ms. Hellfire' (2.9) indicates that they still have much to learn.[6] In 'All Halliwell's Eve' they learn that magic and magical rituals have as much to do with knowledge as with 'natural' powers: Prue, Piper, and Phoebe are sent back to the seventeenth century to rescue a young woman named Charlotte and her soon-to-be-born daughter from the influence of the evil witch Ruth Cobb (who in turn gets support from the also time-travelling Cole/Belthazor). Stripped of their powers because, as the audience later learns, their ancestor Melinda Warren is the baby they were sent to save,[7] the sisters have to learn how to use the magic and power inherent in nature, how to use rituals and ritualized acts.

They learn about the power and wisdom of women; they learn how to use a broomstick to sweep evil from one's path, how to centre one's magic with the help of a conical hat. They learn that 'there is magic all around you', especially on All Hallow's Eve. They also gain a new appreciation for this wisdom and their heritage as well as their sexual and cultural identity as women – or, in the words of the midwife Eva: 'Wisdom gives us power. Power frightens the fearful and the ignorant'. Prue's initial scepticism about her destiny by then has turned into wholehearted affirmation: 'We were born witches. That makes us innately magical.'

This episode marks a turning point in the show. The sisters finally accept that they need more than their innate powers to fight evil. They accept that to perform their vanquishing rituals successfully they need knowledge: the knowledge of how to use the forces inherent in nature and the knowledge of how to use 'ritual' effectively in their fight. It emerges that they are really 'fast learners': at the end of 'All Halliwell's Eve' Phoebe flies through the air on a broomstick, 'embracing the cliché' of the witch and finally embracing their heritage. So, when Paige is called upon to restore the Power of Three after Prue's death, Piper's insistence that their half-sister studies herb lore makes it more than evident that they really have learned their lesson. Phoebe explains, 'Paige, Piper and I had to learn how to be witches the hard way, and it took . . . well, it took too long. We need you to get there faster. Our lives may depend on it' ('Enter the Demon', 4.4).[8]

This raises the question of why the sisters needed such a long time to embrace this lesson. One answer might be found in the way the sisters received their powers in the first place. When Phoebe, shortly after returning to her ancestral/maternal home, finds the Book of Shadows and reads the incantation, there is no special setting, there are no prearranged objects, no altar, and no intent beyond natural curiosity and deeply ingrained stubbornness – at least at first.

The spirit board that spells 'attic', the closed and then mysteriously opening door to the attic, the light illuminating the trunk that holds the book, the trunk suddenly glowing from the inside: all these elements contribute to create, for the observer, a sense of not only anticipation but of a sacral area. According to 'ritual studies' the perspective and intent of the observer are enough to make a simple act into a ritual. In other words, these elements create the 'material plane' for what is about to come, for the incantation that awakens the sisters' inherited powers.

> Hear now the words of the witches,
> The secrets we hid in the night.

> The oldest of gods are invoked here.
> The great work of magic is sought.
> In this night and in this hour,
> I call upon the ancient power.
> Bring your powers to we sisters three.
> We want the power.
> Give us the power.[9]

Here the 'verbal plane' is not supplemented by a 'kinetic plane' and no specific entity is invoked but the 'oldest of Gods' and the 'Ancient power' that remain nameless. The syntax shows no devotional elements but with the repeated exclamation marks an imperative with only the barest hint of courtesy. That indicates a position of strength and independence not found in the introductory scene. As soon as the words are spoken, the audience witnesses that they really had an effect, thus validating it as an immediately successful ritual act: the chandelier on the ground floor begins to jingle and glow, and the images of the sisters in the photograph taken by their grandmother shortly before her death move closer together, symbolizing their belonging – or as Piper later says, 'it made us sisters again'[10] – and their collective power.

Though Phoebe has an instinctive inkling of the possibilities these words could entail,[11] she does not yet know that she just performed a ritual that has been in the making for several hundred years, from the beginning of the Halliwell line with Melinda Warren in the late seventeenth century. It was she who put the first spell in the Book of Shadows and it thus can be assumed that she also wrote the empowering incantation. While spending the night reading the book, Phoebe learns that Melinda foretold of the coming of the Charmed Ones, 'the most powerful witches the world has ever known', and Melinda gave them the legacy of protecting the innocent.[12] They thus are thrust into a new situation and are forced to adapt their sense of self and their expectations to this changed reality.

'The Power of Three Will Set Us Free'
– Between Initiation and Acceptance

The incantation Phoebe read did, however, only activate the powers with which the sisters were born. They quickly learn that their individual powers alone are not sufficient to fight demons and warlocks; they have to use the Power of Three.

In 'Something Wicca This Way Comes' the Charmed Ones only can defeat Jeremy by using the 'verbal' and the 'kinetic plane', by repeatedly chanting what their mother inscribed on the back of the spirit board: 'The Power of Three will set us free',[13] by taking each other's hands and thus creating some sort of protective circle, by standing united against him, with the attic as a given 'material plane'. In this episode they have to repeat the spell thirteen times to make it work.[14] In 'Witch Trial' (2.1) the demon Abraxas steals the Book of Shadows and brings Jeremy back. This time, at the beginning of Season Two and supposedly one year after becoming witches, the sisters only need to perform three repetitions, and they utter these via speakerphone. The vanquishing ritual is thus reduced to the 'verbal plane' only, which on the one hand shows their growing mastery in the use of their collective powers but on the other hand hints of arrogance.

'Witch Trial' does have another even more ritually relevant function in the show. Moments before Abraxas steals the Book of Shadows it opens to a page entitled 'Rite of Passage' – and that is what the episode really is about: to teach the sisters about the true essence, the core of the Power of Three. It indirectly evokes one of the groundbreaking classics of 'ritual studies', *Les rites de passage* by Arnold van Gennep, first published in 1909. As an ethnologist and cultural anthropologist, his main interest was in rituals of initiation, rites of passage. He postulated that almost every ritual consists, simply put, of three parts: separation from 'normality', a period of transition, and the entrance in a new, modified 'normality'.[15]

Put on a grand scale, becoming witches signifies the sisters' separation from 'normality', the first season functions as a period of transition Gennep called *rites de marge* and with 'Witch Trial' the sisters enter a new 'normality'. Throughout the first season they only occasionally invoke the Power of Three – 'Dominus Trinum', as the Book of Shadows calls it – but now they learn to see themselves as a unity, they learn 'to be as one' and finally recognize the symbolism of the triquetra on the cover of the Book of Shadows; they actively affirm the legacy of the Warren/Halliwell witches. The 'power of one' the Book of Shadows spoke about at the beginning of the episode turned out to be the Power of Three used as one.

By performing this *rite d'agrégation* at the end of the episode the sisters also return to a more traditional form of ritualistic behaviour than at the beginning. They consciously set the 'material plane' by choosing a location already seen and blessed as sacred, the altar stone in the park. By taking each other's hands and repeatedly chanting the empowering incantation together (which previously only had been spoken once and by Phoebe alone), they actively reclaim their heritage by enacting the 'kinetic' and the 'verbal plane'. Their adherence to what, with the show's introductory scene, has been established as 'typical' ritualistic behaviour thus validates the Book of Shadows, and with the book, the wisdom and power of their ancestors.[16] Consequently, at the end of the episode, the sisters are rewarded by the appearance of their late grandmother, and – despite the earlier summoning of Melinda and their trip to the past – it is only from then on that they can rely on the power and the help of their fore-mothers.

A striking example can be found in Season Four's episode 'Charmed and Dangerous' (4.13), when Piper, Phoebe and Paige call upon the powers and strength of the witches before them to destroy the Source: 'Prudence, Patricia, Penelope, Melinda, Astrid, Helena, Laura and Grace, Halliwell witches stand strong beside us, vanquish this evil from time and space'. They call upon their ancestors (though not all of them are explicitly named), thus actively affirming a long line of strong female role models. More than once they invoke the help of their mother and grandmother as just two examples. In 'Happily Ever After' (5.3) their grandmother Penny Halliwell helps them to save the fairy tales as we know them and thus the future of good magic, and in 'Witchstock' (6.11) she helps Leo and Chris to fight a 'magical blob' while the sisters are once again in the past – this time the 1960s – to save their present.[17] The importance of this family tradition is further emphasized by the Wiccaning ceremonies for Piper's sons, Wyatt and Chris, performed by their great-grandmother, Penny Halliwell.

> I call forth from space and time
> Matriarchs from the Halliwell line,
> Mothers, daughters, sisters, friends,
> Our family spirit without end,
> To gather now in this sacred place
> And help us bring this child to grace.[18]

We Are Witches, Dear. We Can Do Anything'
– Between Legacy and Individuality

After they had learned how to perform vanquishing and other rituals, accepted their legacy and embraced the familial tradition, one would think that the Charmed Ones could settle into some sort of routine; and in a way they do. They use the Power of Three with true virtuosity but they also become rather complacent, taking their power for granted and unwittingly giving their opponents many opportunities.

Each of the four sisters at one point or another is unable to accept the 'new reality', the new 'normality' they found and seemingly embraced at the end of 'Witch Trial'. Their preconceived notions of a 'normal life', a life without magic and an ordinary heterosexual family unit, and their dogged determination to reclaim such a life whatever the cost leads one to believe that they failed the 'rite of passage' after all.

This last subsection of the chapter will try to shed light on the dynamic between the acceptance of the Halliwell/Warren legacy and the use of ritual either to reject or embrace this heritage. Though Prue is the first to voice her respective concerns in 'Something Wicca This Way Comes' and again in 'Witch Trial' after Andy's death,[19] the sister who has the biggest problems with their Wiccan destiny is definitely Piper.[20]

In the aftermath of Piper being infected with a tropical fever in 'Awakened' (2.12) her doctor, Curtis Williamson, becomes obsessed with her quick and unexplained recovery that 'makes no clinical sense'.[21] He continues his research by injecting three chimpanzees with the blood of the sisters and accidentally gets infected himself.[22] Dr Williamson learns quickly how to use the new powers but, as Leo predicted, he is unable really to handle them. In his need to save lives, starting with the life of his sister, Williamson not only harms others by using criminals as involuntary organ donors, he loses perspective of right and wrong, and becomes a murderer. Williamson is no longer an innocent whom the sisters have to protect but a dangerous foe whom they have no choice but to kill when he refuses to relinquish his/their powers.[23]

Despite this example, the Charmed Ones' longing for a normal life gets stronger through the years and seasons and culminates in Season Seven's episode 'Charmageddon' (7.13). To escape their familial legacy, Piper, Phoebe and Paige help the Avatars to perform a complicated but all in all anticlimactic ritual to create a world where the dichotomy of good and evil, supposedly, no longer exists. Thus they no longer have to choose between their old, pre-witched 'normality' and the ritualistic demands of their demon-fighting existence. They use ritual to escape the use of ritual; they use ritual to negate the very basis of ritualized acts. This 'extreme make-over' comes at a very high price, the price of free will and deep emotions.[24] Only when the sisters threaten to side with Zankou and the rest of the underworld do the Avatars consent to undo the changes, with the notable exception of Paige's boyfriend.

In 'Charmageddon' Piper and her sisters use ritual to escape their familial destiny and undo their mistake by using their supernatural powers. In 'Witch Trial' it worked the other way: they used ritual to reclaim that same legacy. In any case, their use of ritual is guided by the sisters' intentions and feelings, just as a routine act depends upon the perception and/or the intent of the performers to become a ritual – one only has to think of the many times the Charmed Ones get drawn into something through a ritual performed by one of their enemies. In this sense, the rituals enacted in *Charmed* do not have a worth in and of themselves but are only filled with meaning according to the needs of the participants and the audience.[25]

To put it bluntly, the success of the rituals performed by the Charmed Ones, and thus their track record against the forces of evil, are inextricably linked with the degree of their acceptance of their destiny. This explains why in 'Once Upon a Time' (3.3) the Power of Three spell Prue has written does not work at first: Piper has a hard time coping with the fact that the Elders have taken Leo away from her. Only after she manages to put her personal problems aside does the spell work, and they can save Kate and the Fairy Princess Thistle.

In 'Power Outage' (3.7) the connection becomes painfully obvious when Cole/Belthazor incites the demon Andras to amplify the sisters' negative emotions. Insignificant disagreements and frustrations quickly grow to incredible proportions in their minds, and they end up using their powers against each other, thus breaking apart the triquetra and severing the Power of Three. Not only do they lose their collective power, but they also lose their individual powers because – as Leo explains – their 'powers are routed in [their] bond as sisters' and the book is 'an extension' of their bond.[26] To reclaim their power they have to work through their differences and prove that they are once again a united front by facing Belthazor together.

In the end, the Power of Three, the fact that they are sisters standing together, is more important than their needs as women (even in Season Eight), their performance of rituals, and their necessary or recreational use of their individual powers.[27] Rituals, as well as the sisters' powers, are in this regard nothing more but a means to an end – and all in all it might be the Halliwells' unity as sisters and best friends that make the show so successful with a female audience. They are, however, an indispensable means to an end because it is not the awakening of their individual powers that brings them back together after their estrangement before and after their grandmother's death, it is the need to perform rituals, to exercise the Power of Three that 'makes them sisters again'.

'We are witches, dear. We can do anything'. These words of encouragement are spoken by Penny Halliwell to her granddaughters in 'That '70s Episode' (1.17). These words may come from the past, but they are nonetheless characteristic of the overall message of the show. Women respecting the forces of nature and tradition, and women who stand together can do anything.

The Power of Three as Communitas

Moments of Subversion on Charmed

VALERIE CARROLL

3

*C*HARMED IS BOTH a text of compliance and a text of resistance. Like many portrayals of females on television, *Charmed* simultaneously presents women as agents and victims of patriarchal power, power that uses social rewards and punishments to define females stereotypically as subordinate. The sisters on *Charmed*, Prue, Piper, Phoebe and Paige, are caught in the disciplinary power of patriarchy, which persuades females to diminish their own power by focusing on non-threatening aspects such as physical appearance and romantic heterosexual relationships. If this were all that *Charmed* portrayed then it would be redundant to write about the show. Numerous feminist scholars and writers have examined the way that portrayals in US popular culture present women who police themselves to conform to patriarchal standards of stereotypical female behaviour. However, while it is true that *Charmed* embraces the stereotypical ideals of females, it is imperative to recognize that it also presents moments of subversion to patriarchal and dominating power. The fact that these subversive moments are embedded within the series, sometimes hidden from plain view, makes *Charmed* a powerful portrayal of resistance.

Subversive moments appear by reading the first seven seasons of *Charmed* as a narrative that questions, analyses and offers alternatives to current societal views about women, power, social institutions and knowledge. This evidence begins with the first episode of *Charmed*, where subversion is enacted through the portrayal of what John Fiske names *communitas*: an alternative community in which outsiders can develop 'self-identities denied them by the dominant power structure'.[1] Within the *Charmed communitas* the sisters form and control their identities by employing alternative knowledges and practices including care ethics, witchcraft and female-headed family structures to resist identities and roles imposed upon women by a patriarchal dominant power.

Power

Within American culture, patriarchy is a dominating power. Patriarchy refers to a social system that associates dominant roles, values and ideals with the masculine while simultaneously associating subordinate roles, values and ideals with the feminine. This obviously gives the most benefits to the male and the least to the female. However, other dominating powers coexist and mutually reinforce patriarchy, for example domination based on race and class. To use Michel Foucault's construct, these mutually reinforcing power structures are referred to as *disciplinary power* or the structured relationship between the dominant and subordinate groups where the dominant and powerful in a culture control predominantly by training subordinates to act in a manner that benefits the powerful. That is, disciplinary power trains subordinate or marginalized groups and individuals through social rewards and punishments to police themselves into acting, believing and knowing in a way that benefits the powerful. Foucault's disciplinary power is a 'permanent coercion' which creates 'automatic docility' of subordinate groups.[2] The most insidious aspects of disciplinary power is that this training is naturalized; it is made to seem as though the actions or beliefs of the culture are normal and even inherent in humans rather than socially constructed.

One example of this training of the marginalized is evident in the patriarchal construction of romance infused within US culture. Patriarchy teaches women early in life that a heterosexual romantic relationship is their ultimate goal and the source of ultimate happiness.[3] This benefits the powerful, in this case the male, because it means that women focus heavily on heterosexual romance rather than on other aspects of life like political power and equality. In *Charmed*, it means a reining-in of female power because the patriarchal construction of romance defines women as subordinate. The very images we have of romance establish the female as the less powerful – think of the muscular man holding the passive damsel in his arms on romantic novel covers. Moreover, if romance is the ultimate goal for females and female power (be it political, economic or physical) prevents the attainment of this goal, the implication is that females should relinquish or at least hide their own power. The romance narrative as a disciplinary power technique is internalized by females as natural and commonsensical rather than a social construction that benefits patriarchal power.[4] The sisters on *Charmed* portray the internalization of the patriarchal construction of romance through their intense focus on heterosexual romantic relationships as absolutely imperative to life. Time after time, the sisters state that they 'cannot give up on love' and that they want a 'normal life'.[5] What this means is an overwhelming desire for a heterosexual romance *and* it means they are willing to hide or give up their own vast and important magical power to achieve this romantic ideal. All the sisters continually focus on romance, but Piper is the best representative of the relationship between patriarchal constructions of romance.

Piper repeatedly expresses her desire for what she calls a 'normal life'. By normal, she means having a heterosexual romantic relationship. Again and again, she has proclaimed her desire to give up her powers so she can have a date, a boyfriend and eventually a 'real' marriage and family with Leo.[6] Piper's willingness to give up her power demonstrates the incompatibility of female power with romance as patriarchy constructs it. Piper's desires represent a gendered belief that establishes female power as fundamentally incompatible with, and thereby preventative of, romantic love. Her willingness to give up power in order to have a romantic relationship and a 'normal' life values a heterosexual romance above other goals. This desire is incongruent with her power as a witch, a position in which she is not subordinate to the men in her life. Piper's relationship dilemmas are thus a small aspect of the way that the series is both a victim and an agent of patriarchal power. It reflects the reality for women in US culture where females are indeed expected to focus on the attainment of the romantic ideal to the detriment of their own power. It is also a teaching story about gendered expectations and roles. As such, Piper's relationships are a part of disciplinary power's training of female subordination to make it seem natural that females should be willing and even eager to give up power in order to attain romance.

In contrast, other teaching stories on *Charmed* portray resistance, and even subversion to disciplinary/patriarchal power. These stories show how the marginalized can and do resist that power. The cultural theorist John Fiske, expanding on Foucault's work, developed a theoretical construct to explain how individuals and groups deemed subordinates in a culture engage in resistance strategies and practices against dominant disciplinary power. 'Localizing power' refers to subordinate groups, individuals and practices that resist – but never overthrow – the disciplinary power of dominant groups. Localizing power serves as a means of self-preservation and self-identification by employing resistant strategies to attempt to defend against, as best they can, the power of dominant social groups that positions them lower in the hierarchy and defines them as subordinate.[7]

We see both the disciplinary power and the first moments of subversion in the premiere episode of *Charmed*. In this episode, 'Something Wicca This Way Comes' (1.1), Prue and Piper have internalized dominant beliefs and ideals. In fact, they both live a rather mundane life. Prue has a career as museum curator and Piper is attempting to gain employment as a chef. Piper has a boyfriend and Prue an ex-fiancé. They own a house that comes with all the expectations of home ownership, like waiting for the electrician to come to mend the lights. All in all it is a commonplace, mainstream existence. However, once Phoebe, the youngest, returns, the establishment of the sisters as outsiders becomes clear. Of the three sisters, Phoebe is the farthest outside the mainstream. She is a college drop-out who has failed to 'make it' in New York. She returns to the family home because she has lost everything except one bag of belongings and a bicycle. Prue does not approve.[8]

The first episode of *Charmed* presents a conflict between the mainstream and the marginalized through the estrangement of Prue and Phoebe. As mentioned before, Prue represents the establishment order. As an established professional woman, she is the most integrated, the most successful, and the most 'responsible' of the three sisters. Phoebe is the opposite: she is the least rewarded and the most disciplined because, as an unemployed college drop-out, she does not conform to cultural expectations. She has the most conflicts with authority. For example, we learn in a later episode that the police caught Phoebe shoplifting.[9] Moreover, for the first several seasons, Phoebe cannot get and keep a job. Phoebe represents the subordinate and outsider; while her outsider status is in many ways voluntary – she chooses to be a 'free spirit' – she is still symbolically the subordinate outsider.

What is important about Phoebe is that while she is the most marginalized, she also is the one with the clearest vision of the sisters as outsiders and subordinates as well as of the sisters' destiny as the Charmed Ones. This clear vision manifests itself literally by the fact that Phoebe has the power of premonition. While this assignation is most likely ironic since, as Prue explained, 'the girl has no vision, no sense of the future', it also represents Phoebe's 'outsider within' status.[10] Phoebe exists both within and on the margins of the mainstream; because she is both inside and outside her fictional culture, she can more clearly understand and critique the dominant social order. That is, those who exist both within and outside a culture can often see the mainstream power structures and disciplinary techniques more clearly (while conversely, the mainstream never has to enter the margins).[11]

Phoebe, with her clear vision, wholly embraces the idea and reality of being a witch by casting the spell that awakens the sisters' powers. Moreover, she pushes the sisters to accept that power. Conversely, Prue, the representative of the dominant social order in this episode, resists her designation as a witch. In the end, all the sisters, more or less, accept the 'reality' of their status as witches, and in doing so establish themselves as outsiders in this fictional society, a society that does not accept witches. Moreover, in this first episode, we see the beginnings of the development of outsider strategies of resistance and more moments of subversion, especially in the development of *communitas*.

Communitas

With the sisters established as localizing power, the alternative social structure of *communitas* begins its organic growth. Although *communitas* and community share the same Latin root, *communis*, *communitas* is more than just a community. According to Fiske, a *communitas* is a defensive social group made up of the marginalized. It is, 'a social formation whose main, if not only purpose is to produce identities and relationships that are in the control of its members by the means that are denied to them by the dominant social order'.[12] On *Charmed*, the *communitas* of the sister witches is a localizing defensive social formation that challenges and defends against disciplinary power's techniques of control. For the sisters, their *communitas* establishes a social space where they can develop their sense of connection and their destinies as Charmed Ones.

The sisters may be genetically related, but in the first episode they are not a family or even a community. In the first part of the episode, the camera provides a close-up of a photograph where the sisters stand apart from each other, symbolizing their estrangement. However, once the sisters awaken their power, another camera close-up shows the picture shifting: they magically move closer to one another. This movement shows that they are indeed the Charmed Ones, witches, and 'protectors of the innocent'.[13] By the end of the episode, Prue, Piper and Phoebe come together to vanquish a warlock who tries to steal their powers. The spell that finally works is one left by their mother – 'the power of three will set us free'.[14] In the final scene, the sisters walk up the steps to the house, now their home. Each sister's initial reasons for living in the house no longer matter, for now they share a common purpose. The house is now the site of a *communitas* of three, one in which the sisters work cooperatively, bound to each other through choice and common interests.

Within the *Charmed communitas*, the sisters' power stems from their emotional bonds to each other individually and as a group. Their love for each other as individual sisters ties them to each other, but it is the Power of Three that makes them charmed. Although they each have individual magical powers, they must work together to vanquish particularly powerful evil forces. These bonds are important to their magic, and when these bonds break – as in the episode, 'Power Outage' (3.7) – all the sisters' magical powers, individual and group, disappear. In this episode, the demon Belthazor tries to kill the sisters by employing a hate demon to cause the sisters to fight amongst themselves. The sisters use their powers against each other, which destroys their emotional bonds, and thereby their magical powers. To regain their powers, they have to reestablish and reinforce their bonds as sisters and as a group. Once they have done so, they destroy the hate demon and wound Belthazor.[15]

This episode of *Charmed* shows the importance of the sisters' *communitas*. They are strongest when they are together, relying on their emotional bonds. Using their powers against one another destroys their *communitas* because it ruptures the trust needed for it to develop and exist. Because there is no set structure, rules or hierarchy – no discipline to make individuals conform – the only way that *communitas* survives is through the willingness of individuals to be members. That willingness, in turn, is a product of the emotional ties and support networks found in *communitas*. When the sisters use their power against each other, they break that trust and thus destroy the *communitas*.[16]

The *Charmed communitas*, like other localized *communitas*, provides support and connections for the localized: it provides a social location not structured by disciplinary power, and as such it is a potential threat to that power. Disciplinary power needs to prevent the construction of self-defined groups to maintain its dominant power. One technique of discipline is to set individuals by race, gender, class and religion – amongst other categories – against each other. This disciplinary power technique prevents coalitions and alliances of the marginalized, which could threaten the power of dominant groups and individuals. *Communitas* is defensive against disciplinary power because it provides a social formation that is about the group ties that unite the marginalized. As a defensive strategy, the development of the *communitas* on *Charmed* is a space in which the sisters can develop identities not deemed proper by the dominant power. On *Charmed*, the improper identities concern females, female ideals and female power.

The sisters' resistant identity emerges from the feminine. In patriarchal culture, female power threatens the dominant power.

Despite the considerable advances of women's rights during recent decades, the USA is still a patriarchal culture that considers the female (rather than individual females) subordinate. One proposed feminist method for increasing the power of the female is for women to become more like men by taking on characteristics stereotypically associated with the male – ambition, competitiveness and physical strength. This focus has been criticized by many other feminists as devaluing the meaning of female itself as well as offering only a superficial solution to gender inequality.[17] Like these feminist critics, *Charmed* rejects the devaluing of the female outright. As if drawing from cultural feminist philosophy that seeks to flip the gender narrative and value those denigrated female traits, *Charmed* values the feminine.

In this *communitas*, the female is the source of power for the sisters. The sisters tap into a long history of female power manifested though witchcraft and originating from the maternal line. Each generation of women in their family passes on the power as well as the knowledge needed to maintain that power. In fact, the very first spell used by the sisters to defeat evil comes from their mother. However, the *Charmed communitas* is not simply female because the main participants are women. The naming of the sisters' mission or destiny also points to the creation of female space. They are the 'protectors of the innocent'. This simple phrase tells much about the way their destiny is established along female lines. That is, unlike many other fictional heroes with special powers, the sisters fight to protect actual individuals, the innocent. They are not fighting for the abstract morality or vengeance, or even, 'truth, justice, and the American way'.[18] Instead, the sisters, like the cultural feminist's valuing of the feminine, use the traits of caring and nurturing as their guiding moral voice, an ethic of care.

The ethic of care or care ethics is the 'female moral voice' that emerges because of a distinct female need for relationships developed early in life.[19] As a moral structure, the focus of care ethics is on reducing actual suffering and harm. Unlike more abstract and universal moral voices, often described as the male-associated ethic of justice, care ethics is concerned with flesh-and-blood individuals. Because the ethic of justice focuses on abstract rules and laws as its guiding force, it may mean that one may have to sacrifice individuals for an abstract principle. The ethic of care, however, does not sacrifice the real people for a principle.[20]

For the sisters, there is a general principle that their magical powers cannot be used for 'personal gain' or to 'punish the guilty'.[21] However, the sisters constantly break these rules to help those who are suffering. In the episode 'Ex Libris' (2.19), Prue uses magic to help a grieving father find justice for his slain daughter by using a ghost seen only by the sisters to convince the murderer to confess.[22] In 'Charmed and Dangerous' (4.13), Paige magically hides the bruises of a beaten woman so she can go to court to win custody of her son.[23] Moreover, *Charmed* presents the ethics of justice as a foil for the sisters in the characters of the Elders. The Elders are ethereal beings who govern by a specific set of rules that determine how and when they help the sisters, or any humans for that matter. The Elders represent the moral voice based on abstract principles and authority. While historically the morality based on abstract principles and universal truths has been much valued, in *Charmed* it is instead a difficulty to overcome.

The sisters in *Charmed* develop a *communitas* as a female space and employ the ethics of care to structure the morality of that space. While care ethics are one kind of alternative knowledge and practice employed as a resistance strategy against dominant power, others are presented as well.

Alternative Knowledges/Practices

The sisters' *communitas* is a site that symbolically represents the enacting of alternative knowledges/practices, which are tools the marginalized can use to resist disciplinary power. Alternative knowledges and practices, according to Fiske, are defensive measures employed by the localized as ways of explaining and interacting with reality that are outside the accepted or dominant norms. The production of alternative knowledges and practices is a marginalized resistance strategy that attempts to break the dominant social order's definitions of reality by offering alternative interpretations and actions.[24] Witchcraft is a resistant alternative knowledge/practice experienced and enacted within the *communitas* and beyond, grounded in the ethics of care, to protect the innocent. Witchcraft and magic are tools that the sisters use to provide explanations about what is really happening and a course of action to fight against those that would harm the innocent.

As an alternative knowledge/practice and resistance tool, witchcraft on *Charmed* symbolically and literally empowers the sisters. Within the fictional universe of *Charmed*, the agents of domination – the police, the military, the FBI, the news media – do not understand what is really happening. Throughout the series, witchcraft, magic and the supernatural serve as the actual explanation for murder, riots and general mayhem. While the police, agents of dominant power, define riots and civil disturbances, the Charmed Ones know that the Four Horsemen of the Apocalypse are causing the unrest.[25] While dominant social order officials see murder, the sisters know that a fear demon is magically bringing slasher movie characters to life.[26] While the police see suicide and hostage taking, the sisters know that a demon is infecting people with the seven deadly sins.[27] Because the sisters have the tool of alternative knowledges/practices, they know what the actual causes are and save the day: they can defeat the four horsemen, they can trick the fear demon into magically entering a movie and being burned by the projector light, they can infect another demon with the deadly sin of pride. In short, their alternative knowledge/practice of witchcraft allows them to be more effective than official agents of social control, whose vision is narrowly defined by disciplinary ways of knowing. Magic and witchcraft are better and more truthful ways of understanding the fictional world of *Charmed*. The sisters' use of witchcraft is a resistance measure against the dominant knowledge held by the police, the press and the other agents of domination.

On *Charmed*, the accepted belief in and performance of witchcraft is an alternative knowledge/practice that is resistive because it portrays a reality and way of dealing with that reality outside the norms and definitions of the disciplined mainstream.[28] In the fictional world of *Charmed*, and in non-fictional America, witchcraft is not a mainstream, accepted belief system or practice. Witchcraft as an alternative knowledge/practice empowers those outsiders using it because it contradicts the official version of reality and because, as an alternative, it is beyond the control of disciplinary power, which can only attempt to thwart or discredit it.

Another alternative knowledge/practice on *Charmed* is the presentation of extended, female-headed families. Traditionally and stereotypically, males are the heads of families; however, on *Charmed* the females are the heads of the family. Males are relatively absent, including the father, Victor, who abandoned his daughters when they were small children. He occasionally shows up in the series to worry over the sisters and to try to get them to relinquish their powers. For example, the first time we learn of the father is when he returns to steal the Book of Shadows, a book that contains the compiled magical wisdom of all the sisters' female ancestors. Although Victor does not succeed, he continues trying to convince the sisters to give up their powers given by the females of the family.[29]

The traditional male of the nuclear family is absent not only in the daily lives of the sisters, but also on the supernatural plane. Whenever the sisters summon their ancestors' help, they summon females, going all the way back to the original witch, Melinda Warren at Salem. After Prue dies, she joins the litany of ancestors to be summoned in a magical crisis. The *communitas* of ancestors is not only a network of support for the sisters' magic, but is also a way for the dead family members to experience events like a marriage or Wiccaning, a kind of magical baptism.[30] Thus, this *communitas* of living and dead not only helps in the Charmed Ones' missions, but also strengthens family bonds beyond the grave.

Although the sisters and their maternal ancestors are a very female-focused family, there are numerous boyfriends/husbands who move in and out of the sisters' lives. However, the males that become part of the *communitas* are those who connect in a care-giving capacity to *all* the sisters, rather than just one. Of all the males involved with the sisters, Leo is the only one emotionally connected to all the sisters. However, there are issues with his inclusion in the *Charmed communitas*.[31] Leo is an agent of the disciplinary power and he struggles with the conflict between the ethic of care and the ethic of justice.

Leo is the Charmed Ones' Whitelighter, whose duty is to help and protect the witches. He does this not only because they are his assigned 'charges', but also because he is emotionally tied to Piper as her boyfriend and then later as her husband. While he connects with the *Charmed communitas* and all the sisters, he works for and eventually becomes an Elder, defenders of the abstract principle focused ethic of justice. For Leo to truly become a member of the sisters' *communitas*, he must relinquish his alliance to disciplinary power and embrace those of the *communitas*.

For Leo, this change in alliance, the move from an ethic of justice to an ethic of care, the move from agent of disciplinary power to the localized resistant is a difficult passage. In the beginning, he is tied to the sisters only as their Whitelighter, guardian over them and protector of new witches. However, as the series progresses, Leo becomes more closely tied to Piper, finally becoming her husband and father of her children. The focus on relationship and emotional ties is what grounds Leo in the sisters' *communitas*. This focus is not just tied to Piper but to all the sisters.

Leo defies the Elders on many occasions to help the sisters. For example, he saves Piper's life, healing her illness despite the fact that the Elders forbid it. As punishment, Leo's 'wings' are clipped and he becomes mortal.[32] Once mortal he is able to have a 'normal' relationship with Piper. However, even here the ties to all the sisters, to the *communitas* as a whole, take precedence. He gives up his chance at a normal life with Piper to save Prue.[33] Acts grounded in care ethics, while about saving actual individuals, are also about caring for the group as a whole. Leo sacrifices his own desires in order to save Prue, the Power of Three, and the sisters' *communitas*. Saving Prue is about his emotional ties, not romantic love; saving the Power of Three by saving Prue is an act of care for this fictional world where the sisters protect the innocent. Finally, saving the sisters' *communitas* by saving Prue is about protecting all the sisters, including Piper, from the loss of a sister and an integral part of the sisterly bonds. Leo does eventually become an Elder, but even when he fully immersed in the disciplinary culture and focused on the ethic of justice he eventually gives up this power to remain part of the *communitas*. It should be noted that Leo's ability to join the *communitas* fully, albeit inconsistently throughout the series, might have something to do with his own outsider status in this fictional world. After all, he is dead, the ultimate marginalization. However, Leo does belong to the *communitas* because, as the sisters are, he is emotionally bound to the members and he is morally guided by care ethics. While the *Charmed communitas* is a female space, Leo as a male can be included if he values the feminine.

Conclusion

The *Charmed communitas* is a female space governed by care ethics and one that employs alternative knowledges and practices like witchcraft and female-headed families. However, *Charmed* is also a text of compliance. Like all other marginalized and outsider groups and individuals, the localizing power in *Charmed* can only resist domination and can never fully remove itself from disciplinary culture. Along with the resistance is support for dominant disciplinary power, like the focus of females on physical appearance and romantic heterosexual relationships. *Charmed* was created in a disciplinary patriarchal society and therefore cannot fully remove the disciplinary patriarchal aspects from itself.

That *Charmed* is an agent of domination that promotes the self-policing and compliance of the marginalized to support dominant power does not diminish its importance as a resistance text. In fact, having the resistant themes embedded within dominant hegemony may make them even more powerful. Furthermore, this is the fate of localizing power. It can never fully resist, but it can carve out a space where self-identity and interpersonal relationships provide respite from disciplinary power and strengthen the individual to continue their own resistance strategies.

Finally, *Charmed* provides an alternative knowledge to the audience as well. Here is a teaching narrative about three women who are able to tap into a special power, one historically associated with the female, and one that is resistant to disciplinary patriarchal power. This is an alternative knowledge in and of itself: it is symbolically a portrayal of latent female power. The heroes are female. Their power comes from the maternal line, and their ethics are the female-associated care ethics. The audience shares this special knowledge, knowledge where females, stereotypically the 'weaker sex', are powerful heroes that protect people.

PART TWO

Feminist Power

'I Just Want to Be Normal Again'

Power and Gender in Charmed

CATRIONA MILLER

𝕴N 2003, TELEVISION Week noted that TV was becoming the 'place for spunky gals' and the co-CEO of Warner Brothers Network was pondering his responsibility to 'show positive female images on screen'.[1] Charmed is a WB show that by 2003 was already enjoying success. Indeed, according to Brad Kern, executive producer, the premiere of Charmed 'shattered the record for the highest ratings ever for a WB series'.[2]

Charmed tells the story of the Halliwell sisters – Prue (Shannen Doherty, Seasons One to Three), Piper (Holly Marie Combs), Phoebe (Alyssa Milano) and Paige (Rose McGowan, Seasons Four to Eight) – who are the Charmed Ones, young women who inherit magical powers and battle demons and warlocks to protect the innocent. The sisters are attractive, feisty and active, and the fantasy[3] scenario allows the heroines to explore an ostensible agenda of empowerment and 'girl power'. As one fifteen-year-old put it, 'It is extremely refreshing to see a new feminine power taking over TV in the forms of Buffy and the Charmed Ladies'.[4]

When looking more closely at Charmed, however, many of the ideas, images and narrative tropes, which appear to invite engagement only at a superficial level, turn out to be far more complex and ambiguous. It is a dense and perhaps contradictory text. This chapter will attempt to unravel some of these contradictions, with particular emphasis on the deployment of power within the text. First it will delineate a Foucauldian perspective on power, and then explore how this illuminates the competing discourses at work in the text, thus bringing into question the easy assumption that it is a straightforwardly feminist text.

Foucault and the Deployment of Power

Foucault suggests that traditionally power has been formulated as 'that which represses. Power represses nature, the instincts, a class, individuals'.[5] Power has been seen as something that some have and others do not. The aristocracy have power, commoners do not; men have power, women do not; the rich have power, the poor do not. In this schema, power comes from the top down, through the institutions of the State.

Foucault, however, contests this view and, indeed, turns it on its head, suggesting that power is not something that should be sought in the institutions and structures that overtly govern our society. Rather than being the *source* of power, these institutions are in fact merely the end points of power. As he says, 'Power's condition of possibility . . . must not be sought in the primary existence of a central point . . . it is the moving substrate of force relations . . .' that constantly engenders states of power that are always local and unstable.[6]

Charmed is not a highbrow, high-culture programme and it would not normally be considered intellectual art. It is not important in that way. On the other hand, *Charmed* has been a very popular programme and from that perspective the workings of power and control within the show's narrative are of interest because there would appear to be competing discourses[7] of power at work in the show. As Angela McRobbie points out, 'relations of power are indeed made and re-made within texts of enjoyment and rituals of relaxation and abandonment'.[8] It is perhaps within the least serious of texts that the deployment of power can be seen most clearly.

Fantasy is a genre that is patently 'unreal' and deals openly and frankly with strange subject matter, but does so with a freedom that other genres are not permitted. The fantastic imagery and symbolism employed in horror and fantasy explores the deployment of power, utilizing much of the same kind of symbols and code as dreams, myth and fairy tales: chronology is unreliable, landscapes can change in the blink of an eye, seeing is not necessarily believing, and transformation and ambiguity abound.

For instance, *Charmed* treats linear time in a cavalier fashion, regularly sending the girls backwards and forwards in time, and it allows for multiple appearances by characters who are either dead or not yet born.[9] *Charmed* also boldly utilizes a wide variety of the imagery of mythology, legend, fairy tale and some religion. The Charmed Ones face demons[10] (an iconography from many religions), Titans[11] (Greek mythology), Lady Godiva[12] (legend), leprechauns[13] and fairies[14] (fairy tale) amongst others. The Charmed Ones' fears have a way of literally coming to life, and these mischievous, destructive and dangerous figures may then be played with in a concrete way, becoming a matter of life and death, at least in the context of the show's narrative. This fantasy scenario of the show, which freely poaches mythologies, legends and symbolism from around the world, allows the Halliwell sisters to interact physically with their demons and fears. However, this use of 'unreal' imagery should not divert attention from the reality of the discourses that it is exploring and, as suggested, *Charmed* gives a picture of a number of contested discourses in contemporary society.

The Halliwell sisters are presented as being active protagonists in their own drama and seem to have agency and power, but the question that might be asked is, not how the sisters use their power, but how power is deployed more generally within the confines of the show's narrative. Foucault proposes that we do not look for power to be obvious or concentrated, (i.e. in the hands of the show's heroines) but diffuse and contingent. Power is 'the name that one attributes to a complex strategical [sic] situation in a particular society'.[15] Thus, it could be suggested that the influence of *Charmed* lies in the fact that it illustrates for its audience how power might be deployed around, against, or by them, for power begins from local centres, a back-and-forth process that is far from being static or fixed, but which is 'subject to constant modifications and continual shifts'.[16]

For instance, we do not need to look for the moments when the sisters come up against the institutions of the State – such as the Center for Disease Control;[17] Detective Sheridan (Jenya Lano) and the police,[18] or Agent Murphy (Brandon Quinn) and Homeland Security.[19] These are not really the institutions that control the Charmed Ones. In fact, power transactions take place at the moments when one human being says 'No' or 'Yes' to another. Power is deployed around the Charmed Ones by their boyfriends, husbands, Whitelighters and demons, in the individual points of contact, in one-to-one contacts. These are the points at which subjects are 'gradually, progressively, really and materially constituted through a multiplicity of organisms, forces, energies, materials, desires, thoughts etc'.[20] Thus we can better begin to understand the complexity of the *Charmed* text. It articulates a constant and shifting negotiation of power within its narrative. There is constant questioning, constant admissions and interpretations of the Charmed Ones, their role, their personalities and their 'destiny'.

Power, in Foucault's depiction, is net-like in organization and therefore does not ultimately rest with one person or institution or group or discourse, and as such it does not move in only one direction, quite the opposite in fact. Individuals are 'always in the position of simultaneously undergoing and exercising this power. They are not only its inert or consenting target: they are also the elements of its articulation. In other words, individuals are the vehicles of power, as well as its points of application'.[21] These individual interactions reproduce discourse, while at the same time acting upon the individuals who interact and so the Charmed Ones are acted upon and at the same time exercise power over others.

The relationship of the Charmed Ones to the Elders, for example, is particularly fraught. The Elders (senior Whitelighters, or angels) are supposed to guide and protect the Charmed Ones. For example, in 'Morality Bites' (2.2) the sisters are sent into the future. As Leo (Brian Krause), their personal Whitelighter and later Piper's husband, tells them after they return, 'You three were given a glimpse of your future to learn a valuable lesson. And I'm glad that you learnt it too because I know they wouldn't have brought you back if you hadn't'. This is the first time the Elders exert themselves openly, although the presence of Leo from the very start of the series argues for their tacit presence. Their guidance (or interference) however, gradually becomes more overt. In 'Magic Hour' (3.2), for instance, the Elders remove Leo at the moment when he is about to marry Piper, and not until she 'learns her lesson' (that innocents must come first) is he restored. The Elders continue to interfere (or guide) in this fashion even after Season Five, when most of them are killed.[22] The Charmed Ones, however, at the same time, often defy the Elders. In 'Blinded by the Whitelighter' (3.11) another Whitelighter, Natalie (Audrey Wasilewski) is put in charge of the sisters, but when Natalie is killed the Charmed Ones only save the day because they break the rules and have Leo orb them 'upstairs' to the Elders and vanquish the warlock.

This is the micro-mechanism of power at an individual level, which, according to Foucault, is then built up into a more global power. The micro-mechanisms of power described in the individual character choices within the narrative context of the show articulate part of a complex patchwork of discourses that make up our culture and society; personal choice is thus implicated in the workings of power on a macro level. The individual character choices are illustrative of a number of discourses of power at work in *Charmed*, all of which are competing with each other, and so the Elders circumscribe the power of the Charmed Ones, while at the same time the sisters resist that control. But this control goes beyond the characters as the discourses implicated exist beyond the confines of the show.

There are, for instance, a number of competing feminist discourses illustrated in the series, not, it must be said, a single feminist discourse, as it is difficult (impossible?) in the twenty-first century to argue that such a thing exists. There is also a discourse of patriarchy articulated within the text, and possibilities of both resistance and perhaps surrender are suggested. These discourses of feminism and patriarchy are particularly closely intertwined within this show, as one would expect, but there is one other discourse set out: consumer capitalism. Although this is less clearly enunciated within its narrative, it is implied within the programme's visual styling, and examining the place of the show within a wider production context suggests that the show is a vehicle for a range of commodities, both actual (with a use value) and symbolic (brands and lifestyles) marketed at niche audiences.

These discourses (feminism, patriarchy and consumer capitalism) are not even internally consistent and so it is unlikely that there will be coherence in their representation within the text. It is a complex melange of discourses with no uniformity of tactical aims and functions. As Foucault's understanding of the workings of power would suggest, discontinuity, volatility and negotiation are the rule rather than stability or consistency. As will be discussed more fully below, feminism(s) may be deployed in order to prop up a commodity capitalist agenda (i.e. to sell things to girls), but feminism(s) itself may contain the seeds of a resistance to patriarchy. Herein, perhaps, lies the source of the inherent disorder and inconsistent nature of the text, and the rest of the chapter will attempt to follow through some of the workings of these discourses.

Feminist Discourse(s)

Feminism is probably the discourse most heavily foregrounded in *Charmed*. The three sisters are the centre of the show and the narrative quite clearly revolves around them. They are action heroines, physical, articulate and strong willed. They certainly appear to be the 'spunky gals' that the WB network was looking for and one way in which the show invokes a feminist spin for the show is in invoking the strong female symbol of the witch. However, the symbolism of the witch is not entirely straightforward and this serves to illustrate the complexity of the feminist discourse(s) at work in the text.

In folklore, witches have been traditionally characterized as 'cannibals, sorceresses, murderesses and destroyers of male potency'.[23] From a more historical perspective, a witch has been depicted as a 'female who practises *maleficium*, the art of doing harm by occult means. In league with the Devil and associated with wild and desolate places, she was thought to ... possess the power of flight, so as to attend a coven of her fellows, where they fed on the human flesh.'[24] Or at least, so the witch hunters of the fifteenth, sixteenth and seventeenth centuries appear to have thought.

Such images of women engaged in malevolent magic are a far cry from the depiction of the Charmed Ones, who are shown as being young, cute and sassy. Their power is magical and comes from a long line of female witches starting with ancestor Melinda Warren,[25] who seems to be every bit as young, cute and sassy as the sisters, and so the witch imagery upon which the show draws is not 'simply' the witch of fairy tale, or even of history.

The idea that the image of the witch might be a positive role model stems from the reclamation of the symbolism of the witch by second-wave feminists.[26] Second-wave feminism can be characterized as interested in consciousness raising, civil liberties for women and highlighting the dominance of patriarchy in society. One of the ways it did this was to question traditional depictions of women, such as the imagery of the evil witch. Mary Daly, for example speaks of understanding the witch burnings as 'embedded in contemporary androcratic Western-dominated society, on whose boundaries Hags and Crones are struggling to survive today'.[27] Witches, for Daly, were 'women living outside the control of the patriarchal family, women who presented an option – an option of "eccentricity" and of "indigestibility"'.[28] Daly goes on to suggest that witches were healers, counsellors, wise women and teachers, with qualities of independence, strength, wisdom and learning.[29] It seems that the second-wave feminists were trying to unearth a subjugated knowledge[30] of the wise woman who was persecuted by the mainstream religion of the day. They were trying to rediscover a discourse that might lie outside patriarchy and patriarchally assigned gender characteristics.[31] In this context we might read the Halliwell sisters as spunky gals in a rediscovered, unearthed tradition of female knowledge. However, there is another feminist discourse at work in *Charmed*, because the trouble is that the Charmed Ones, if feminist, appear to be more postfeminist than second wave.

The second-wave attitude to witches wanted to claim them as a feminist icon[32] – dangerous, powerful, bloody, sexual – but *Charmed*, positioned as a prime-time show for a teen and young adult audience on a mainstream network, is rather more conservative. The Halliwell sisters are respectable, clean and proper. They are groomed to perfection, with permanently glossy hair, accessorized, coordinated and sanitized. Their 'dilemmas' do not extend, for example, to their appearances. The 'powerful and painfully unruly witch of the second-wave feminist reclamation'[33] has been banished and 'magic is harnessed to the production of a clean and orderly (ladylike) self'.[34]

In a postfeminist perspective, the 'emphasis . . . is on exploring the lifestyle choices and pleasures of women rather than on outlining agendas for more direct recognisable kinds of social activism',[35] while the second-wavers were seen as 'hopelessly outdated and stifling, only offering women a rigidly delimited set of "politically" correct behaviours and beliefs, that is, where everything about one's personal life was and is ostensibly prescribed'.[36] This debate between second-wavers and postfeminists seems to be one discussion around which *Charmed* circles.

The girls are constantly in a quandary over 'fun and boys' on the one hand, and their 'duty' to protect innocents on the other, and, as suggested, the appearances of the three sisters are part of the coding of this dilemma. In the aforementioned episode, 'Blinded by the Whitelighter' (3.11), when Leo is temporarily replaced by Natalie, the Whitelighter who disapproves of the girls' rule-breaking behaviour, this includes their clothing. She tells them 'You need outfits that are loose and move. That means no more braless, strapless, fearless attire'. To which Prue replies, 'Okay, but then I have nothing to wear'.

The question of appearance and visual styling is an integral part of the show and perhaps fundamentally brings into question its feminist credentials, for although the feminist agenda appear to be at the forefront of *Charmed*, there is a competing discourse that works to place more fixed boundaries around the power of the Halliwell sisters. Throughout all eight seasons, the sisters remain unsure about their priorities, a dichotomy most often expressed by Piper. Early in Season One, she says:

> Our whole lives we've been like everybody else – rushing off to work, going out on bad dates, buying shoes, then suddenly you wake up one day and everything is different. We're witches now. And I don't know if that's a good thing or a bad thing . . . I just want to be normal again, as messed up as that was. That too much to ask for?[37]

A central problematic for a fully feminist reading of the show is that the instant the sisters acquire their magical powers (for 'powers', read 'power') they do not want it. As Piper says in the second episode, 'A toast to the Power of Three – whether we like it or not!'[38] Foucault suggests that 'the particular elements of the knowledge that one seeks to disinter are no sooner accredited and put into circulation, than they run the risk of recodification, recolonisation',[39] and it raises the suggestion that another of the discourses competing in *Charmed* is that of patriarchy.

Patriarchal Discourse

Patriarchy is a 'system ruled over by men whose authority is enforced through social, political, economic and religious institutions . . . it is an ideology that permeates every area of culture'.[40] Its presence can be seen in *Charmed*, although the deployment of its power to circumscribe the authority of the sisters is both overt and covert. Overtly, and perhaps a little crudely, in terms of the show's narrative, it can be seen that the Halliwell sisters are victims of a large number of attacks by male demons and warlocks.[41] With the exception of Season Six, between 70% and 75% of the various demons, warlocks, beasts, creatures and so on that attack the Charmed Ones and seek to gain their power are male. In the remaining 25% of episodes, around 14% of attacks were from female demons, witches, or other magical creatures and the remaining 11% were either gender-neutral beings,[42] or the Charmed Ones were the source of the attack itself,[43] or were dealing with personal problems.

Those on the side of 'Good', however, as discussed above, are also implicated in the restriction of the Charmed Ones. The Elders' role in the sisters' lives is paternalistic to say the least. To return to Season One, one key episode, 'Wicca Envy' (1.10), undercuts the source of the Charmed Ones' power and their appearance of agency. The sisters have been blackmailed into giving up their powers, but Leo simply (and secretly) waves his hands and restores their magic to them, presumably at the behest of the still hidden Elders. Thus, in a sense, their powers no longer emanate from Melinda Warren, but from Leo and the Elders. Indeed, their power is seen to be at the sufferance of the Elders, as Phoebe is stripped of her powers in Season Six.[44] In a further interesting development, it appears that, in the future, it is Wyatt, the son of Piper, who will have *real* power. He is the first-born son of the Charmed Ones and, even as a child, has the power to bring back the Source of All Evil.[45] Once again, this calls into question the power of the Charmed Ones.

Apart from the Charmed Ones themselves, powerful women seem to be missing from the text. As Rachel Moseley points out, it 'seems significant that mothers – the generational connection to 1970s feminism – are dead or absent'.[46] Patty Halliwell (Finola Hughes), the sisters' mother, died when the girls were young – Phoebe has hardly any memory of her and Paige has none at all. Penny (Grams) Halliwell (Jennifer Rhodes) brought the girls up single-handedly, apparently keeping their father at bay. The mother and the grandmother are both present, in that they feature as characters, and yet absent in that these characters are ghosts and so limited in their influence.[47]

However, a patriarchal discourse also confines the potential of the Charmed Ones in a more covert fashion. As the magazine *Cult Times* put it, 'When it comes to affairs of the heart, the Charmed Ones are cursed. Over eight seasons on their show boyfriends and spouses have come, gone, died, and even been vanquished'.[48] Right from the beginning of the series, witchcraft is seen to come between the sisters and their love lives and it seems as if a simple equation is at work – having power equals not having a boyfriend, husband or father of children – or at least the question of a relationship becomes exceptionally difficult and awkward. Being 'normal' seems to mean not having power, but having access to men.

In the very first episode, Piper has a boyfriend called Jeremy (Eric Scott Woods) who turns out to be a warlock. He arranged to meet her at the hospital where her grandmother was dying and the fact that she acquired power meant that her boyfriend wanted to murder her. In Season Two, Prue is shown a future in which she is exceptionally successful in the business world, but does not have a husband or children.[49] This is instrumental in her decision to leave her high-flying job at Bucklands. In Season Eight, Phoebe becomes obsessed with her desire to have a child, dashing off for a weekend with current paramour Dex Lawson (Jason Lewis) because she's ovulating.[50] Paige, meantime, struggles to balance work and magic, quitting her job, as Prue had done before her.[51] She 'strives to achieve the balance she knows a superwitch can attain – love, family, friends and a satisfying career'.[52] Possibly in that order.

In Season Three, the sisters' grandmother (who has had perhaps more than her fair share of husbands) admits that this is a problem for Halliwell women. 'The Charmed Ones are destined for greatness, but that fact doesn't keep a girl warm on a cold winter's night'.[53] It is also worth noting that a high percentage of the female demons and monsters that attack the sisters have become monstrous because they were crossed in love, such as the wendigo[54] who ate her lover's heart, the siren[55] who was burned for having affairs with married men, or the ghostly lover with unfinished business.[56]

To lack love, or to have love taken away, in terms of the show's narrative, seems to render a woman monstrous, and it is perhaps not surprising, therefore, that the three surviving sisters are desperate for love and are given a conventionally happy ending. Piper remains married to Leo, the (ex)angel. Phoebe has landed Coop (Victor Webster), one of the Cupids who has helped to 'keep her heart open', and Paige, perhaps the least witchy of the trio, being part-Whitelighter, is marrying a mortal, Henry (Ivan Sergei), and they all either have children or are promised them.

So it appears that, despite the fact that this show is in the fantasy genre and thus (in theory) capable of imagining life outside the patriarchal envelope, the Charmed Ones appear caught in the mechanisms of repression of patriarchal power. They are attacked by male demons and warlocks who want their power, they are manipulated by the Elders, and shown cautionary tales of monstrous women who have been crossed in love. These are the 'closely linked grid of disciplinary coercions'[57] that constitute the patriarchal discourse in this narrative, and in the end the sexuality of the Halliwell sisters is respectably contained within reproduction and thereby rendered 'safe'. These witches are not the 'indigestible' women outside the patriarchal fold conjured by Mary Daly.

While feminism(s) and patriarchy seem to be the most visible discourses at work in *Charmed* there is another discourse operating, albeit in a more hidden way.

Consumer Discourse

The *Charmed* creation is successful because it is very marketable. It is a successful product that possesses the kind of strong visual styling that permits branding across a number of products, reflecting the multimedia nature of the corporations that produce and distribute the show.[58]

The show is produced by Spelling Television Inc., a Paramount/Viacom Company. This puts the show into the portfolio of one of the world's largest media corporations. Paramount/Viacom has interests that span television, film, print media, production facilities and so on, and *Charmed* was shown on the Warner Brothers Television Network in the United States.[59] WBTV is part of the Time Warner Company, which, likewise, has a very large portfolio of businesses related to entertainment, and the company says of itself that it is 'one of the leading and most diversified licensing and merchandising organisations in the world'.[60] They include in their grouping theme parks, comics, toys and hold some patents on DVD players. So for example, *The Book of Three: The Official Companion to the Hit Show* is published by Simon & Schuster, which is part of the Paramount/Viacom group. The marketability of *Charmed* goes beyond the programme itself. The *Charmed* product exists to be sold to networks, to be sold as DVDs, and it also exists to sell other consumer merchandise such as books, soundtrack albums, board games, travel mugs and so on, and if nothing else the product placement within the show would make this clear.[61]

This should not be a surprise. After all, as Foucault points out, power works to maintain a status quo, it doesn't seek to destroy, it seeks to maintain itself, and thus perpetuate itself. The consumer capitalist discourse puts other discourses to work in order to enlarge capital. If producing a feminist gloss will help to sell the show, and bring in its target demographic, then it will be deployed. It may even be possible to suggest, in a wider context, that postfeminism is a commodified version of feminism, more amenable to a capitalist agenda. For instance, the sisters celebrate their sense of sisterly unity by indulging in yoga, pedicures, shopping and lunch. As Piper says, 'Any day that brings new shoes is a good day'.[62] Capitalism thus puts feminism to work in making money.[63]

Although *Charmed*, like other television shows, can be seen in this consumer context, it is interesting that Wicca[64] itself has come in for similar analysis. It has been suggested that rather than being the revival of a pre-Christian goddess religion, Wicca is instead a postmodern pastiche of religion, largely created in the twentieth century.[65] This religion is available for purchase in the form of commodities such as books, candles and other paraphernalia and in effect, 'white Witchcraft is a marketing label for a type of Witchcraft consistent with consumer capitalism',[66] as many of the spell books sold 'advocate change through empowering prosperity and inner harmony rather than countercultural living'.[67]

As suggested above, the show invokes witchcraft and the symbolism of the witch to give the show a feminist gloss, and yet it makes no attempt to refer to 'real' Wiccan practices and traditions. It is interesting that *The Book of Three* says nothing much about Wicca at all, sticking closely only to what is said in the show itself. It includes some spells from the series, such as little verses and perhaps some brief instructions. For instance, to scry[68] it suggests that one 'Light a candle. Before the flame subsides, let the wax from the candle drip onto the crystal. Once consecrated, scry with the crystal for the one who is sought.'[69] By way of contrast, Janet and Stewart Farrar in *The Witches' Way* give three pages of detailed instructions.[70] *Charmed* works hard to be innocuous and palatable, one might even suggest that it was a 'diet-version' of Wicca.

Charmed is a marketing opportunity that invokes a version of feminism, perhaps postfeminism, that is compatible with consumer capitalism, for the show does not just sell goods, it also sells symbols and ideas. Thus *Charmed* is a marketing vehicle, not just for itself, but for Wicca, and its technologies of the self, all of which sit very well with the corporatization of the media and its multimedia interests. It seems a long way from Mary Daly's invitation to the 'Wild Witch in all women'[71] to get moving against the pseudo-feminism promoted by the patriarchs. Being a product of the early twenty-first century, perhaps

Charmed is not capable of that kind of clarity, as the net-like nature of power relations is all too obviously revealed in its narrative.

Charmed is not simply about an empowering of young women, although it might do that. It is not simply a revalorization of patriarchal family values, although it might do that. And it is not simply a marketing tool for itself and for Wicca, although it might do that too.

Conclusion

Power operates through complex, overlapping and even contradictory mechanisms that are capable of producing both subjugation and resistance. *Charmed* sits between power and its opposition and is therefore both empowering, and, at least from a second-wave feminist perspective, hinting more than a little at collaboration. It is full of messy contradictions and changes in perspective and perhaps what it possibly argues for most is the development of negotiating skills in young adults today.

Ultimately, the multi-faceted nature of the text and the uncertainty inherent within its narrative is best interpreted from a Foucauldian perspective, where the discourse of power itself is understood as constantly altered, modified and transformed. As Foucault says, 'We must make allowance for the complex and unstable process whereby discourse can be both an instrument of power and an effect of power, but also a hindrance, a stumbling block, a point of resistance and a starting point for an opposing strategy. Discourse transmits and produces power, but also undermines and exposes it.'[72] *Charmed* appears to be a site of negotiation between these powerful discourses that shape contemporary society.

The Power of Two – Plus One

RANDALL CLARK

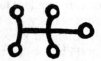

SHANNEN DOHERTY'S UNEXPECTED departure at the end of the third season of *Charmed* had a significant impact on the series. With a series star gone and a leading character to be replaced, every element of *Charmed* would be affected: content, production, promotion and fan response. The introduction of Paige Matthews, as portrayed by Rose McGowan, had an equally substantial effect on the program. With the family dynamic and power structure between the three leading characters now completely redefined, a new interpretation of *Charmed* was now not only possible but unavoidable. An examination of the final episode featuring Prudence and the first episodes featuring Paige will show how this pivotal point in the series' history resulted in an entirely new way of reading *Charmed*.

If one views *Charmed* as one continuous narrative rather than as a series of individual television episodes, one can see that the introduction of Paige altered the overall narrative thrust of the programme. For its first three years, *Charmed* had been the story of three sisters who first discovered that they were witches, then came to terms with that fact as they learned about their new powers and attempted to discern exactly what responsibilities came with these abilities. It had also been the story of three sisters learning to accept and respect one another as Prudence, the sensible, reliable and dependable sister, came into conflict with Phoebe, the immature sister, with Piper both literally and figuratively the sister in the middle. The feminist overtones were obvious: the issues that the series' female characters faced as witches, including acquiring and using power, defining their identities and finding their role in a male-dominated society, paralleled the issues that they faced as mortal women.

The death of Prue and the introduction of Paige brought an unusual change to the narrative; it is not uncommon for a television series to undergo a sweeping change after a few years, simply to keep things fresh, but initially the change in *Charmed* did not so much send the story in a bold new direction as it did mandate that the story of the first three years be retold.[1] The first several episodes of Season Four once again focus on three sisters who are witches, but the story is now about two experienced witches guiding the third as she learns what they already know – it is difficult to maintain life as a normal human when one is a witch and the powers must be used wisely. It is now the story of two sisters who lost the older sister who had always been their anchor, of how those sisters learn to adapt to their new roles and of an orphan who learns that she has a family. The feminist overtones remain present but have by necessity changed, since Piper is now married – to her Whitelighter, no less – and Phoebe has attended college and fallen in love with Cole, a demon. Responsible Prue has been replaced by Paige, a younger, less traditional woman with a history of juvenile problems. Adding Paige to the series certainly redefined what was acceptable behaviour for a Halliwell sister, both as a witch and as a woman. The sisters are less confined by rules and more aggressive than they were in the episodes featuring Prue, particularly the first episodes that parallel the beginning of the Paige storyline, the episodes in which they are learning about their powers and one sister – first Phoebe, then Paige – is being accepted by the other two.

The differences between Prue and Paige are so evident that even a casual viewer of *Charmed* can see them, but the relationship between the two sisters, who never meet or even appear in the same episode, is surprisingly complex and layered. Although it might initially appear that the producers of the series simply decided to replace Prue with a character that is her exact opposite, that is actually a facile reading of the programme. Still, the contrast between Prue and Paige is substantive enough that it is helpful to examine them. Prudence was the oldest sister and, as the sisters' mother died when they were young and their father was largely absent, she took on the responsibility of caring for Piper and Phoebe, almost becoming a surrogate parent. The youngest of the sisters, Paige was technically orphaned as a child as her father was a Whitelighter and Patty – her mother as well as being the mother of Piper, Prue and Phoebe – died while Paige was an infant; Paige's history is explained to Phoebe and Piper by the ghost of Patty in the episode 'Charmed Again' (4.1): 'When you were very little, something happened', Patty's ghost says. She explains that she conceived a child with her Whitelighter and that the girls never knew because they were toddlers and 'just thought Mommy got a little fat'. Afraid of what the Elders might do to a half-Whitelighter infant, Patty and her Whitelighter left Paige for adoption at a local church. Paige's childhood and adulthood, therefore, turned out to be very different from Prue's; rather than assuming a role of responsibility as Prue did,

Paige drank, smoked, cut class and caused her adoptive parents much despair. Paige even believes for years that she was responsible for their deaths in an automobile accident.

Personally, Prue is a stickler for rules; Paige breaks them. This specific difference is highlighted in the third episode with Paige, 'Hell Hath No Fury' (4.3), in which Paige steals the Book of Shadows and uses it to help her co-workers, including a young man who turns out to be quite handsome once Paige uses magic to clear up his severe acne. When, at the episode's conclusion, Piper reminds Paige that 'there are rules', Paige responds, 'You're married to your Whitelighter and Phoebe is shacking up with a demon. Can't my friend just stay cute?'. It is hard to imagine Prue ever making a statement like that. Paige's irresponsible nature is particularly stressed in *Charmed Again*, the first of the *Charmed* novels to feature her character. Paige is introduced to readers in a scene in which she is making out with her boyfriend in the copy room; a subsequent passage states that

> Work versus pleasure had always been a bit of an issue for Paige. It didn't matter what that pleasure was – partying into the wee hours, eating lollipops until her teeth screamed in protest, making out with her latest boyfriend . . . As soon as any pleasure reared its pretty head, Paige had a way of forgetting about responsibilities. What could she say? She was a free spirit, and she definitely walked her own path.[2]

Of course, since the early Paige episodes are loosely reworking the first *Charmed* episodes anyway, this is familiar material; *Charmed* fans had been through much of this with Phoebe in the first season – she also was more interested in men than in a career, willing to bend the rules surrounding the use of magic and frequently reprimanded by her older sister. But there are some important differences here. Paige, for all her irresponsible inclinations, actually works as a social worker, a demanding job that requires a great commitment from her; she is even tempted to use her powers to help an abused child in 'Charmed Again II' (4.2). Furthermore, even before she learns that she is a witch, Paige is attempting to change. She has quit drinking; more importantly, she has graduated from the University of California and become a social worker, in part to atone for her bad behaviour as a teenager, and if this is her motive for becoming a social worker, surely it is partly her motivation for agreeing to act as one of the Charmed Ones and fight evil.

Paige and Prue are also quite different in appearance and demeanour. Prue is a professional who dresses as such. Paige's wardrobe could charitably be described as 'non-conformist'; she shows up for a custody hearing with an exposed midriff and wears a denim miniskirt to Prue's funeral. Paige's jet-black hair and bright red lipstick give her a Goth look that Prue, of course, never had, and Paige's habit of sucking lollipops – something that Piper strongly urges her to give up, claiming to be concerned about Paige's dental health – is implicitly sexual. This contrast is reinforced by the actresses who portray Prue and Paige and the persona that each brought to the television screen. Shannen Doherty had a long history of playing well-behaved children on wholesome television series *Our House* and *Little House on the Prairie* before she achieved fame as Brenda Walsh on *Beverly Hills 90210*; Brenda, though not a goody-goody, was a relatively nice girl. Doherty herself had a reputation as difficult to work with and impulsive, a reputation that was reinforced by her sudden departure from *Charmed*;[3] still, her TV image made it easy to accept her as responsible Prudence Halliwell.

Rose McGowan, on the other hand, was probably best known for her gruesome death scene in the first *Scream* (Wes Craven, 1996) movie and her role as a scheming high-school student who kills a close friend in *Jawbreaker* (Darren Stein, 1999); she was also widely recognized as the former girlfriend of rock singer Marilyn Manson. By casting McGowan as Paige rather than choosing a more mainstream actress (Jennifer Love Hewitt, for example, had been mentioned in several news stories as a possibility), the producers of *Charmed* guaranteed that Paige would be perceived as edgier and more rebellious than Prue even before the first episode with Paige had been filmed. If nothing else, the first episodes with Paige showed *Charmed*'s audience something they had never seen before, a flawed character that was rooted in the alternative culture and who managed to do good, an image valuable from a feminist perspective as it helps challenge some of the dominant portrayals of women, even young women, on television at the time.

It would be incorrect, however, to view the replacement of Prue by Paige as some sort of equation in which X was replaced by Y, thus yielding a different result. Paige and Prue are half-sisters, so at the very least they have blood in common but in truth they have a great deal more. Paige is indeed Prue's opposite but she is also a sort of alter ego for Prue, the person Prue might have been but never dared let herself become. Prue's frustration with her own persona shows in a few episodes, most notably the sixteenth episode of the series, 'Which Prue is it Anyway?' (1.16), in which a spell creates two extra Prues. These two do the things that the real Prue has wanted to do but suppressed, beginning with her using all the hot water in the shower, escalating to flirting with attractive men and culminating in her throwing caution aside and confronting a demon herself, without Piper and Phoebe to back her up. Similarly, in 'Just Harried' (3.15), Prue astral projects a double of herself who gets into such a vicious confrontation with a biker outside a bar that Prue is suspected of his murder. The double is free to do as it pleases while Prue lies in a dream state and cannot be awakened; her mother explains that Prue feels trapped and wants to escape.

Both of these episodes suggest that Prue is subconsciously rebelling against the constraints of being the responsible oldest sister. Two other episodes suggest that not only would Prue like to be a different person, but that Paige represents the sort of person that Prue, in her most reckless moments, would have liked to be. A first season episode that is actually titled 'The Fourth Sister' (1.7) stands as an interesting prefiguring of the introduction of Paige to the series. Aviva, a troubled girl who lives in the Halliwells' neighbourhood, knows through her own experiments with magic that the Halliwells are witches and approaches them about joining them to perform Wicca. When Prue turns Aviva away, Aviva attempts to manipulate Phoebe into practising magic with her. Aviva never actually becomes the 'fourth sister' – that is left to Paige – but it is clear that if she had, it would have been at Prue's expense; at one point, Phoebe even lends her one of Prue's dresses.

A somewhat similar situation occurs in 'All Hell Breaks Loose' (3.22), the final episode to feature Prue. After Piper and Prue have been shown on television destroying a demon, the entire world knows that the Halliwells are witches. One young woman, calling herself a witch, enters the Halliwell home in an attempt to join what she believes to be their coven. Prue not only rejects the woman, she uses her powers to send her flying out of the home. The woman retaliates later by shooting and killing Piper; this in turn leads to time being turned back and to Prue's death. What is significant is that neither of these young women, confused loners with connections to Gothic culture, have anything in common with Prue, but they are not that far removed from Paige.

Paige really is Prue's alter ego, the part of herself that Prue pushes away or represses and which she strongly perceives as a threat to her. Paige can replace Prue, but at the same time, a little of Prue will exist inside of Paige. She feels compelled to attend Prue's funeral simply because she read Prue's obituary. Later, when Phoebe asks why Paige was at the funeral, Paige's explanation is, 'I feel like part of me lost her too'. In the novel *Charmed Again* she adds, 'It was just part of my trying to find out who I really was, I guess.'[4] The novel also explicitly states a significant connection between Prue and Paige. When Phoebe first sees Paige, at Prue's funeral, 'she saw a young woman in a cream-colored vintage jacket, a woman who so resembled her dead sister, Phoebe felt a thread of ice shoot into her chest. The Snow-White pale skin, the glossy black hair, the full lips and fine cheekbones – all of Prue's best qualities were there.'[5] *All of Prue's best qualities were there.* Paige is part Prue, just as Prue is part Paige, and over the first several episodes featuring Paige we will see how she matures and learns to use her powers responsibly, becoming more like Prudence while still retaining her own identity.

What is particularly significant here is that Paige is actually a more powerful character than Prue. The difference in powers is especially important to a feminist reading of *Charmed*. The women of *Charmed* were never given great physical abilities; Phoebe's martial arts abilities were learned, not the result of magic, and Piper's ability to blow things up was never completely under her control. When compared to the most obvious referent, the active female characters on the series *Buffy the Vampire Slayer*, the women on *Charmed* may appear passive and reactive; for the protagonists of a series and graced with supernatural abilities, they seem to spend an unusual amount of time running away from menaces and screaming, 'Leo!' The truth is that Phoebe and Piper, though strong women on many levels, are less physically powerful than Prue; their abilities – having visions and freezing persons and objects – do not really involve physicality and do not allow those sisters to do much more than react to something that is happening to them. Prue, who is telekinetic, has a more aggressive power. She can move things, which gives her an element of control and causality that her sisters lack. Paige has the same ability as Prue, but with a key difference. Because she is half-Whitelighter, her powers work a bit differently – the objects that she moves come directly to her, giving her an even greater amount of control. She also has the ability to orb; in fact, her first act of magic is instinctively to orb when a demon attacks her in 'Charmed Again'. Later she discovers that she had orbed once before, when still in high school, and that is what allowed her to survive the automobile accident that killed her adoptive parents. When one compares Paige's orbing to Prue's first use of magic, which was to make a pen leak and ruin the shirt of her co-worker and former lover in the series' pilot, the contrast between the two is obvious. Paige is more self-reliant than Prue, automatically taking care of herself. Furthermore, her Whitelighter heritage allows Paige to sense the presence of evil so that she can seek it out, rather than waiting for evil to come to the sisters as Prue had always done. Piper and Phoebe do not immediately accept this change in their usual procedure – in 'Size Matters' (4.5) Leo has to convince them to pay attention to Paige's instincts – but it works well for the sisters.

Paige's powers and her personality mean that while she will go through the same learning experiences as her sisters did, her experiences will not be the same as theirs. Paige is wilder when she discovers her powers than even Phoebe ever was; this is witchcraft in a primal form. As a result, while Paige possesses a great potential for empowerment, she is also more vulnerable than the other Halliwells were at the same point in the development of their powers. She is open to temptation, which the Source realizes can be used against her to prevent the Power of Three from being reconstituted. In 'Hell Hath No Fury' a demon attempts to get her to use her powers improperly by possessing the body of a man accused of abusing his son and taunting Paige. The man is in fact merely covering up for the boy's mother, who is abusing him, so if Paige had succumbed she would not only have broken the rules regarding use of witchcraft, she would also have punished an innocent man. She also would have kept the Power of Three from ever being restored simply by failing to join her sisters during an allocated amount of time.

Even after Paige has become one of the Charmed Ones, her character flaws continue to cause problems. As noted earlier, in 'Hell Hath No Fury' she steals the Book of Shadows to perform magic at work, including giving herself much bigger breasts; again, even Phoebe at her most outlandish would not have done such a thing. In the episode 'Enter the Demon' (4.4) she accidentally casts a spell that causes her to switch bodies with Phoebe. This happens partly because of Paige's natural curiosity about what it would be like to be Phoebe, but also happens simply because of another of Paige's weak points: she was too impatient to cast the spell properly. When Phoebe asks, 'What did you do?', Paige's immediate instinct is to deny – 'Why do you automatically assume it was something I did?' – but almost at the same time she accepts responsibility for her mistake: 'It was an accident, I swear. I just wanted to know what it was like to be you and somehow the potion I was working on just sort of blew up.' Paige will overcome many of her flaws eventually, just as the others did, but she will never be as grounded a character as Prue was and this further causes the Paige episodes to be open to an analysis different to the Prue ones; watching Paige's highly imperfect character use her great abilities makes for a narrative different to the one in which great powers are used by steady and reliable Prue. Paige presents an internal struggle that Prue never seemed to have deal with.

Complicating the change from Prue–Piper–Phoebe to Piper–Phoebe to Piper–Phoebe–Paige is the fact that Piper and Phoebe need Paige more than she needs them. Without them she is an orphan who has long harboured vague suspicions that she might be related to the Halliwells, but the last major upheaval in Paige's life came when her parents were killed while she was in high school; she has had time to complete a college degree and begin her career in social work, so she has also had time to get used to her life as it is. The death of Prue not only brings major changes to Piper and Phoebe, it brings their very identities into question; without their sister they are still witches but they will never again wield the Power of Three. Whether they even want to might be debatable – Phoebe seems to want to, Piper initially does not – but there is no denying that without Paige, life as Charmed Ones cannot continue.

Even though Paige feels drawn to the Halliwells – in the novel *Charmed Again* she is so obsessed with them that she actually wonders whether she might be turning into a 'freaky stalker' – she is not anxious to join them and understandably reacts negatively when Piper and Phoebe get her to cast their first spell together in 'Charmed Again'. 'What have you guys turned me into?' she shouts before leaving the Halliwell home. Even after she has accepted the fact that she is a witch, Paige does not embrace the life of a Charmed One. 'Sometimes I feel like they want me to be Prue', she complains to Leo in 'A Knight to Remember' (4.6). She even resists moving into Halliwell Manor, hoping to preserve some part of her own private life. Finally, Piper and Phoebe make her understand that she is welcome there and that it is safer for all of them if they are together, but in a nice bit of symbolism, after Paige moves in, she takes Prue's old room and redecorates it to suit herself.

The addition of Paige to the Halliwell family is difficult for Paige, of course, but it is not easy for Piper or Phoebe either, and Piper in particular has a difficult time adjusting to the loss of Prue and the discovery of a new sister. With Prue gone, Piper has lost her primary support. 'She's been there my whole life', Piper tells Leo shortly before Prudence's funeral in 'Charmed Again'. 'I've always had a big sister. And I don't know how to live without one'. Furthermore, Prudence's death means that Piper is now the oldest sister. It is a role that brings with it responsibilities that she has never had to face and it is a role for which she feels extremely ill suited. 'I didn't ask for this big sister gig', she says in 'Hell Hath No Fury'; 'Frankly, it sucks'. Attempting to cope with her loss and her new responsibilities, Piper first resorts to anger – or, as she puts it in 'Charmed Again', 'I am not angry. I am pissed off'. She is angry that Prue is dead; she is also angry that Leo saved her, his wife, instead of saving Prue. Just as Paige's flaws make her vulnerable to demons, so does Piper's anger and grief open her to a supernatural threat. In 'Hell Hath No Fury', because of her rage she temporarily becomes a Fury and comes very close to killing Paige and Cole. Paige returns Piper to her normal state by helping her recognize and deal with her anger. Confronting her at Prue's burial spot, Paige tells Piper, 'It's all right to hate her. You should hate her. When my parents died I hated them for it. I was alone and I hated them. It's okay to hate Prue.' Although Piper has had a difficult time accepting Paige, this conversation apparently has a great effect on her; not only does it cure her of being a Fury, it also gets her to visit Paige at work and identify herself as Paige's sister.

As she mourns, Piper goes through something like a state of denial regarding Prue's death. Her grandmother explains that this is why the sisters can see her and their deceased mother but not Prue; even viewing her spirit would cause Piper to refuse to accept that Prue is gone. Piper even rejects Paige because – she tells Phoebe – everyone around them is at great risk and she cannot bear the thought of losing another sister. A particularly significant episode depicting Piper after Prudence's death is 'Brain Drain' (4.7). Attending a friend's baby shower has caused Piper to long even more than before for a normal life (especially now that she has a half-sister who is living proof that human beings and Whitelighters can procreate). The Source takes advantage of her feelings and places her into a dream state in which she believes that she is in a mental institution and all the events of the past three years have merely been a delusion. Piper fails to resist the Source's spell because her desire to have a normal life almost outweighs her identity as a Charmed One. Only the intervention of Phoebe and Paige prevents her from surrendering the Charmed Ones' powers to the Source.

In attempting to cope with the loss of Prue and to become her replacement, Piper makes the error of imitating Prue. What she at first fails to recognize is that she is not replicating Prue's behaviour and her attempts to emulate her are simply putting everyone at risk. In 'Hell Hath No Fury' she has taken Phoebe and Cole out hunting for demons; even Cole sees this as a reckless move and a failed attempt to imitate Prue, but Piper insists she is merely being 'proactive'. 'Regardless of the consequences,' Cole quotes her, 'Now you sound like Prue'. Phoebe actually mocks Piper when she insists in 'A Paige from the Past' (4.10) that when it comes to personal lives, 'The Charmed Ones come first'; all Piper can offer in her own defence is that 'It always worked when Prue said it'. Eventually Piper will realize that she can replace Prue without becoming Prue; as she explains to Paige in 'Hell Hath No Fury', 'I'm best in the kitchen. Prue was the one who liked to chase demons'.

Phoebe must also adapt to the introduction of Paige into the Halliwell family, but she seems to have an easier time with it than Piper does. Phoebe does not suddenly have to take on the responsibilities of 'big sister'; the arrival of Paige moves Phoebe up to Piper's old place as middle sister and it is much easier to mediate than to lead, especially if one mediates the way Phoebe does, which is by keeping things secret. In two of the first episodes with Paige, 'Hell Hath No Fury' and 'Enter the Demon', Paige does something wrong – stealing the Book of Shadows in the former, swapping bodies with Phoebe in the latter – and convinces Phoebe not to tell Piper. Phoebe gets to be a confidante while Piper makes rules. It is also easier for Phoebe to adjust because she had anyway been making a conscious effort to change and is less set in her ways than is Piper. When Phoebe first meets Paige she has a premonition of her being attacked by a demon, which puts her in a position of caring for Paige's safety from their first contact, which in turn gives her a feeling of sympathy toward Paige that Piper never felt.

In addition, as the youngest child – and the one who was away from home for many years – Phoebe always felt a bit alienated from her sisters and was more inclined to reach out to others. The same instinct that allows her to see the good in Cole and which almost led her to accept the false 'fourth sister', Aviva, causes her to accept the genuine fourth sister, Paige. Certainly she is more welcoming to Paige than Piper is. In the episode 'A Knight to Remember', Paige learns that she was an evil witch in a previous life. When Paige asks, 'Does this mean I'm evil?' Piper immediately replies in the affirmative, while Phoebe says, 'No, just your past self. You've grown and evolved. We all have. That's what we do'. She is speaking from experience, of course. At the end of 'Charmed Again II', Paige has accepted her place as a Halliwell sister and comes to Piper's club. After a brief awkward conversation with Piper, Phoebe, Cole and Leo she turns to leave. Leo asks her to stay; it is a troubling scene because that offer should have come from one of her sisters, both because it would show that they have accepted Paige as their own and because it is their decision to make. Significantly, in the novelization *Charmed Again* that line is reassigned to Phoebe.

Although *Charmed* was to run for five more years after the Paige character was added, the initial narrative arc of Paige's being accepted into the Halliwell family can be said to conclude with the tenth episode featuring Paige, 'A Paige from the Past'. Leo sends Paige into the past so that she can learn about the death of her adoptive parents. Still inclined to break the rules, Paige tries to change the past but cannot. This episode ends with Paige accepting fate; as a reward, Leo briefly allows her parents to come from Heaven and say that they know what she has become and that they are proud of her. In a way this scene sums up what had been the dominant theme of the first half of the fourth season, and a prominent theme throughout the eight years of *Charmed*: the Halliwells cannot escape their destiny. Paige learns that in this episode, and having gained closure to her parents' death, she is ready to become a Halliwell sister and a Charmed One. Piper and Phoebe, for their part, now truly have another sister and have also accepted destiny. The Power of Three is restored.

There is no way of knowing how *Charmed* would have progressed had Shannen Doherty not left the series, but it is undeniable that the presence of Paige and the casting of Rose McGowan provided for a brand new interpretation of the series. Paige brought a hipper, even a more genuine edge to a typically glossy Aaron Spelling production, transforming a programme about three sisters who cast spells and fought evil to a series about three sisters whom viewers could actually see dealing with the things that women deal with in society, while they also cast spells and fought evil. In particular, the first ten episodes featuring Paige allowed characters to change and grow in front the audience. Finally, the addition of a more powerful female to the series caused the other female characters to develop a little bit and become stronger themselves.[6] If *Charmed* is about the Power of Three, then Prue gave them the original three, but Paige is the one who really gave them the power.

Charming the Elders

Girl Power for Second-Wave Feminists

SUSAN J. WOLFE

EARS BEFORE I had the opportunity to watch *The L-Word*, I became hooked by *Charmed*.[1] I am a sixty-year-old lesbian feminist. I know that many of the women who were my sisters in the second wave of the women's movement would be surprised that I watch the show. *Charmed* is very heterosexual in content and not openly political; the wars its stars wage against the forces of evil are fictional. The word 'patriarchal' does not occur at all and the word 'sexist' figures only briefly in its plots or dialogue. On first viewing, my lesbian-feminist friends might regard it as a pastiche, a sort of *Charlie's Angels* meets *The X-Files*, in which three beautiful, young women combat supernatural villains.

Moreover, *Charmed*'s intended audience is clearly younger women, women who can easily identify with the attractive, twenty-something Halliwell sisters. The sisters – Prudence (Prue), played by Shannen Doherty, Piper, played by Holly Marie Combs, and Phoebe, played by Alyssa Milano (and after Prue's death in Season Three, their half-sister Paige Matthews, played by Rose McGowan), are always made-up and coiffed; Alyssa Milano, in particular, sometimes sports several hairdos in a single episode. Prue, Phoebe and Paige wear the latest fashions, bared midriffs, off-the-shoulder halter tops, and designer dresses. (In 'I've Got You Under My Skin', 1.2, for instance, Prue remarks that Phoebe is wearing an Armani dress; in other episodes, they speak of their taste in expensive shoes.) Their careers are enviable, either glamorous or socially significant: Piper owns and manages P3, a club that books popular rock groups; Prue leaves a job evaluating antiques and artworks for Buckland Auction House to become a photographer who shoots celebrity portraits; Phoebe is an advice columnist; Paige is a social worker who eventually runs a school for children with magical talents. Moreover, the sisters are not only sexy but sexually active, taking for granted their right to sexual gratification. For the three Charmed Ones, the sexual revolution is over and the battle has been won.

The challenges faced by the Halliwell sisters are typical of those confronted by ambitious, young, heterosexual women. Each wants to find a Mr Right and settle down with him eventually; at the same time, each recognizes the need to support herself and tries to find meaningful, preferably lucrative, work. Because their greatest power lies in the Power of Three, the combined power arising from their bonds as sisters, they live in the same house, and sometimes squabble over household responsibilities. However, they must balance their ordinary needs and desires against their extraordinary mission, the neverending battle against evil in the shape of demons, warlocks, ancient gods and other supernatural forces. As early as the second episode of the series, Prue remarks on the conflict between their personal lives and their destiny; in response to Phoebe's relieved statement that their powers are good, Prue replies, 'Yeah – good for everything but our love lives, unfortunately'. In order to fight evil, the sisters must continually hone their abilities, writing new spells, concocting new potions, mastering their powers, and, in Phoebe's case, practising kickboxing.

In short, though Piper is careful to refer to the Charmed Ones as 'women', they are the embodiment of Girl Power, sexy, beautiful young women who can and do still 'kick ass'. They are constructed to appeal to third-wave feminists, the twenty- and thirty-year-old women pursuing individual solutions, seeking personal freedoms. Consistent with third-generation feminism, the sisters do not engage feminist causes. In their case, their shared destiny and the need to conceal their identities isolate them from the non-magical community. Thus they cannot, as Piper Halliwell sometimes objects, lead 'normal lives' at all, much less participate in political movements. Hence, though the mundane problems they face are common ones for women of Generation X, they seek individual solutions to them. Because of both their destiny and their strong personalities, they are positioned, then, as power feminists. Arguing that the third-generation's emphasis on autonomy explains young feminists' rejection of second-generation feminism, Astrid Henry cites Naomi Wolf's *Fire with Fire*, stating that

> . . . the feminism she advocates [is] that which '[e]ncourages a woman to claim her individual voice rather than merging her voice in a collective identity.' Wolf gives us a clue about what individuality represents for many third-wave feminists: it is the antithesis of 'merging her voice in a collective identity . . .' Wolf's description suggests that in order

to retain – or even to gain – one's identity and autonomy, one must unmerge, move away, break free.[2]

This, of course, is precisely what the Charmed Ones cannot do. The Power of Three is a joint power: 'The Power of Three will set us free' is the strongest charm they have.

Yet so much of the series appears to run counter to everything I espoused as a second-wave feminist – a need for broad social and political change to achieve justice for all women, refusal to adhere to feminine stereotypes, rejection of institutionalized heterosexuality and monogamy – that I initially wondered why I was drawn to the show. What could it possibly say to me?

Once I began a more critical viewing of *Charmed*, I realized that my earlier concerns were ill founded. In fact, in focusing on the might and power of individual women and on the bonds that strengthen them further, *Charmed* incorporates many ideas that second-wave feminists – particularly radical and lesbian feminists – worked to establish. In the first place, despite the show's references to guardian angels and demons, pre-Christian rites and rituals as well as relics of a goddess-worshipping paganism punctuate many of its episodes. Second, the Halliwells are a female line; they trace their ancestry and derive their abilities from their foremothers. Third, the sisters understand the need to provide for themselves, their children and each other, with or without male assistance; they find means of sustaining their lives together. Last and most important, perhaps, the sisters are deeply loyal to one another, often (though not always) choosing each other, remaining together despite the men in their lives.

During the 1970s, many radical feminists and lesbian feminists railed against patriarchy, or institutionalized male dominance, including not only male power but the customs that supported it, such as patronymics (naming after the father), patrilineal inheritance (goods passed from father to son) and patrifocal religion (the worship of a male deity). Many of us chose to change our names, choosing new ones based on nature or using our mothers' given names. Some of us embraced paganism and Wicca. We were certain that men were not the superior sex, and that the myth of male superiority must have been enforced throughout many of the world's histories. Patriarchal history, we felt, had erased the history of women's past power, and we read eagerly art historian Merlin Stone's *When God Was a Woman* (1976), which claimed that the Canaanites were peaceful goddess-worshippers demonized by the Israelites, who substituted male-centred monotheism for the earlier religion; and librarian Elizabeth Gould Davis' *The First Sex* (1971), which argued that a peaceful, agrarian, matriarchal culture had been destroyed by violent, nomadic tribes that subsequently inverted the older stories. According to Davis, cultures that had celebrated women's sexuality and revered their ability to bear children were replaced by the Christian view that women were the source of evil in the world. We read, too, Marxist anthropologist Evelyn Reed's *Women's Evolution* (1975), an account of the anthropological cover-up of the universality of the matriarchal stage that preceded patriarchy in all early societies.

These books and others assured us that familial lines had once been mother-lines, with names and responsibilities passed from mother to daughter. The mother-lines traced themselves back to a mother-goddess, a Creatress of all. Some goddesses, such as Isis, Brigid, Ceridwen and Hecate, forms of the Great Goddess, had three aspects, traditionally termed the Maiden, the Mother and the Crone; the first is a representation of new beginnings, the second a source of life and compassion and the third a repository of a lifetime of wisdom. These aspects, which were otherwise apportioned among separate goddesses, had dominion over all life, fortune, and death.[3]

While it contains no overt references to goddesses, *Charmed* is replete with symbols and rituals derived from goddess-worship and, of course, witchcraft. For instance, the triquetra, the three interlocking circles on the cover of the Book of Shadows, is an ancient symbol for the triple goddess as Maiden/Mother/Crone. The interlocking circles represent life, death and rebirth as well as the three elements that symbolize these stages, earth, air and water. The triquetra figures importantly in *Charmed*, for the Halliwell sisters acquire their powers only when Phoebe reads the incantation from the book, 'Bring your powers to we sisters three. We want the power. Give us the power' ('Something Wicca This Way Comes', 1.1). Moreover, the cat that mysteriously appears at Halliwell Manor, later discovered to be the witches' familiar, wears the same symbol on the collar around her neck, and both the cover of the book and the cat appear in the opening credits to each show. When, in 'Power Outage' (3.7), Andras, the demon of rage, provokes sufficient anger in each of the three to cause them to attack one another, the circles of the triquetra on the Book of Shadows draw apart, symbolizing the division among them as each discovers she has lost her powers. When they acknowledge each other's contributions to the family and their own faults, the circles join again and their powers are restored. As their Whitelighter Leo remarks, 'Your powers are rooted in your bond as sisters'; the triquetra, the sign of the triple goddess, is not only a reflection of these powers but mystically linked to them.

Piper, whose marriage to Leo has faced strong opposition from the Powers That Be, is finally joined with him in a hand-fasting, originally a Celtic pagan ritual. Although the ritual is said to have been conducted by a Celtic high priest or priestess in the past, it is fitting that a high priestess performs the ceremony in *Charmed* ('Just Harried', 3.15) and that Penelope 'Penny' Halliwell, Grams, who raised the girls after their mother's death, serves as high priestess. The fact that it is Leo marrying into the Halliwell line rather than Piper marrying into his is clear; although Leo has brought his Whitelighter robes as formal attire, Phoebe informs Leo that he will wear something 'more traditional' – a rented tux. Although the tuxedo has no connection to ancient religions, it is significant that Leo is 'enrobed', readied for the ritual, by his wife's sister and that the hand-fasting takes place in the Halliwell mansion, with the family of the 'bride', but not of the groom, present. Even Patty, their deceased mother, attends, having been released by the Elders for the ceremony.

The importance of matrilineal inheritance to the Halliwell line is clear during Piper's first pregnancy. Piper, her sisters and Grams anticipate the child will be a girl; the Halliwells, as Grams observes after Wyatt's birth, always have girls. Summoned for a Wiccaning ('Necromancing the Stone', 5.21), the welcoming of a child into the family line, Grams is surprised and very disappointed that the new baby is male; she asks Piper what she did wrong, and asserts that men who possess magical powers cannot handle them because magic is 'too strong' for them. Grams initially refuses to perform the ceremony; indeed, she seems reluctant even to hold the baby, a fact that does not go unnoticed by her granddaughters.

Eventually she relents after vanquishing the Necromancer, a man who appears at each Wiccaning in order to steal the powers of the entire Halliwell line. The Necromancer, Grams' former lover, is in love with her still; he seduces her, placing her spirit in thrall, and tries to persuade her to join him in appropriating the Halliwell magic so that they can be together forever. However, placed under a truth spell by Paige, Grams admits that her greatest love is that which she holds for her family. Her attitude toward Wyatt's gender softens, and she proceeds with the Wiccaning. To do so, she summons forth the matriarchs of the Halliwell line, whose ghostly spirits join her:

> I call forth from space and time
> Matriarchs from the Halliwell line,
> Mothers, daughters, sisters, friends,
> Our family spirit without end,
> To gather now in this sacred place
> And help us bring this child to grace.[4]

She pledges that the family will stand forever with Wyatt, stating, 'He is one of us and because of that, we will bless him with all the goodness that we are.' Grams then welcomes him to the family as a descendant of the *female* line, and concludes 'Blessed be', the traditional Wiccan words of greeting and blessing.

The two major plots of 'Necromancing the Stone' are the conflict between yet another evil being bent on acquiring the Halliwell gifts for his own, and an inversion of the typical patriarchal desire for a male child to 'carry on the family name'. As is evident from the summoning spell, the Halliwells are matriarchal; the family name and its gifts are typically inherited by its women. Thus, Wyatt derives only his birth name from father Leo Wyatt's last; his family name, like his mother's, is Halliwell. Asked by Piper whether the baby should carry her name or his father's, Leo responds, 'No, it's definitely Halliwell. Demons fear it, good magic respects it, and I want what's best for him' ('Baby's First Demon', 5.16). 'Necromancing the Stone' not only emphasizes lineal descent, however, but the importance of all the connections among the members of the Halliwell clan, aunts and cousins as well as mothers and daughters, all descended from Melinda Warren.

Such is the power of the family line that it figures in vanquishing the most powerful of demons, the Source of All Evil. In 'Charmed and Dangerous' (4.13) the Source has broken an age-old compact between good and evil by incorporating the Hollow, a vapour that allows him to absorb the powers of the sisters. Their own spell fails, too, as does a force-field generated by a crystal circle and the sisters determine that they must draw upon the strength of the entire Halliwell line in order to vanquish him. Piper, Phoebe and Paige utter the spell: 'Prudence, Patricia, Penelope, Melinda, Astrid, Helena, Laura and Grace. Halliwell Witches, stand strong beside us. Vanquish this evil from time and space', and it succeeds; the Source screams, bursts into flame and explodes. The spell that draws on the entire matrilineal clan is, then, their strongest spell, stronger even than the Power of Three, a spell that draws the women, 'mothers, daughters, sisters, friends', in the same summoning spell used for Wyatt's Wiccaning.

The fact that *Charmed* seems to have absorbed many of the cultural trappings of second-wave lesbian feminism comforts me even as the independence of the women who dominate its fictional universe inspires me. There are even one or two episodes that can and must be read as supporting the tenets of second-wave feminism, must be read, that is, as commenting on the inequities that women face and the constant need for women to prove themselves men's equals in public spheres. In 'House Call' (5.13) and 'Soul Survivor' (6.7), for instance, the sisters confront supernatural opponents as they always do; however, a separate plot bridging the episodes is the rivalry between Phoebe and fellow columnist Spencer Ricks, whose sexism is so blatant as to be almost anachronistic.

For me, Ricks' name evokes that of Bobby Riggs, the 1939 Wimbledon champion who challenged two of tennis's reigning queens, Margaret Court and Billie Jean King, to matches in 1973. King, who had already won six women's singles championships at Wimbledon and who was seeded No. 1 for five years, was something of a feminist icon, credited with having made it acceptable for women to excel at something besides motherhood, and instrumental in the formation of the Women's Tennis Association. Her match with Riggs, won handily by King before an audience of fifty million people, was termed 'The Battle of the Sexes', and King, according to columnist Larry Schwartz, 'was carried out on the Astrodome court like Cleopatra, in a gold litter held aloft by four muscular men dressed as ancient slaves'. Riggs was wheeled in on a rickshaw pulled by sexy models in tight outfits, 'Bobby's Bosom Buddies'.

Bobby Riggs, who was a self-confessed 'male chauvinist pig', is an excellent model for Spencer Ricks, whose comments Phoebe terms 'chauvinistic crap' in 'House Call'. A full-page ad states, 'Ask Phoebe says, every woman needs to find her inner goddess, correct? Spencer Ricks says, that's fine, as long as she cooks and cleans'. Phoebe's boss, Elise, regards the sexist ad as a clever ploy to boost circulation and soon hires Ricks to capitalize on the interested readership he has garnered. One day Phoebe enters her office to find Ricks sitting in her chair, with his feet on her desk, thus symbolically usurping her position. He greets her as 'Phoeble', and when she insists that he vacate her space, his rejoins, 'Jeez, keep your panties on'. As he passes her, he gives her figure the once-over. Then, although they are supposed to share Phoebe's column, providing competing responses to Phoebe's correspondents, he dismisses all the letters with the derogatory comment that they are 'pile of drivel. . . . It's like a freaking PMS convention', finally calling their writers 'a bunch of whiny chicks'. After Phoebe tosses a potion at him, temporarily transforming him into a turkey, he finally selects a letter from a male writer who wonders whether he should bother inviting a 'girl' who 'is flat as a board' on a date. Phoebe throws another vial at Ricks, this time transforming the sexist pig into an actual pig.

Overt political statements are few and far between in *Charmed*. There are no other campaigns for equal rights beyond the Halliwell household, no marches, picketing or letters to editors and legislators. Evidently the family has never participated in political movements. Even when the sisters travel back in time to find grandmother Penny as a hippie advocating love as the solution to the world's problems ('Witchstock', 6.11), there is no mention of the anti-war activities of the 1960s. The women of *Charmed* do express many of the same concerns as liberal second-wave feminists did: the desire to have others acknowledge the contributions of homemakers, the difficulty of finding quality day-care, the right to satisfying sex-lives. But the problems they face, while common to many heterosexual women, are framed in unique terms and require individual solutions (in the way that third-wave feminists do).

In 'The Power of Two' (1.20), for example, Phoebe, asked to pick up Prue's dry-cleaning on her way back from the market and asked by Piper to talk to the gardener about the weeds, responds between clenched teeth, 'Sure. I'll just add it to my *list*'. Then, after Piper and Prue leave, Phoebe sighs, 'I'm not even married and already I'm a housewife.' Phoebe, experiencing the dissatisfaction identified as 'the problem that has no name' by Betty Friedan in *The Feminine Mystique* (a book credited as the catalyst for second-wave feminism) and resenting the fact that her sisters seem to take her for granted, accompanies a friend on a tour to Alcatraz instead. Returning from work, Prue is upset to discover that the household tasks have not been performed. In the argument that ensues, both sisters admit that neither considers domestic chores to be work. Phoebe angrily asserts that Prue 'and Piper just assume I'll do things around the house because . . . I don't have a real job', and expresses the frustrations of all homemakers when she asks, 'When's the last time you went shopping, did the vacuuming, waited around all day for the cable guy?' Although she accuses Prue and Piper of giving her 'absolutely no credit for everything I do around here', Phoebe also admits, 'But I want a job – I want a *real* job. I'm the one that's upset with myself for not working for a living . . . I work around the house.'

Unlike women who came of age in the 1950s, however, Phoebe identifies the source of her dissatisfaction. And unlike many of the husbands of the 1950s and 1960s, Prue apologizes, expressing her gratitude to Phoebe, 'I never realized how much I probably do take you for granted, and not just for what you do around the house, either' ('The Power of Two', 1.20). In other episodes, it is clear that the series has also incorporated the hard-earned wisdom of second-wave feminists, articulated by Friedan in *The Second Stage*: far from liberating themselves from the family, women who entered the workforce retained the domestic and child-rearing responsibilities they had before and exhausted themselves, or deferred marriage and motherhood only to regret their choices later in life.

The Charmed Ones, forced both to engage demons and to work outside the home at ordinary jobs, all while attempting to lead satisfying personal lives, continually fight to maintain balance in their lives. Occasionally, Prue, and later Paige, become overly absorbed in demon hunting. In the Season Two finale, 'Be Careful What You Witch For' (2.22), for example, Prue, justifying a date she has made with 'dull Dick', states, 'Yeah, well, all demon hunting and no play has made me less picky. I gotta figure out a way to put some more balance into my life.' In 'Siren Song' (5.4) Paige, so enthusiastic about witchcraft that Piper feels ignored, retorts, 'Look, I gave up a promising career so I could focus on the craft, and, no offence, Piper, I still got a lot to learn, which means I can't just sit around the house chit-chatting.'

In fact, the word 'job' is ambiguous in *Charmed*, referring to both supernatural responsibilities and positions that generate income. Hence, when Piper complains to her husband Leo that she is, 'sick and tired of focusing on everything but *us*. I feel like I'm going through this whole pregnancy thing by myself and I do not like it,' Leo responds, 'What am I supposed to do? I have a *job*,' referring to his Whitelighter mission. Indeed, Piper is the sister who complains most consistently that 'It's never-ending – I mean, we have no lives' ('How to Make a Quilt Out of Americans', 2.17); as early as the series' second episode, 'I've Got You under My Skin', she states, 'I just want to be normal again . . . Is that too much to ask for?' In fact, when, in 'My Three Witches' (6.6), a demon accesses the sisters' innermost desires and creates alternate realities in which they can experience them, Piper finds herself without powers, leading a completely 'normal' existence, while Paige finds herself in a world in which her powers are respected and knowledge of them widespread.

Ultimately, of course, the Charmed Ones can never truly relinquish their powers until there is another generation to succeed them, in the future outlined in the series finale, 'Forever Charmed' (8.22). They have, as Whitelighter Leo and future son Chris often remind them, a sacred duty, a destiny; they have been given their powers 'for a reason'. However much she yearns for 'a normal life', then, Piper promises Prue and Phoebe that she will not surrender her powers until the others decide to do so ('How to Make a Quilt out of Americans').

Nor can any of the sisters envision truly abandoning the others. Piper's determination to remain a witch as long as her sisters do is rooted in more than the knowledge that theirs is a Power of Three; it is rooted in the strength of her love for her sisters, which is, after all, the source of all their powers (as Leo remarks in 'Power Outage'). Moreover, when witchcraft appears to conflict with Piper's love for her sisters, she attempts to fight her destiny (in 'Charmed Again', 4.1, for instance, after Prue has been killed). Phoebe is also intensely devoted to her sisters; the Demon of Fear, Barbas, identifies her dread of losing a sister as Phoebe's greatest fear ('From Fear to Eternity', 1.13), and she eventually chooses to vanquish Cole, a man she describes as the love of her life, rather than sacrifice her family and her heritage in 'Centennial Charmed' (5.12). In the same episode, Paige, who had earlier discussed moving out of the manor, decides firmly against leaving, 'Well, you know, maybe when I'm married or pregnant or hopefully both at the same time. We're sisters; we shouldn't split up until we absolutely have to. You know that, right?'

The sisters do know that. Although each may temporarily leave, only death separates one sister permanently from the others. They relish one another's successes, cherish Piper's children, and (with the exception of Paige's entirely warranted suspicion of Cole) support each other in the choices that they make. Despite their complaints about fighting demons, they also often seem to rejoice when they all share in hand-to-hand combat (as they do in the great courtroom fight scene in 'The Honeymoon's Over', 3.1). Confronted with a choice between an important mission that threatens many and saving the life of a sister, between honour and loyalty, loyalty to a sister often triumphs.

Charmed, like *The L-Word*, appears to present us with a community (albeit a smaller and consanguinial one) of women whose courage and strength derive from the intensity of the connections among them. Hence, while the sisters lead a relentlessly heterosexual existence, they still live along what Adrienne Rich has termed 'the lesbian continuum'. For Rich, lesbian identity is not restricted solely to those who enjoy romantic or erotic relationships with other women. Instead, it is shared by those who participate in a range of woman-identified experiences and is the result of primary intensities among women. In placing female friendship and comradeship along the lesbian continuum, Rich draws upon the work of Audre Lorde. Lorde redefined the concept of the female erotic, considering it to be a diffuse energy that is not confined to specific body parts but is present in the sharing of work and of 'joy, whether physical, emotional, or psychic'. Drawing upon that energy, according to Lorde and Rich, makes us less willing to accept powerlessness, resignation and despair; it is that energy that sustains the Charmed Ones.

The sisterhood that unites the women of *Charmed* is not solely derived from their shared lineage, then, but from the power and energy they derive from the other things they share: their work and their joys, their everyday lives, their fight against the powers of evil. Were we to deconstruct *Charmed* as a lesbian feminist series, we might, dare I say, read the powers of evil as standing in for the various hegemonies that seek to govern and restrict the choices we make as women, and the Charmed Ones as feminists par excellence, contesting the various social forces that oppress, repress and restrict women.

The women of *Charmed* are third-wave feminists, feminine and fashion-savvy and, true, they seem to embrace the goals of marriage and motherhood much as I did before my feminist days. At the same time, they demonstrate that women together can fight battles on a global scale and that, together, our power can be truly magical. They may even inspire budding fourth-wave feminists to become martial artists. Hence, though I am a second-wave feminist in my heart, I find there is much to be said for a series that reflects the ordinary lives of young women – lives filled with love, sex, heartbreak, birth, death and work who are also karate-kicking, fireball-throwing female heroes.

Old Myths, New Powers

Images of Second-Wave and Third-Wave Feminism in Charmed

KARIN BEELER

VER THE COURSE of eight seasons, WB's telefantasy[1] series *Charmed* incorporated many allusions to ancient myths and fairy tales. One could argue that the use of familiar myths or archetypal figures in this series, combined with the screen appeal of young, attractive and accomplished witches, may help explain the enduring popularity of the series[2] not only in the United States but around the world. Season Five of *Charmed* is particularly rich in its depiction of the Charmed Ones in the contexts of Greek mythology and European fairy tales.[3] The Charmed Ones become Greek goddesses of love, war and the home in 'Oh My Goddess' (5.22 and 5.23), they relive the stories of fairytale characters such as Little Red Riding Hood, Cinderella and Snow White in 'Happily Ever After' (5.3) and Phoebe becomes a mermaid in 'A Witch's Tail' (5.1 and 5.2). Although the use of myths and fairy tales in *Charmed* is interesting in its own right, what is worth further examination is how mythic figures and fairytale characters in the series are incorporated as a way of showing an intergenerational conflict between the Charmed Ones and an 'older' or ancient generation of feminine power. In addition to resisting patriarchal forces as symbolized by the Elders or the Source of All Evil and various male demons, the sisters must contend with an assortment of older, female characters including an evil witch, a sea hag and representations of the crone. The focus on the juxtaposition of ancient feminine forces against the younger, modern generation of the Charmed Ones may be viewed as a symbolic representation of differences between second- and third-wave feminism. In *Charmed* traditional or earlier myths may have some value, and how women interact with one another across generational lines can be important, yet the series still critiques an earlier expression of feminist power: second-wave feminism.

As a series that began in 1998 and ran for eight seasons until 2006, *Charmed* is a third-wave feminist or postfeminist[4] series that articulates certain conflicts between second- and third-wave feminist perspectives. These conflicts are illustrated through the control that representatives of the older feminine order exercise over the Charmed Ones. The vanquishing of 'older' female forces by the young upstarts may be viewed as a third-wave feminist desire to express a new brand of feminism that is youth oriented. The interaction between young and 'old'[5] does not only problematize the use of myth and archetype in the series, but it also reveals how *Charmed* can be interpreted as a site for the generational and philosophical differences between second- and third-wave feminism. However, this tension is not only articulated through characters who appear to belong to an 'older' generation or feminine order, but may also be expressed through the Charmed Ones themselves as they may embody this interplay between second- and third-wave feminist beliefs.

Initially, it appears that *Charmed* adheres to a simplistic television formula for telefantasy – the simple binary opposition of good versus evil, the basic dichotomy of European fairy tales. It is no coincidence that many of the demonic forces in *Charmed* happen to be 'masculine', thus facilitating a reading of *Charmed* as a series about three women who consistently defeat patriarchal forces. Yet the series actually sends an important message about the representation of some of its 'mythic women' even though the sisters achieve a mythic status of their own as they challenge the negative connotations of the term 'witch'. While the very foundation of the series is based on the re-fashioning of the term witch – a term that historically and mythically has had negative connotations as a result of patriarchally constructed narratives[6] – the Charmed Ones still engage in battle with other 'witch' figures, thus problematizing the notion of what it means to be a witch. They defeat witch-like figures that are presented as 'older' evil forces: the evil witch in 'Happily Ever After', a sea hag in 'A Witch's Tail', an old crone in 'Sense and Sense Ability' (5.20), a siren in 'Siren Song' (5.4) and the Furies in 'Hell Hath No Fury' (4.3). All of these figures have 'witch'-like characteristics and symbolize ancient forces that may be juxtaposed against the younger generation of modern witches represented by the Halliwell witches.

In order to view the representation of mythical women and interactions in *Charmed* as a generational or philosophical debate, it is necessary to describe some of the distinctions between second- and third-wave feminism. Second-wave feminism, the movement of the

1960s to the 1980s, has been understood as a debate about equality, feminist activism, 'equal access to the workforce' and criticism of patriarchy.[7] Third-wave feminism emerged in the 1990s and has continued into the twenty-first century. Third-wavers have their own struggles, but one of these struggles consists of third-wave feminists trying to distinguish themselves from the earlier generation of the second wave. As a result, third-wave activism does not 'always look "activist" enough to second-wave feminists'.[8] Furthermore, women of the third wave have often embodied an individualistic spirit that appears to counter the 'collective movement ethos' of second-wave feminism that developed in the 1960s, the era of 'flower power'.

One of the key ways of distinguishing between second- and third-wave feminists has been through the use of the generational metaphor. Astrid Henry indicates that the term third wave has 'frequently been employed as a kind of shorthand for a generational difference among feminists, one based on chronological age'.[9] The Charmed Ones are young women who project various third-wave or postfeminist images or beliefs; they reflect a generation's belief in a pleasure-seeking feminism that celebrates the feminine body and fashion as a way of distancing themselves from the image of 'dowdy'[10] second-wave feminists; as third-wavers, the Charmed Ones are shown questioning the second-wave feminists' obsession with career-driven lives (Phoebe's difficulty holding onto a lasting career) and through a figure like Piper, *Charmed* demonstrates the third wave's validation of domestic life. In addition, third-wavers have rejected an earlier image of feminism as anti-male;[11] this is a stereotype or caricature of feminism that has often been associated with second-wave feminists. Third-wave feminists, however, have acknowledged that this stereotype was 'instrumental in forming [their] ideas of what it would mean to be [third-wave] feminists' and argued that there 'must be a place for men and positive nonoppressive "masculinities" in a feminist politics for the 1990s'.[12]

Like other popular telefantasy series created during the age of third-wave feminism (e.g. *Buffy the Vampire Slayer, Dark Angel*), *Charmed* presents young women who project the image of the sexy, fashion-conscious warrior heroine whose views often represent a departure from the feminism of second-wave activists. These female characters have often been discussed as 'kick ass' heroines who offer a new form of female empowerment[13] that is an alternative to a second-wave feminist activist notion such as promoting social equality in the workforce.

Since young third-wave feminists often reject the views of their feminist mothers, it is not uncommon for the 'mothers' of these third-wave female heroes to be 'absent' in the series. For example, in *Buffy the Vampire Slayer*, Buffy's mother dies, leaving Buffy to become the new, 'hip' parental figure who also happens to be a vampire slayer. In *Charmed*, the sisters do not have a living mother or grandmother; they only encounter them in ghost or 'mythical' form.[14] In many ways, the defeat of other feminine figures in the storyline can be viewed as a desire to articulate a new brand of feminine empowerment through the displacement of an older, feminine (second-wave feminist) order, whether this older order is represented by mythical figures such as the Furies ('Hell Hath No Fury') or by the Charmed Ones' maternal figures (their mother Patty and their grandmother Penelope). While the Charmed Ones draw on their mother and grandmother for some assistance and recognize the importance of past connections (e.g. through their witch ancestor, Melinda Warrick), they ultimately develop their own way of handling conflict or evil. The vanquishing of the crone and the sea hag, Piper's displacement of Grams (the crone-wolf figure in 'Happily Ever After') and the defeat of the siren and Furies may all be construed as the Charmed Ones' overthrow of an older feminine order. Yet what is even more interesting is that *Charmed* does not simply present this conflict between old and new through completely different 'generations' of women; sometimes one of the 'third-wave' Charmed Ones can even express the struggle between the values of second- and third-wave feminism.

Charmed articulates the differences or the conflicts between second- and third-wave feminism by depicting the third wave's criticism of the second wave's embrace of ageing. Mary Daly is one of many second-wave feminists who have validated the hag or the crone figures. She indicates that the terms hag and crone were used to describe women on the boundaries of patriarchal society during her time: 'Hags and Crones are struggling to survive today'.[15] Patriarchal systems had positioned these women on the boundaries of society, but a feminist critic like Daly tried to reclaim these terms by investing them with positive characteristics. However, these figures are generally presented in a less than sympathetic way in *Charmed*, thus suggesting a younger generation's critique of the these figures, perhaps because of the third-wave feminists' celebration of youth, fashion and physical appearance. In 'A Witch's Tail, Parts 1 and 2', the ancient force consists of the sea hag who tries to give a mermaid to a demon and to rob her of her immortality. The sea hag or sea witch is a figure who appears in the well-known Hans Christian Andersen story 'The Little Mermaid' (1836); because of the hag's involvement in the death of sailors who perished at sea, these hags are similar to the sirens of Greek mythology. Narratives about hags often present the old and the ugly juxtaposed against images of a young woman in love. In 'A Witch's Tail' the 'hag' has red hair and is probably about fifty, so she is older than the Charmed

Ones. It is significant that the hag's age is also equated with evil. Piper asks whether the hag is an 'old woman hag' or an 'evil magic hag' and Mylie the mermaid's response is that 'she's kind of both'. If the hag symbolizes an older feminine order, then the association of the hag with evil might be even more disturbing for second-wave feminists, who have embraced the archetypes of the hag or the crone. However, if she is branded as evil by Piper, Phoebe and Paige, then these third-wave feminist witches can easily justify her destruction.

The storyline of 'A Witch's Tail' also involves another mythical creature, a mermaid, who serves as a youthful counterpoint to the hag[16] and as a fitting symbol for the youth-oriented culture of third-wave feminism. Mylie, the mermaid is in search of love from a mortal or she will lose her immortality to the sea hag. It is significant that Phoebe, one of the Charmed Ones, is transformed into a mermaid. Phoebe's reluctance to return to a world of responsibility where she fights evil shows her desire to escape painful aspects of her life, including the memory of her former relationship with her demon lover, Cole. Yet the hag and the mermaid may also be analysed in the context of the generational division between second- and third-wave feminists because Phoebe, who becomes a mermaid, vanquishes the hag by throwing an auger shell at the hag. The shell attaches itself to the hag and she disintegrates. Phoebe's destruction of the hag suggests an inability to tolerate the aged or their influence on the lives of the 'young', and may symbolize the third-wave feminist rejection of second-wave feminists as 'dowdy' or 'asexual' women who try to control a younger generation's freedom of expression, as mentioned above. Her desire to become a mermaid may also be viewed as a third-wave interest in suppressing the effects of age, thus promoting an image of feminism as 'sexy, attractive, and fun'[17] – a desire that is perpetuated through images of seemingly ageless icons like Madonna who have been celebrated by third wavers.[18]

Like the hag, the crone is perceived as an adversarial figure in *Charmed*. In 'Sense and Sense Ability', the older feminine order is represented by a crone who robs the Charmed Ones of their senses; they become blind (Piper), deaf (Phoebe) and mute (Paige). The metaphor for control over a new generation of women is quite graphic in this episode, as the old dominates the new through the suppression of the young women's senses. The silencing of third-wave feminist or postfeminist expression by the 'old guard' of second-wave feminists has been discussed in a variety of feminist forums[19] and serves as an interesting parallel to how the third-wave Charmed Ones are 'controlled' by an older generation. The domination of the new by the old in 'Sense and Sense Ability' becomes even more significant as the crone tries to kidnap Piper's baby and enacts the abduction of a child by a witch, an event that occurs in fairy tales. Here age is once again equated with evil in the world of *Charmed*; the three sisters eventually defeat this manifestation of an ancient, evil 'witch' figure with their vanquishing potion, in part because they have been able to develop a collective sixth sense to compensate for the absence of one of their regular senses. They successfully vanquish the crone, and free Leo, after Piper says 'Do you want to see real power, lady?', thus establishing the superiority of the Charmed Ones' brand of feminine power. A third-wave supplanting of the second-wave establishment occurs once again, this time with Piper's liberation of a masculine figure from the evil crone's power just to illustrate that women can stand by their men, unlike an earlier generation of women (second-wave feminists), who were often perceived as anti-male.

The generational distinction between second- and third-wave feminism takes an even more surprising turn when Grams, the sisters' grandmother, is transformed into a threatening wolf-like grandmother and Piper is cast in the role of Little Red Riding Hood in 'Happily Ever After'. In this episode both the 'evil witch' and Grams function as older women who represent an older, threatening feminine order. The 'evil witch' is clearly evil, but Grams, whose body has been invaded by wolf (she has ingested the wolf – a reversal of the traditional fairy tale), is even more dangerous since she is a wolf in grandmother's clothing. If the Charmed Ones are third-wave feminists, then the evil witch and Grams, both of whom appear to be in their fifties, could serve as second-wave feminists who threaten the third-wavers.

The evil witch also harks back to figures of the evil stepmother in 'Snow White' and other fairy tales, whose image is threatened by the younger and more beautiful daughter figure. This evil witch tries to eliminate the younger generation of Charmed Ones in order to maintain her position as the most powerful witch. Here an interesting analogy may be drawn between this battle of women in fairy tales and the differences between second- and third-wave feminists. The second-wavers have been critical of third-wavers for expressing their brand of feminism.[20] The fact that the evil witch (a stand-in for disapproving second-wave feminists) is vanquished by Piper in this episode indicates that the older feminine order is displaced by the newer. Grams presents a more complicated view of the archetypal feminine identity of the maternal. She is part of the Charmed Ones' past, and offers knowledge and wisdom that the Charmed Ones can access. Many third-wave feminists acknowledge their indebtedness to second-wave feminist accomplishments,[21] while still distinguishing themselves from second-wave feminism. Grams or Penelope Halliwell's link to second-wave feminism is actually represented in 'Witchstock' (6.11), where she is a flower child, a woman of the 1960s, the heyday of second-wave feminism.[22] This episode mentions 1967 and the title is a clear echo of the Woodstock lovefest period. Gram's brand of feminism is evident in the statement she makes about men after she has lost her soulmate, Alan: 'No one will ever compare to him. I'll probably end up hating men'.[23] Her words highlight the peace activism and the 'anti-male' attitudes often associated with second-wave feminism.

How then does Grams function in 'Happily Ever After' in relation to the Charmed Ones if the younger witches incorporate third-wave values? Grams becomes 'demonized' in this episode because she harbours a wolf within her. This image of the wolf-like crone suggests that second-wave feminists are perceived as dangerous by third-wavers because they appear to promote maternal solidarity with their feminist 'daughters', but may threaten the third wave's freedom of expression. While the 'real' Grams is still 'rescued' by Piper and actually 'survives' the magical 'possession', she is also symbolically killed by Piper so that Piper can assert her own third-wave feminist identity. The simultaneous retention and displacement of Grams reveal the kinds of contradictions at work in third-wave feminism – a form of feminism that is indebted to an earlier generation, yet defines itself as distinct in so many ways. Has Piper therefore completely eradicated tradition in her life? Not necessarily, since Grams is still present, but it is significant that her grandmother is only a ghost. Like second-wave feminists, Piper has resisted one form of traditional patriarchal knowledge (that Little Red Riding Hood needs to be rescued by the woodsman), but she has rewritten the Little Red Riding Hood narrative in a unique third-wave feminist manner. Piper does not shoot the wolf – which would be an effective way of killing the wolf in one kind of feminist fashion – instead she literally explodes the myth or fairy tale from the inside out. She lets Grams the wolf swallow her, and uses her superhuman powers to blow things up to kill the 'wolf within Grams', thus freeing herself and Grams.

While some of the representations of the old feminine order in *Charmed* actually incorporate older-looking women like Grams or the evil witch in 'Happily Ever After' or the crone as a way of emphasizing a clear generational separation between the Charmed Ones and older women, several images of these 'ancient' women still consist of female characters who appear to be under forty. This incorporation of relatively young-looking, yet mythically ancient, women is not surprising given *Charmed*'s target audience or fan base of younger viewers. American television shows and films have long been guilty of glorifying youth, and this also seems to apply to the representation of supernatural female characters in *Charmed*. Thus in *Charmed* the battle between generations, and between second- and third-wave feminism may often be incorporated in a more subtle way through the use of mythical characters whose appearance is superficially youthful (perhaps to appeal to a fan base raised in the era of third-wave feminism) but whose mythical contexts convey the sense of an older feminine order.

The mythical siren is one example of how an ancient figure is incorporated into *Charmed* as a commentary on the Charmed Ones' interaction with an 'older' feminine force. 'Siren Song' also reflects what has been presented as a difference in how second- and third-wave feminists view men in the context of feminism. In this episode the siren may not be depicted as an 'ancient' character in chronological terms, but her vengeful man-hating quality links her to one of the qualities ascribed to second-wave feminists. Paige describes the reasons behind the siren's vengeful nature. The latter was persecuted for her 'sin' of adultery in a fashion consistent with the burning of other 'witches' in history:

> ... as a mortal the siren fell in love with a married man but when they were caught the man was held blameless ... The village women cheered as they burned her to death and her rage turned her into a siren, a vengeful demon who seduces married men with her song, then destroys the couples with the very flame that consumed her.[24]

This image of the siren as witch in *Charmed* is somewhat of a departure from the conventional depiction of the sirens in Greek myth as temptresses without a specific history, but it preserves the portrayal of the siren as a 'destroyer' of men[25] – a stereotype of second-wave feminism as anti-male, and an association that has resulted in the third wave distancing itself from second-wave feminism. Thus, even though the siren may not appear older than the Charmed Ones, she represents an older kind of 'feminine' power that happens to be coded as 'demonic' and vengeful.

While other feminine forces in *Charmed* reinforce the age differentiation between the Charmed Ones and these supernatural feminine forces, it is important to look beyond a purely chronologically oriented distinction, especially since the genre of *Charmed* is fantasy. Astrid Henry has argued that the term 'third wave' should not only be limited to a difference based on chronological age, but must also be seen as 'representing the desire of those who embrace it to signal a 'new' feminism that is distinct from the second wave'.[26] In 'Siren Song' the Charmed Ones' desire to vanquish the siren paradoxically reflects a movement away from a destructive, anti-male feminine force, to one that signals cooperation between the sexes. This is illustrated through Phoebe and Leo's joint work on a vanquishing spell:

> *Phoebe:*   Hey, let's hear the spell, Leo, we've got a siren to vanquish.
> *Leo:*   'Oh singing lady of the dusk, who preys on men turns love to lust, we hearken ye.' . . .
> *Phoebe:*   'We hearken ye'? What, are we trying to summon a leprechaun here?
> *Leo:*   I told you I wasn't very good at this.
> *Phoebe:*   Give me that. It's okay, honey, we'll just rewrite that last line.

Even though Phoebe jokes about Leo's wording of the spell, the spell is created in the spirit of cooperation.

Third-wave feminists have pointed out some other inflexible aspects of second-wave feminism, and these are suggested through the image of the siren in *Charmed*. The siren's own history of oppression suggests that she lived in a time with a puritanical mindset and expression of sexuality conflicted with this time. This representation has parallels with what Astrid Henry identifies as second-wave feminism's 'ideological battle over the meaning of sexuality', which included debates about whether 'sexual freedom and pleasure were central to women's political liberation' or whether 'sex was primarily a site of oppression and danger to women'.[27] The destruction of the siren represents the destruction of this polarized debate in the sense that third-wave feminists 'see their sexual freedom as a fundamental right' and wish to move away from an anti-male image of feminism that is implicated in the mythical siren's destruction of men.[28] The third-wave feminist interaction with men is further facilitated in *Charmed* by the fact that Piper and Leo swap powers during this episode and are given a rare glimpse of how the other half lives. Thus, even though Leo appears to be the one who destroys the siren by blowing her up, he is in fact in possession of Piper's powers, so one could argue that Piper and Leo have jointly accomplished the vanquishing, thus contributing to the third wave's acceptance of having men become part of feminist work and part of a new third-wave feminist mythology.

The battle between second- and third-wave feminism is presented in an even more unusual way when this particular conflict occurs within the body and psyche of a Charmed One. In 'Hell Hath No Fury' the Furies are the representatives of the older order. They were goddesses of vengeance in Greek mythology, 'portrayed as ugly women with snakes entwined in their hair, and were pitiless to those mortals who had wrongly shed blood'.[29] They make a comeback in *Charmed* as three wild women who exhale smoke and bear snake-like swirls on their faces:

> *Phoebe:*   Okay, uh, Fury smoke kills bad guys, right? But in good
>   people, it looks for a portal of unexpressed fury.
> *Paige:*   And?
> *Phoebe:*   It builds until it consumes your humanity and it turns you
>   into a Fury.[30]

Piper actually becomes one of these Furies and may be viewed as a third-wave feminist who has been controlled by an ancient force. Cole, Phoebe's demon boyfriend, kills two of the Furies with a fireball, and Piper returns to her former self when Paige tells Piper that her rage is the result of the feelings of abandonment she experienced after the death of her sister Prue.[31] As ancient forces who control Piper, the Furies may also symbolize a quality that has often been associated with second-wave feminism: anger. 'Angry feminism' is thus associated with the ancient Furies and with the oldest sister Prue. During the first three seasons of *Charmed* Prue actually functioned as a parental figure who struggled with the responsibilities she had to undertake as the oldest; thus, even though she appears to be a third-wave feminist in generational terms, Prue incorporates the independence and career-driven ideals that some third wavers have undoubtedly 'inherited' from the second wave. 'Hell Hath No Fury' demonstrates how the ancient is not necessarily equated with the advanced age of a completely different 'generation', but reveals how even a slightly older sister such as Prue can incorporate some of the values of an older generation – and by extension the values of second-wave feminism – despite her chronological affiliation with the generation of third-wave women. The images of Prue as a third-wave feminist who still retains some second-wave characteristics, and Piper's transformation into a Fury indicate how the sisters themselves can serve as a site of contest between second- and third-wave feminism: the battle between past and present forces.[32]

Charmed uses 'older' or ancient female characters from myths and fairy tales to highlight the interaction of these older women with the Charmed Ones, a younger generation of beautiful and powerful witches. If Prue, Piper, Phoebe and Paige symbolize the expression of third-wave feminist images and beliefs, then figures such as the sea hag, the crone, the evil witch, the siren and the Furies become stand-ins for an older generation of feminine power: second-wave feminism. The fact that these forces try to control, silence or abduct the Charmed Ones or their loved ones (including the men in their lives), dictates that they must be vanquished according to the moral order of the fantasy world and according to the centrality of the third-wave feminist perspective in the series. In order for the third-wave feminist Charmed

Ones to remain powerful, they must resist these ancient forces. Thus *Charmed* appears to demonize the older generation of women through the integration of figures from myth and fairy tale. The suppression of the 'old' by the new is not limited to the realm of supernatural strangers but also applies to the sisters' mother and grandmother. Patty and Penelope Halliwell remain ghosts in the series, and may symbolize the image of second-wave feminism as a movement from the past. Grams is further demonized in a mythic and in a feminist sense; she is presented as a crone/wolf figure (under the influence of an evil witch's spell) and is also a second-wave feminist grandmother. This representation of the older generation ensures that the younger generation of witches is given the moral right to express their brand of feminism, which often displaces an earlier kind of feminism.

While some of the representations of ancient feminine forces in *Charmed* appear to be based on caricatures, this is not at all unusual for a fantasy series that presents 'evil' and 'good' with broad strokes. Third-wave feminists have acknowledged that the development of their distinct brand of feminism has occurred in response to caricatures or stereotypical images of second-wave feminism; in a similar fashion, the Charmed Ones resist one stereotype associated with a second-wave feminism – the anti-male position – and instead attempt to integrate men into their feminist circle. While *Charmed* demonstrates that the third-wave feminism embodied by the Charmed Ones may occasionally incorporate some elements of second-wave feminism (e.g. Prue's concern with her career), the frequent rejection of older women, as reinforced by mythical and fairytale images, suggests a rejection of an older generation's validity and reflects a younger generation's fear of ageing. The celebration of youth and the eradication of 'evil' older women thus ensure that third-wave feminism maintains the moral and feminist high ground in the series. This kind of third-wave power may be liberating for a new generation of feminists, but it is rather troubling for anyone who might be considered a second-wave crone in today's youth-driven culture.

Postfeminism Without Limits?

Charmed, *Horror and Sartorial Style*

ALISON PEIRSE

T HIS CHAPTER REPRESENTS the convergence of two interests: the study of horror film aesthetics in the contemporary television series and the representation of postfeminism in popular culture. Through an analysis of costume and make-up, narrative and editing patterns in three episodes in *Charmed* Season Four, this chapter explores the way that postfeminism, interpreted through horror film aesthetics, is presented as monstrous and excessive. As such, the horror mentioned in the chapter title refers not only refers to the series' regular horror film references, but also to the horror *of* postfeminism. The latter half of Season Four depicts Paige and Phoebe extending beyond their regular 'sexy and powerful' demeanours and expressing their bodies through key horror film tropes including the lesbian vampire and the possessed womb. Even though the sisters grow increasingly monstrous they do not lose their sexual allure, their clothing grows more skimpy and revealing and the excessive femininity characteristic of postfeminism is thus taken to its logical conclusion. Additionally, this chapter posits that the hyper-postfeminism modelled by Phoebe and Paige's monstrous bodies is textually constructed as aberrant. When the Source is vanquished at the end of Season Four, patriarchal authority restores the Charmed Ones to their 'natural' states in order to establish clear patriarchal limitations for the representation of postfeminism.

Reading postfeminism in relation to the television series *The X-Files* (1993–2002), Linda Badley argues that the term suggests 'a progressive movement, a sexual politics and a group identity, feminism is over, its goals accomplished, leaving in its wake the assumption of gender equity and cultural heterogeneity . . .'[1] However, Badley points out that it is in fact a backlash to late 1960s and early 1970s feminism as it rejects the suggestion that women are oppressed and is 'a compromise with patriarchal culture that reinstates "family values" and individualism'.[2] Likewise, Angela McRobbie reads a dual meaning in postfeminism. First, it 'positively draws on and invokes feminism as that which can be taken into account, to suggest that equality is achieved, in order to install a whole repertoire of new meanings which emphasise that it is no longer needed, it is a spent force'.[3] McRobbie then points out that this 'taken into accountness permits all the more thorough dismantling of feminist politics and the discrediting of the occasionally voiced need for its renewal'.[4] This dualism between progression and rejection of feminism for young women embodied in postfeminism can also be seen in Sarah Projansky and Leah R. Vande Berg's feminist reading of the television series *Sabrina, the Teenage Witch* (1996–2003). They argue that the programme 'offers empowering representations of independent girls who have access to equality and engage in cross-gender behaviour *and* that it simultaneously contains those representations within narratives that emphasize beauty, male attention, and taking responsibility for others'.[5] They suggest that there is a tension in the programme between feminism and female suppression, the two concepts work in conjunction with each other, and that 'the series simultaneously empowers *and* contains Sabrina'.[6] According to Vande Berg and Projansky, Sabrina expects gender equality, and the series is commendably fluid in its constructions of gender and sexual boundaries. However, despite the series' continual attempts to negotiate a wide-ranging feminist position, its 'affirmation of traditional patriarchal feminine concerns with physical beauty, acquisition of heterosexual male attention, and responsibility for others undermines Sabrina's access to independence and contains her feminist potential as a role model'.[7]

This disjunction between a supposedly emancipatory postfeminist position, coupled with the restitution of traditional patriarchal values and female containment, is equally apparent in *Charmed*. There are two crucial factors that allow the series to be read as postfeminist. The first is that the sisters are granted magical powers that create supernaturally powerful female bodies. These powers include Paige's 'orbing' ability, Phoebe's premonitions and levitations, and Piper's ability to both blow up and freeze other characters. These powers allow them to repel and destroy a wide variety of supernatural attackers; as a result, they are also able to control the spaces and places that they inhabit from multiple demonic attacks. Furthermore, in accordance with the postfeminist rejection of second-wave feminism and demand for femininity, postfeminism in *Charmed* is constructed through the 'women's choice to engage in heterosexually attractive bodily behaviour'.[8] The series celebrates the beautiful female body, and Phoebe and Paige in particular are represented as extremely feminine and sexually appealing, often adorned with skimpy clothing, dark hair dye and heavy, seductive make-up. Dee Amy-Chinn notes that 'the excessive performance of femininity is often seen as a trope of postfeminism'[9] and thus, postfeminism for the Charmed Ones is a combination of wielding immense, often violent power that kills demons (predominantly male), while clearly displaying overt female sexuality. In her study of the teen witch in television programmes including *Charmed* and films such as *Carrie* (Brian De Palma, 1976), Rachel Moseley argues that the texts are postfeminist as 'their investment is in the conjunction of conventional femininities with power'.[10] This chapter analyses *Charmed* through the rubric of postfeminism. This will be achieved through a close reading of how femininity is expressed in the clothing, make-up and hair of the sisters, how power is expressed through their bodies in their magical abilities and, most importantly, how the combination of excessive femininity and excessive power embodied by Paige and Phoebe in Season Four leads to the creation of a horror film rhetoric.

Interestingly, Phoebe and Paige's appearance is in direct contrast to older sister Piper's appearance, which is low key and naturalistic. The sisters' disjunctive sartorial style is clearly displayed in the opening scene of 'Bite Me' (4.18) when they vanquish a harpy. Paige has frosted pink nails and wears pale pink lipstick that matches her candy-striped top, matching pink belt and jeans. The effect is sexy but also young and casual. The pastel colours reinforce the characterization of Paige as the youngest and most naive. In contrast, middle sister Phoebe is far more glamorous. She wears heavy make-up, her eyes are defined with black kohl and she has tied up her dark brown hair, revealing a sharp razor-cut fringe. Her glossy hair and make-up are complemented by a low-cut black dress that almost reveals her breasts. Like Paige, Phoebe is dressed sexually, but whereas Paige is innocent, Phoebe's well-cut black clothing and perfect make-up signifies her as older and powerful. In contrast, Piper's appearance is particularly low key. Her make-up is minimal, she wears a plain blue t-shirt and jeans with an unadorned black belt, and her natural brown hair falls loosely around her face. The excessive detailing in costume and make-up is specific to the female bodies in *Charmed* and the male bodies have little attention devoted to them.

Jane Gaines writes on the connections between costume and narrative in film that 'although all characters, regardless of gender, are conceived as "costumed" in motion pictures, a woman's dress and demeanour, much more than a man's, indexes psychology; if costume represents interiority, it is she who is turned inside out on screen'.[11] The male bodies in *Charmed* do perform in coded costume, but the codes operate at the level of simple dualisms and do not offer the symbolic significance of the female costumes and appearances. Whitelighter Leo wears a variety of bland, beige clothing that signifies his goodness. The Source of All Evil and Phoebe's husband Cole is continually costumed in shades of sharp-suited black to symbolize his inherently evil nature. Even in 'Bite Me' the handsome young male vampire Rowan wears plain black clothing that draws little attention to individual sartorial style. In this way, *Charmed* constructs an explicit connection between clothing, identity and gender. The female body is figured through excessive femininity, specifically through clothing and make-up. Each of the sisters' costumes displays the intended perception of the women and sets up the triangulated relationship between earth mother Piper, the glamorous and powerful Phoebe, and the innocent-but-sexy child Paige.

Empowerment/Containment: Charmed*'s Postfeminist Female Monsters*

As suggested above, the postfeminist stance has its problems and in *Charmed* the postfeminist trope of being 'powerful *and* sexy' is a site of constant negotiation and anxiety. This anxiety becomes manifest in Season Four through constant narrative, thematic and visual references to the horror film genre. The horror film aesthetic is usually generated through the transformation of the sisters' bodies: in 'Bite Me' Paige becomes a lesbian vampire, while in 'We're Off to See the Wizard' (4.19) and 'Long Live the Queen' (4.20) pregnant Phoebe is a fireball-throwing Queen of the Underworld married to the Source of All Evil. In 'Womb Raider' (4.21) Phoebe is then possessed by her monstrous and demonic foetus. Most importantly, while Phoebe and Paige grow monstrous they lose none of their physical allure. As postfeminist female monsters their clothing grows skimpier, their hair more styled and their make-up even heavier. They embody excessive femininity taken to its logical conclusion. Only the mother-figure and older sister Piper, reinforced by both the space she inhabits (the kitchen) and her visually pure appearance (minimal make-up, natural hair colour and long flowing clothing) avoids the lure of hyper-postfeminism. As such, the iconography of the horror film is invested upon the feminine bodies of Paige and Phoebe to make them concomitantly powerful *and* sexy, evil *and* excessive. In these episodes femininity is displayed as excessive and monstrous, and while earth-mother Piper stays at home in the kitchen chopping fresh fruit and pining for babies with Leo,

Paige and Phoebe negotiate some of the key tenets of the horror film's monstrous-feminine: the lesbian vampire, possessed monster and monstrous womb.[12]

The postfeminist trope of excessive femininity, coupled with an allegiance to the horror film in both narrative and sartorial style, produces a conflicting sense of empowerment and containment for the sisters. The empowerment is briefly depicted as Paige and Phoebe revel in their new evil roles and additional powers, including Paige being able to fly and Phoebe throwing fireballs. The containment is far more pervasive and occurs as the episodes focus on disempowering these evil female monsters. The disempowerment is achieved through destroying their 'Other' evil families – the vampire collective and the Source – and returning the sisters to the manor with Piper. In fact, it is predominantly through Piper's 'pure' and cleansing actions that both Phoebe and Paige are saved. While *Charmed* appears to be a progressive and feminine text, in fact it imposes clear patriarchal limitations according to the presentation, behaviour and sexual proclivities of the Halliwell sisters. It condemns Phoebe and Paige's excessive femininity and divergent desires as aberrant. A detailed reading of 'Bite Me' will begin to provide evidence for these suggestions.

The Vampiric Body: Eroticisation, Homosexuality and Abjection

Writing on costume in sound films, Gaines proposes that 'the use of bold design, enlarged detail, and exaggerated shapes was consistently defended not as aesthetic interest in and of itself but as the need to make a character statement'.[13] In accordance with this, in 'Bite Me' the beautiful vampire queen's costume is highly indicative of her purpose in the episode as both seductress and destroyer. The conscious eroticization of her look is achieved through her revealing black mesh dress and strategically placed red sequins. The red sequin choker circling her pale neck is a continuation of her sartorial style and a reminder of the wound in her throat and vampiric status. Her plump lips are coloured a deep glossy red and her heavy black eye make-up mirrors her straight black hair. The constant recurrence of red throughout her costume symbolizes not only blood and danger, but also passion and sensuality. The queen is flanked by three beautiful and nubile young women, who are narcissistically matched in dresses of revealing red satin. The silent girls brush her hair, paint her nails and stroke her adoringly. A lesbian sensibility is evident in the homoerotic set-up between the queen and her young female slaves; the lesbian vampire is a dangerous and illicit creature: 'as well as transforming her victims into blood-sucking creatures of the night (she does not necessarily destroy her victims), she also threatens to seduce the daughters of patriarchy away from their proper gender roles'.[14] The lesbian vampire is a common theme of the horror film, and 'Bite Me' plays to several of its mainstream conventions. The vampire queen and her subjects represent the myth of the female vampire and her lesbian associates, so beloved of the vampire film, and Hammer Horror in particular. When Paige later joins the queen's ranks, the fantasy of the lesbian vampire turning the innocent young woman, as evidenced in *The Vampire Lovers* (Roy Ward Baker, 1970) is complete.

After introducing the vampire queen, the following scene is situated at the manor, where Piper is standing at the sink drying up pots and pans. There is a distinct contrast between the two worlds – the sensual and decadent lair of the vampires, and the domesticated space of Piper. Throughout the series Piper is represented in terms of the kitchen and domestic space. After Prue's death at the close of Season Three, Piper has taken over the role of oldest sister and replacement mother-figure. Sartorial style further reinforces Piper as a simple and maternal character. As she dries the pots she is wearing a black polo-neck jumper that covers her upper body. Her hair is tied back, her make-up is barely discernible and she wears plain gold hoop earrings. Piper complains to Leo that she is lonely as she moves around the kitchen carrying out a series of household tasks. The banal domesticity of Leo and Piper is reinforced as Leo reminds Piper they are trying for a baby.

Recently there have been a number of useful journal articles about new domesticity and its associations with postfeminism, such as Joanne Hollows' insightful study of British cookery writer and television presenter Nigella Lawson.[15] However, this chapter suggests that the construction of Piper as the sensible sister who simply wishes to be a stay-at-home mother emphatically goes against the postfeminist position. Piper longs for the pre-feminist housewife existence where she cooks, cleans and raises children, a place where her Wiccan duties and active powers are not welcome. This wish is reinforced by regularly situating her within the manor undertaking domestic duties, or shopping, or inviting people to stop for food. The 'natural' and 'inevitable' coding of her character's actions and the eventual return of the other sisters to the manor suggests that Piper's longings are the proper order of things. This proves to be an unhealthy patriarchal disjunction lurking just under the surface of the series' postfeminist veneer.

Later in 'Bite Me' the vampire queen arranges for the handsome young male vampire Rowan to attack Paige and convert her to vampirism. Notably, Rowan is the only male vampire in the episode, which reinforces the suggestion of a lesbian vampire collective. The attack is arranged to take place when Paige leaves Piper's club, P3. The attack has multiple moments of connection and reflection from the horror film, both in terms of its construction and thematic resonances. The danger is established through several horror conventions: Paige leaves the club alone, late at night, and she hurries through a deserted car park. The scene alternates between an overhead extreme long-shot 'watching' Paige in the car park and a long-shot level with Paige framed in the centre of the shot. The P3 club music fades and Paige hears a bat shriek. She walks quickly to her car. A single bat swoops down and bites her, knocking her to the floor. As she lies on the tarmac a swarm of bats fly in and undertake a frenzied and violent attack on her body. The assault has strong moments of thematic resonance with the infamous attack scene in the attic on Melanie Daniels (Tippi Hedren) in *The Birds* (Alfred Hitchcock, 1963), while the frenzied editing has structural resonance with murder of Marion Crane (Janet Leigh) in the shower in *Psycho* (Alfred Hitchcock, 1960).

The first eight shots of the scene as Paige moves across the car park are relatively long distance and last between three and five seconds. However, as Paige lies on the tarmac the scene is fragmented into fourteen shots that last around one second or less. These fourteen shots break down into three repeated images: a medium close-up of Paige lying on the floor screaming and flailing her arms, an extreme close-up of various parts of Paige's bloodied body being actually bitten by the bats, and a continuation of the original overhead long shot, depicting the bat's point of view. After forty-two seconds of biting and bleeding and violent attack, Paige passes out unconscious. The bats whirl away into the night sky.

There are two crucial observations to draw from this scene. The first is regarding point of view and identification mechanisms. Of the twenty-four total shots in the sequence, ten of them are from the same disembodied and roaming point of view. As Rowan was ordered to attack Paige, these shots can be interpreted as Rowan's ocular view. Accordingly, the viewer is positioned from the vampire's point of view, and as a result, the viewer does not identify with Paige as the victim. Only one shot, lasting less than one second, is constructed from Paige's point of view. Consequently, the scene is coded through the sadistic point of view of the vampire, rather than a masochistic alignment with the victim, and in this way the identification is not with *being* the victim, but a frenzied pleasure in *viewing* the victim that is concomitant with the position of the vampire. This blood-thirsty positioning and pleasure in viewing Paige's transgressed body in bleeding close-up goes some way to undermining the postfeminist and progressive positioning of the show, for the scene takes a clear pleasure in transgressing and punishing the female body. This is castigation for Paige's attempts to break away from the dyadic sisterly trio and go on a date; Paige had arranged to meet Rowan at P3 and had only left on her own because he did not show up. As the conclusion of this chapter suggests, the entire series of *Charmed* systematically undermines the sisters' rights to external relationships, motherhood and careers. Most particularly, the end of Season Four stops all three sisters from obtaining 'Other' families or family members, and concludes by destroying the sisters' babies and lovers to keep the Charmed Ones locked in an infantilized relationship with each other in the domestic space of the manor.

The second fundamental point in analysing the attack is that Paige's body is regularly framed in extreme close-up being bitten, with blood flowing across her skin. In particular, there are four close-ups of Paige's arm and armpit, framed in extreme close-up and lasting less than one second, where the smooth skin of her body is transgressed by a bat puncturing her skin. The skin is clearly depressed as the bat's white fangs press down hard on her flesh. As a consequence of this bodily transgression, Paige becomes coded as abject. One particular way abjection is coded in relation to the human subject is through the notion of the bodily 'border', of the breakdown of the inside and outside of the body. Julia Kristeva suggests that 'any secretion or discharge, anything that leaks out of the feminine or masculine body defiles'.[16] Kristeva argues that we expel wastes such as blood, pus and excrement to retain our 'clean and proper' bodies. However, the horror film – and by extension this episode of *Charmed* – takes great pleasure in *displaying* these moments of bodily border crossing to the viewer. The horror film stages the insides of the body on the outside of the screen world and in *Charmed* this premise is drawn upon to code Paige as the archetypal vampire victim – transgressed, defiled and abject. Paige is no longer a fully constituted subject but riddled with abjection, as blood found on the inside of the body is drained onto the surface of the skin.

Despite the graphic nature of the attack on Paige, there is a clear difference between the abject in the horror film and contemporary horror television such as *Charmed*, *Angel* (1999–2004) and *Supernatural* (2005–), where censorship more severely regulates and restricts the display of blood and gore. This has been noted by Matt Hills and Rebecca Williams in their study of abjection in *Angel*, where they consider how the rhetoric of the horror film is reworked for the television audience. Hills and Williams point out that 'due to discursive constructions of television as a "domestic" or "family" medium, the depiction of "disgusting fluids or revolting images" is arguably far less commonplace in "television horror."'[17] They suggest that abjection does occur in *Angel* but not in the same way as in the horror film. Abjection becomes far less graphic and is restricted in terms of visual and narrative content. While I am certainly in agreement with Hills and Williams' general propositions – copious amounts of actual blood and gore have always been lacking in *Buffy the Vampire Slayer* (1997–2003), *Angel* and *Charmed* – it is interesting that Paige's vampiric attack in 'Bite Me' is depicted as a truly bloody and violent event. The extreme close-ups of her body offer a visual display of abjection that begins to undermine the general textual address of contemporary horror television where 'what is *not* shown is as significant as what is'.[18]

Needles, Make-up and Incest

After the bats have flown away, leaving Paige unconscious on the floor, the scene fades to black. This ominous punctuation indicates both a passage of time and a possible death for Paige. Thankfully (after all, this is *Charmed*) the next scene reveals Paige alive and being treated in hospital, with Phoebe, Piper and Leo arriving to see her. Paige's pale face is disfigured with eleven major punctures that are bruised and swollen with gaping holes. Interestingly, after the fairly subversive moment of bloody attack in contemporary horror television, the abject theme intensifies rather than being disavowed. While Paige's blemished face continues to mark her as abject, the camera zooms into a series of close-ups of a nurse pressing a needle into Paige's arm. The scene is constructed through a series of alternating close-ups of the needle and syringe, and medium shots of Phoebe queasily watching. Writing on the 'low' genres of porn, horror and melodrama, Linda Williams suggests that such films offer moments of correspondence between the bodies on screen and the bodies of the spectators. She claims that there is a perception that 'the body of the spectator is caught up in an almost involuntary mimicry of the emotion or sensation of the body on screen along with the fact that the body displayed is female'.[19] Williams' comments regarding the alignment of the spectator and the victim's body has a clear analogy, except here the scene does not identify us with Paige the victim, but instead with her queasy sister. Phoebe's body mimics the response of the viewer who is forced to watch blood drawn from the vein of her abject sister. Spectatorship analogies between horror film and television become further apparent as the viewer is forced to gaze upon something abject and unpleasant.

There are three extreme close-ups of blood being drawn from Paige. Each shot lasts around one second. The first is of the nurse's gloved hand unpacking the syringe next to Paige's arm, the second focuses on the blue vein on Paige's arm and shows the needle pushing against the skin and actually entering the flesh, while the final extreme close-up is of the barrel of the syringe being pulled back from the needle and filling with blood. Blood is an indicator of the fragile nature of the self and Paige has now been penetrated twice, doubly abject, for 'the wound is a sign of abjection in that it violates the skin which forms a border between the inside and the outside of the body'.[20] This doubled effort to present Paige as abject sets her up for a full transition into a vampire later on in the episode. To emphasize Paige's aberrant ontological status, Phoebe sees the bloody needle and faints.

Later, Paige transforms into a bat and flies to the vampire lair. While she still retains her skimpy pastel-coloured clothing, her make-up has been dramatically enhanced and her dark hair is wound in loose curls. Like Rowan and the queen, her lips are now painted a dark red. Her otherwise fair skin has become translucent and she wears heavy black eye make-up. The combination of Paige's regular clothing with the vampiric make-up suggests a figure in transition and a liminal body that contains both good and evil. The vampire queen instructs Paige to hunt down and bite her sisters, which will seal Paige's conversion and turn Piper and Phoebe into vampires. The vampire girls drape Paige in matching red satin as she sets off to find her sisters. This narcissistic coupling in outfit is another motif of the lesbian vampire film, where 'the female vampires even look alike, further reinforcing the suggestion of narcissistic desire'.[21] Analysing serial television, Eric Freedman insightfully notes that 'characters can be in flux throughout the series where clothing is typically attached to that character's mental/physical attitude relative to a particular crisis in the narrative arc of the programme'.[22] Extending Freedman's useful point regarding clothing and the serial television narrative arc, this chapter argues that cosmetic make-up, as a subset of sartorial style, is essential to the development of characterization and narrative in *Charmed*. This is a postfeminist text that is obsessively constructed around three female bodies. Not only does the clothing of the sisters alter according to the narrative and their mental attitudes, but hair and make-up undertake equally striking revisions, and become important signifiers of crises. Crucially, the excessive increase in femininity and sexually provocative clothing, make-up and hair is twinned with an increasingly deviant aspect to the character's personality.

Paige finds Piper and Phoebe in a graveyard. Paige leans over Phoebe, revealing her fangs and says 'now it's time we really bond as sisters'. The incestuous connotation is clear, especially as Paige is now marked as lesbian by her affinity with the lesbian vampire collective in her clothing, fangs and matching red silk outfit. The fantasy of incestual sex between lesbian vampire Paige and her sister Phoebe follows Tanya Krzywinska's observation that incest on screen has multiple purposes, one of which is when incest is displayed as a form of erotic transgression and titillation and is commonly associated with the sibling relationship.[23] Overtaken by her vampire nature, Paige intends to bite Phoebe and 'turn' her sister in both the vampiric and homosexual sense. However, Leo appears and scorches Paige with holy water and Paige flees from the graveyard. She is followed to the vampire lair by the sisters and Leo. The vampires overwhelm them but the Source arrives. Phoebe stakes Rowan, the Source kills the vampire queen and Paige reverts to her former self. Paige's detachment from the abject is signalled immediately. She wakes up on the floor of the lair, still wearing the red dress but her face is bare and wiped clean. Her renunciation is complete the following morning when she comes downstairs to breakfast at the manor wearing an oversized and shapeless woolly beige cardigan and pigtails: she is both covered up and infantilized in one fell swoop. Paige's vampiric family has been destroyed, as have her lesbian proclivities. She is successfully rehabilitated into the manor and the 'proper' behaviour of a young woman symbolized throughout the series by 'good' sister Piper.

Phoebe's Pregnancy: The Monstrous Womb and the Possessed Body

Writing on the vampire film, Andrea Weiss notes that 'the vampire's thirst for blood and the association of blood with menstruation makes mocking reference to female life-giving capacities, inverting them into life-taking ones'.[24] However, the three consecutive episodes that follow 'Bite Me' revolve around Phoebe's demonic pregnancy. 'Bite Me' concludes with Phoebe discovering that she is pregnant by Cole, and 'We're Off to See the Wizard' ends as pregnant Phoebe renounces her sisters and takes her place at Cole's side as Queen of the Underworld. The following episode, 'Long Live the Queen', begins as Phoebe stares out of the window of the penthouse apartment she now shares with Cole. As the newly-evil queen, Phoebe's make-up and costume are even more decadent and glamorous than usual, reiterating that excessive femininity is aligned with anomalous behaviour. Her heavy and smoky eye make-up is twinned with jet-black hair, a luxurious housecoat and long red nightdress. Later in the episode she stalks around the apartment wearing a sadomasochistic split leather waistcoat with a partially revealed bare chest, fetishistic high heels and a see-through black lace skirt. Phoebe goes into her bedroom and removes the leather waistcoat with her back to the camera. She walks away across the room, her naked back and shoulder tattoo prominently on show. Here the episode suggests that excessive sexuality and evil equals power, and it constructs Phoebe as a desirable but dangerous sexual object. Moseley points out that 'the word "glamour" reveals a relationship between feminine allure and magic, witchcraft and power'.[25] When Phoebe is at her most sexually appealing and most powerful, she is also pregnant and evil. As such, *Charmed* continues to equate female sexuality and motherhood with a monstrosity that produces a reading of postfeminism as excessive and horrific.

The conclusion of 'Long Live the Queen' depicts pregnant Phoebe returning to her sisters and vanquishing Cole. The episode ends at the manor as Phoebe is laid on her bed. She is visually cleansed as she literally cries off her heavy make-up, pools of black mascara staining her cheeks. Her overtly sexual and sadomasochistic clothing has been replaced by an oversized grey sweatshirt that encircles her body. The credits begin as all the sisters curl up together on the bed to comfort Phoebe. Without their 'Other' families, the sisters become childlike and indulge in asexual cuddles and comfort in the safety of the manor. At the core of this analysis is the assertion that *Charmed* depicts postfeminism as having limits. The end of Season Four depicts the Charmed Ones going beyond their regular 'sexy and powerful' depiction and expressing their bodies through key horror film tropes that result in an ever-more heightened sense of sexuality and power. However, this hyper-postfeminism is constructed as aberrant, and a form of patriarchal authority restores the Charmed Ones to their 'natural' states when the Source is vanquished. Paige becomes fully human again and Phoebe vanquishes her evil husband. Concurrently, Paige and Phoebe's dress sense, hair colour and make-up are significantly toned down to mirror the appearance of earth-mother Piper.

The following episode, 'Womb Raider', runs on two parallel lines: Phoebe's increasing inability to keep her unborn demonic baby under control, and the Seer's attempts to steal the baby and carry it herself in order to become the Source. Phoebe, as the embodiment of the monstrous womb, has parallels with several major horror films including *The Brood* (David Cronenberg, 1979), *Demon Seed* (Donald Cammell, 1977) and *Rosemary's Baby* (Roman Polanski, 1968). Importantly, Phoebe becomes hyper-sexualized and evil again through her possession. In her study of gender and the horror film, Carol Clover suggests that in possession films 'moderate slides into excessive; appealingly open becomes monstrously open, emotionally impressionable becomes mentally ill, charmingly pregnant becomes hideously pregnant, and so on'.[26] Eventually, the baby takes complete possession of Phoebe's body. Barbara Creed points out that in possession films 'possession becomes the excuse for legitimizing a display of aberrant feminine behaviour which is depicted as depraved, monstrous, abject – and perversely appealing'.[27] Phoebe's increasing possession by her unborn demonic baby is used to legitimize her increasing irrational and evil behaviour throughout the later episodes of Season Four. In the latter half of 'Womb Raider', possessed Phoebe allows the Seer to take her unborn baby from her. The Seer transfers Phoebe's foetus into her own body and is confirmed as the new Source. However, like Phoebe, the Seer's body becomes unstable and bursts into flames. She cannot contain the baby and the Source's power, and the episode ends as the Seer kills all of the demons at the coronation, the baby and herself through a magical explosion.

In *Charmed*, power and femininity are invested with monstrosity. Horror is created through an allegiance to key tenets of the horror film and the punishment of excessive female bodies garbed in provocative clothing and heavy make-up. As a lesbian vampire and the Queen of the Underworld, Paige and Phoebe received glamorous makeovers that further enhance their already feminine and sexual appearance. Additionally, their powers were significantly enhanced: Paige could fly, she was stronger than her athletic sister Phoebe and developed telepathic ability, while Phoebe was invested with 'upper-level' demonic fire-throwing abilities. However, the detailed reading in this chapter has revealed that such a weighty postfeminist investment in glamour and power has penalties, namely that these investments lead to an untenable excess in femininity, sexuality and horror and must be extinguished. Both Paige and Phoebe's evil female role models, the vampire queen and the Seer, are destroyed by the end of Season Four to compensate for their aberrant and monstrous sexualities.

Postfeminism with Limits: The Destruction of the Monstrous Feminine

'Womb Raider' ends with the Charmed Ones reunited at the manor. Phoebe has lost her husband and baby; Paige has been unsuccessful in going beyond the boundaries of acceptable gender, familial and sexual behaviour as a transgressive and incestuous lesbian vampire; and Piper has been told by the doctor that it would be almost impossible for her to conceive her own child. The sisters have all made varying attempts to create a family unit of their own: Paige attempted this through a vampire collective, Phoebe in her royal domain of the Underworld and Piper through her wish for a child with Leo. All were unsuccessful, and the trio are forced to live together as sisters rather than as mothers. The monstrous sexuality and allure embodied in these four episodes by Paige and Phoebe is renounced, suggesting a clear limitation on how excessively glamorous the sisters are able to become. As Moseley states, the glamorous witch can be pleasurable and fascinating; however, the glamour is also 'emphatically superficial, ephemeral and cosmetic, thus raising significant questions about the representations of gendered power they offer, and the femininities they construct and validate'.[28] As such, Phoebe and Paige's representations at the close of Season Four are problematic: they are stripped of their make-up, their Other families and their overtly sexual appearance. Aberrant sexual proclivities are papered over and the sisters are infantilized and controlled within the maternal space of the manor. The destruction of the horror film's über-sexy monstrous-feminine and the restitution of the power of three as a cogent family unit can be construed as a cautionary note for citing *Charmed* as an unproblematic celebration of postfeminism. The analysis of these episodes reveals that at a certain point, female sexuality and power becomes excessively dangerous and must be destroyed. Paige and Phoebe's beautiful bodies are a warning that postfeminism can be attained but must be constructed and controlled within clearly defined limits. *Charmed* celebrates postfeminism through the emancipation and empowerment of young women through magic while garbed in feminine apparel and sultry eye make-up; it also comes with constraints and boundaries that point to its postfeminist leanings not being entirely intact or stable.

Throughout this chapter theories of postfeminism and the horror film have illuminated key anxieties and tensions around the bodies of the Charmed Ones at the end of Season Four. However, while the series as a whole draws upon horror film aesthetics and narrative, it doesn't follow that film theory is easily transplantable onto the study of a long-running television series. As Freedman points out in his analysis of *Buffy*, there are 'technological and cultural' differences between film and television, and, in particular, that 'the serial format mandates development and regression, a forward and backward trajectory that continuously plays out the female protagonist's empowerment, disempowerment, re-empowerment'.[29] This chapter suggests that this oscillating trajectory of gendered empowerment and containment demonstrated in *Charmed* is particularly effective in the serial television format. It presents the opportunity to depict the female protagonists Paige and Phoebe in a variety of deviant, excessive and monstrous roles that transgress accepted notions of sexuality and sexual behaviour (incest, vampirism, demonic foetuses) before returning them to so-called 'normality', namely living in the manor with Piper. Similarly, Krzywinska suggests that the difference between horror television and the horror film is 'the scope afforded by the series format'.[30] Krzywinska argues that whereas the ninety-minute horror film is a one-off event and need not entice the viewer to tune in again, the 'long running serials allow characters to be drawn in more robust ways, evolving in ways that the format of the horror film cannot accommodate'.[31] As such, the horrific natures of Paige and Phoebe are explored in some depth across Season Four. The trajectory between good and evil depicted in the sisters' actions and sartorial style becomes a complex site of negotiation that would be untenable in a contemporary linear narrative horror film.

PART THREE

Visual Power, Place and Genre

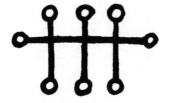

There is Nothing New in the Underworld

Narrative Recurrence and Visual Leitmotivs in Charmed

STAN BEELER

> I would like to now consider the case of a historical period (our own)
> when iteration and repetition seem to dominate the whole world of
> artistic creativity, and in which it is difficult to distinguish between the
> repetition of the media and the repetition of the so-called major arts.[1]

Art and Industry

In the above quotation Umberto Eco indicates that because
contemporary art has taken on the aesthetic values of postmodernism
we must re-evaluate traditional notions of iteration and repetition. This
is especially true when we look at the narrative structure of television
series and serials (both episodic and serialized narrative television).
Eco believes that contemporary art moves beyond the Romantic
distinction between crafts/industry and art. To Romantic sensibilities,
art must be an earthshaking paradigm shift that forces its audience
to reconsider the world, while crafts and industry did not focus on
this desire for something completely new as their overriding concern.
However, the Romantic segregation of art from craft and industry is a
relatively new distinction. For example, art in the Baroque era gave us
musical forms in which,

> the basic melody is given by a psalm, a folk dance or a folk song
> that contemporary listeners were supposed to know by heart. Each
> of the customary three or more variations follows a fixed pattern.
> The pleasure is given both by the recurrence of the same patterns on
> different melodies and by the skill with which the player is supposed

to interpret the many possibilities of reinventing the pieces by a variety of portatos, nonlegatos, staccatos, and so on.[2]

Eco believes that the contemporary television audience has taken on the aesthetic sensibilities of pre-Romantic art and has come to find pleasure in the infinity of variation upon familiar themes. This is a particularly revealing insight into the reasons for the longevity of a series like *Charmed*. Each week the basic narrative format, the character structure of the three powerful young witches, is repeated with elaboration and the standard visual repertoire of the series returns with comforting regularity. Halliwell Manor is constantly present, both externally and internally, in reassuring familiar detail in stock shots that go far beyond the normal function of establishing location. These constants of character and image play out in contrapuntal complexity against a series of fugue-like variations provided by new demons, new lovers and new ethical dilemmas.

Character and Power

The narrative variations in *Charmed* often represent the development of new powers or the loss of former puissance by the three Halliwell sisters – powers logically based upon their original gifts. Yet, this is not a simple juvenile fantasy construction based upon wish fulfilment and the desire to be different. The sisters' powers are the physical manifestations of their emotional and ethical characteristics; consequently the plots present the audience with insights that indicate the sisters' strengths and flaws as they contribute to an inevitable happy resolution. Because this is a definitively third-wave feminist series, the triumphant resolution of all variations upon the theme of Halliwell entails – along with the second-wave feminist goals of career and independence – long-term relationships and children. The twists and turns of the plot are all predicated upon the reassuring character 'development' of the sisters. The fact that one of the sisters, Prudence (Shannen Doherty) only lasted for three of the eight seasons did present some difficulties to an overarching plot structure initially conceived using Prue as the dominant voice in the fugue-like structure of the narrative.[3] When Paige (Rose McGowan) comes into the narrative after Prue's death, the whole complex, yet repetitive, structure of sisterly relationships is altered. Piper is transformed from the middle sister to the eldest, and although Phoebe (Alyssa Milano) becomes the middle sister, in many ways she maintains her plot function as the most immature and therefore irresponsible of the three; she is constantly in need of moral guidance from her siblings. To some extent, Paige serves to replace the mediating function that Piper (Holly Marie Combs) held when she served as a buffer between Prue and Phoebe.

Plot and Structure

The *Charmed* plotlines are normally variants of classical Hollywood narrative structure. That is, the plot is divided into three primary components: the introduction, which presents the problem to be resolved in the episode; the second act, which conveys the complications that are necessary to resolve the problem presented in the introduction; and the third act, which is the climax and resolution of the problem. Television narrative in general, and *Charmed* in particular, is somewhat different to filmic expressions of classical Hollywood structure in several ways. The first, and perhaps the most prominent element is the fact that an hour-long television episode is divided by four commercial breaks that serve the function of splitting the episode up into four acts. The end of an act is often signalled by a small climax in the action that is resolved after the break. Moreover, multiple storylines are commonly present in an average episode; there are at least two and often more. Major narrative lines are referred to as 'A plots', and less important narrative lines are 'B plots'. The development of the plot entails the resolution of some – but not all – of the storylines that are introduced in the first section of each episode.[4] The narrative is built around a basic unit that is about two minutes in length, dealing with each storyline from scene to scene in alternating format.[5] Because television has in recent years chosen to enhance audience loyalty through the use of story arcs lasting longer than a single episode, it is clear that all of the story material presented cannot possibly be resolved in a single episode. *Charmed* is a series built around the lives of three sisters, and therefore the episodes commonly have two or three storylines that are centred around one or more of the sisters, running in parallel.

The Sisters

In the pilot episode of *Charmed*, Phoebe is estranged from her sisters and has just returned from an extended time away from San Francisco. Her mobility, or lack of dedication to the physical location of her native city, is repeated with numerous variations during the course of the eight seasons of the series and is one her defining characteristics. She always seems to toy with the idea of moving away from her sisters, but the consequences of any steps towards realizing these ideas are always unfortunate. It is perceived as a sign of her immaturity, even though in normal North American society maturity is often gauged by willingness to leave home and strike out on one's own. In Seasons Four and Five she moves in with Cole (Julian McMahon), her half-demon boyfriend, first in an apartment in San Francisco and eventually marries him and moves to the Underworld. In Season Six she contemplates moving to Hong Kong with her current boyfriend, Jason. She is given advice by her boss Elise Rothman (Rebecca Balding) that sounds as if it was taken directly from a third-wave feminist manifesto:

> There's a whole generation of women out there who followed the dream, built successful careers, but at the expense of everything else. Now I'm not saying I think they all made mistakes, because some of them are very happy. But some of us aren't. Trust me, you don't want to wake up one day and realize that all you've got is your career.[6]

Phoebe's character is related to matters of the heart, and her recurring plot variations tend to revolve around romantic relationships that often lead to unfortunate events because she is unable to assess her current lover accurately. This libido-driven character structure is occasionally swapped to one or more of the other sisters, but when this happens the device is most noteworthy as a break in the expected pattern rather than a true alteration in character of one of the sisters.

In contrast to Phoebe's mercurial concentration on love and feelings, Piper's character is centred on home and family. Because of this, the plot variations that foreground her role are about long-term relationships and the care and nurturing of her children. In a classic pop-psychology cliché, Piper the mother-figure is initially represented as a chef and then as the mistress of cauldron-based spell making; after all, she is maternal and therefore an association with cooking is obvious. Piper's relationship with Leo, although suffering many ups and downs, lasts for nearly the entire eight seasons of the series. Her variation upon the theme of third-wave feminism is developed around the difficulties entailed in maintaining a life as a working, and occasionally single, mother. Unlike her other two sisters, Piper is not remarkable for her tendency toward short-term relationships; when Piper dates a man it is most often with the possibility of developing a long-term relationship.

Prudence is, perhaps, the most accurately named of the three sisters. Although she is the only one of the Charmed Ones who dies permanently, her general demeanour and character goals are more serious than those of her sisters. Although at first blush Piper's teleological inclination to hearth and family may seem quite serious, the manner in which these drives are expressed indicates a more personal and less altruistic motivation than that espoused by Prue. Prue as the eldest sister is the most socially conscious of the four Charmed Ones and, therefore, perhaps the closest to second-wave feminism in her mannerisms and ethical stance. Plotlines featuring Prudence tend to demonstrate her willingness to sacrifice her own well being and happiness for the greater good of humanity and the magical balance of the universe. As with all of the other sisters, there are plots that represent Prue in a different light, but this is not surprising given the sheer volume of this series. If the sisters only acted completely within the limits of their prescribed character parameters, *Charmed* would have failed to last more than three seasons.

Paige, brought in to maintain the essentially trinitarian structure of the series after Shannen Doherty's departure, demonstrates an interesting combination of character elements that transform the fugue-like plot patterns that were developed during the first three seasons of *Charmed*. Because Phoebe is no longer the youngest sister, many of the ingenuous aspects of her character are taken over by Paige. She is, after all, new to witchcraft as well as being unfamiliar with non-magical aspects of the Halliwell family traditions. Many of the early plots featuring Paige emphasize her need to find her place in the already developed structure of the narrative. As the new 'youngest sister', one would expect Paige to prove more prone to precipitous action than her two older siblings, but, in fact, she is presented as more mature than Phoebe. Paige is always suspicious of Cole and it is clear that her suspicions are well founded. The narratological reasons for Paige's somewhat unexpected maturity are probably based upon the series developer's reluctance to abandon the successful structure of the first three seasons of the series. The fundamental patterns of Phoebe's narrative position have already been established by the time that Paige arrives on the scene, and it would have been a major disruption of the successful template of repetition to alter her role by representing substantial maturation of the character. After all, as Jane Feuer suggests, the characters do not actually develop, they only alter in their relationships to one another.[7] When Paige is introduced, the relationship of the three new Charmed Ones is, by necessity, not quite the same as the original cast. Yet, it was close enough to the original pattern that it did not alienate the established *Charmed* audience. For this reason, although Piper does seem to accept the mantle of eldest sister in a familial context, it is Paige who takes on the job of headmistress of the Magic School and shows the most social concern in a 'big picture' context. She also develops much more potent powers than one would expect of the youngest sister. These aspects of Paige's equivocal position in the Halliwell family are diegetically explained by reference to her father, a Whitelighter. As Whitelighters are the *Charmed* universe's analogue of angels, Paige's half-angelic power and generally unassailable moral position make her role much closer to Prue. The plot structures of the series reflect Paige's position as a highly moral character, by birth as well as by predilection, in the post-Prue reconfiguration.

The Men

Charmed's feminine – if not feminist – bias necessitates that recurring male figures in the series have relatively minor significance in plot developments. Indeed, Leo Wyatt (Brian Krause) and Cole serve as exemplars of specific types of consorts rather than truly active participants in the dance of relationships that is *Charmed*'s central narrative. Leo is the mature, supportive husband whose one true flaw is his excessive dedication to his work. Promotion to Elder takes him away from his familial obligations and allows Piper to function as a not-quite-single mother for a number of seasons. Leo's devotion to the altruistic duties of an Elder serves to highlight Piper's devotion to family above all else.

Cole, on the other hand, is an archetypal man-with-a-secret. At first he hides his demon nature, and when that comes out he hides the fact that he is the Source. No matter what the circumstances, Cole is always hiding something from Phoebe. His duplicitous nature allows him to serve as a plot-foil emphasizing that Phoebe is ruled by her heart. She knows that she has taken up with a bad man, but cannot bring herself to end the relationship under her own power. There are a number of other men who serve as subject material for story arcs over the course of *Charmed*, and the most interesting of these tend not to be potential partners. Darryl Morris (Dorian Gregory) probably appears in the series more often than any other man apart from Leo. He is married (and racially other) and never considered as a potential partner for the sisters.

Character and Narrative Form

It is important to understand clearly the character configurations that are at the heart of *Charmed*'s narrative structures for, as indicated above, *Charmed* plot structures are a bridge between the serial and the purely episodic forms. The serial component of *Charmed*'s plots often manifests itself through the introduction of character development;

through their experiences in fighting evil the sisters learn more about themselves, and, perhaps more importantly, about each other. This highly specific type of character development is dismissed by Jane Feuer as an illusion. She believes that character development in television serials is not necessarily real: '[I]t is not correct to say that characters change in prime-time continuing serials. More often they perpetuate the narrative by continuing to make the same mistakes. Rather, owing to the multiple plot structure, characters' positions shift in relation to other characters.'[8] This denigration of the type of character development affected in serial television is, however, by no means a universally held opinion: 'In fact, many times, character and story are so intertwined that it is difficult to differentiate between them. As a result, television has a unique opportunity to continue character development both on a regularly scheduled basis and over a long period of time.'[9] *Charmed* is a perfect example of the intertwining of character and story; the repetitive nature of the plots shifts the focus from the development of a truly linear narrative and places it upon the embellishment of the three relatively stable character types. Although a Baroque analogue of development is inherent in the narrative, the women of *Charmed* never have the life-altering epiphanies so dear to Romantic narrative structures. Their realizations never really transform their more-or-less fixed relationships; their knowledge is enhanced and their actions in the future are predicated upon this revealed knowledge.

There is, however, one really significant exception to the rule of static characters in fixed relationships in the series; the removal of Prue from the intricate, yet essentially static, narrative structure of *Charmed* necessitated the one great transformation in the dance of family relationships that is the heart of the series. Although perceived at first by many fans as detrimental to the continued viability of the series, it is possible to argue that this introduction of narrative complexity into the plot structure roughly halfway through the course of the series actually aided in the continued maintenance of audience interest. Jason Mittell describes a similar technique which he refers to as 'narrative spectacle' and describes it thus: 'But the boldest moments of narrative spectacle occur when the plot makes unforeseen sharp twists that cause the entire scenario to "reboot", changing the professional and interpersonal dynamics of almost every character.'[10]

Mittell is describing a technique used in the series *Alias* (2001–6). Although the plot reconfigurations in *Alias* are deliberate and clearly designed to enhance the audience's appreciation of the complexity of the narrative, I believe that the transformation of the sisterly relationships that occur in *Charmed* with the departure of Shannen Doherty and the introduction of Rose McGowan inadvertently breathed new life into the series through a tour-de-force of (necessary) narrative reconfiguration. Even though the series remains repetitive in its narrative structure even after this modulation, it gains a new life through the introduction of necessary transformations.

Visual Repetition

Although the plot structures of *Charmed* are remarkably similar to Baroque counterpoint, certain visual elements of the series can be usefully compared to the arch-Romantic composer Richard Wagner's technique[11] of the leitmotiv. Wagner developed the practice of introducing important characters, places and ideas in his massive Romantic operas with characteristic musical themes that served, among other functions, to enhance the unity of the work. In the highly visual world of contemporary narrative television, the repetition of characteristic images has come to serve a similar unifying function. In standard cinematography establishing shots are used to introduce the audience to the location and characters appearing in a subsequent scene. This technique was developed – at least in part – for technical reasons that include reduction in expensive location shooting. Once the location has been established through the use of a familiar landmark, the bulk of the filming can return to the highly controlled and more economical studio. For example, the opening credits of each episode of *Charmed* play over an aerial shot that begins over San Francisco Bay, moves in over the Golden Gate Bridge to the city's down-town where the Transamerica Pyramid features prominently. The geographical positioning of the series is thus accomplished and subsequent scenes are, unless otherwise signalled with a different establishing shot, understood to take place within the environs of the city. However, *Charmed* uses a number of establishing shots that extend substantially beyond this basic cartographic function and provide us with immediate knowledge of the characters' mood and specific plot elements that are to follow. These shots are primarily developed around architectural elements that are not so well known as the standard city signifiers that make up the opening scenes of the series. Of course, the traditional understanding of television, developed in the early years of the medium, suggests that television is 'unsuited to spectacle and visual display'.[12] Because of this understanding of the medium, television analysis often ignores the role that visual elements play in the development of television series' overall impact. These attitudes toward television analysis are founded upon the limitations of technology that had been transcended long before *Charmed* started to air in the 1990s. Of course, the series still depends heavily upon the traditional television mainstays of dialogue and close-up shots of actors emoting, but as an example of telefantasy[13] *Charmed* takes advantage of visual spectacle to both frame and develop its plot. As presented above, *Charmed* is a narrative that depends heavily upon repetition and iteration to develop its audience, so it is not surprising that the same techniques are to be found in the visual spectacle of the series. The establishing scenes and stock location shots that serve as visual leitmotivs in the *Charmed* narrative are carefully chosen to reinforce the contrapuntal structure of the plotlines. The following sections present some of the primary visual elements of the series and attempt to indicate their functions in the repetitive narrative structures at the heart of the series.

The Attic

Perhaps the most persistent of the visual signifiers in *Charmed* is the attic of Halliwell Manor. The attic is an innovative example of *mise-en-scène*, combining signature elements of lighting and colour with a specific decor. The attic is in contrast to the clichéd film and television conceptualization of a cramped and cluttered location with limited lighting, suitable for scenes of horror. The Halliwell Manor has an attic brightly lit with stained-glass windows that evoke the sacred atmosphere of a church, while using abstract patterns of light yellow, blue and green glass rather than the specific images of holy figures more common in church windows. Shots of the Halliwell attic are usually low density, the clutter of disparate objects spread widely apart to give the impression of eclecticism without confusion. The objects in the attic are a jumble of unmatched furniture and shelves that vary from episode to episode and season to season. The floor of the Halliwell attic has plenty of bare space for the drawing of magical designs or placing protective crystals. At least one wall is also bare and serves as a drawing board for large magical symbols that usually result in portals to other times or alternate dimensions.

The attic is the seat of the sisters' mystic power, and when it appears it indicates that the sisters' inherent magical powers are going to manifest themselves. The image of the attic is usually, although not always, combined with images of the Book of Shadows, which is prominently displayed in the attic on a podium, open for reading. In the earlier seasons of *Charmed*, the Book of Shadows is carried from room to room in the manor, but as the series progresses the book seems to take up permanent residence in the attic, adding to the room's aura of mystic power and enhancing the plot connections to the matrilinial derivation of the sisters' power. The general plot of the series indicates that the true heart of the mystic power of the Halliwell Manor is geographic and it is located in the basement. A number of episodes revolve around the positive and negative application of that seat of power. However, the visual cues of the series lead the audience to expect that magic elements reflecting the sisters' power will ensue when the attic serves as an establishing shot.

The Halliwell Manor

External shots of the house that provides a communal living space for the three sisters are, perhaps, the most persistent images of the entire series. The manor is normally shot from a low angle to emphasize the importance of the location to the series. It is also commonly viewed from an angle rather than directly from the front or side. This angle accentuates the building's unique charm, a Victorian remnant that stands out in North American architecture, which tends toward new and featureless buildings in residential areas. Although the actual building that is cast as the Halliwell Manor is located in Los Angeles rather than San Francisco, the quirky appearance of the edifice serves, within the context of the series, to evoke San Francisco's special historical value to American culture. External shots of the house not only indicate that subsequent action takes place inside, they also usually indicate that the narrative will focus more upon the sisters' emotional lives rather than their adventurous careers as witches. In other words, when the manor is the establishing shot, the plot will, at least for a time, deal with the sisters' lives as women who are negotiating the difficult territory of family life and dating.

These are only two examples of the primary visual leitmotivs that are used to enhance narrative continuity in *Charmed*. It is, nevertheless, important to introduce them in order to clarify the ensuing detailed analysis of a single episode of the series.

Narrative Recurrence and Visual Leitmotivs in 'Something Wicca This Way Comes'

In this section I will present a brief analysis of the narrative recurrence and visual leitmotivs as they are set up in the very first episode of *Charmed*. The structure of the analysis relys upon the short (roughly two minutes in length) segments that are the basic element of narrative construction in this series.

'Something Wicca This Way Comes' (1.1) begins with a quick establishing shot of the Golden Gate Bridge in a rainstorm. At this point the visual is simply intended to set the geographical location of the action in San Francisco. The Golden Gate has a long filmic tradition as a signifier of San Francisco. However, there is something more than a simple reference to physical positioning of the plot. This *particular* location is important to the ambience of the series as San Francisco has a long tradition in the USA as a seat of counter-culture. The narrative structure of the series depends heavily upon San Francisco as a place where New Age and Wiccan events are a cultural norm.

The scene then moves to show a witch murdered during a magic ceremony. The face of the murderer is not shown and this serves as the introduction of a plotline that will be completely resolved in this episode; that is, 'who killed the witch?' This establishes the series' pattern of presenting a demonic influence in a plotline that will be resolved – usually through the vanquishing of the demon – by the end of the episode. This 'demon du jour' is the a way of eschewing a completely serialized narrative structure and providing interest for an audience that watches the show only occasionally or in the scrambled order favoured by syndication.

The next scene introduces two of the major characters of the series. Piper and Prue are physically present and their relationship with the absent sister Phoebe is introduced through their dialogue. Piper defends Phoebe while Prue criticizes her. This sets up another plot refrain that will continue throughout Prue's tenure on the series; Piper will defend Phoebe and Prue will be critical. *Charmed* follows the pattern established by a number of television series in the 1990s of starting the episode with a short expositional segment – often called a teaser – running before the series credits. The credits follow the teaser and then there is another short musical selection played over an aerial image of the Golden Gate Bridge and San Francisco skyline at night. This is also part of the pattern for the series. The music that plays after the credits is usually from hip indie bands and serves to orient the show's focus at young – but not too young – people; the kind of people who would recognize the music that follows the credits. In 'Something Wicca This Way Comes' this pattern is not yet established, but the position in the narrative structure is developed with a short scene with more conventional music.

The segment following the credits returns to the initial plotline dealing with the witch's murder. The characters that are introduced are the two detectives Andy Trudeau (Ted King) and Darryl. They reiterate the events of the opening scene and introduce new information; this is not the first murder of a witch in the area and Andy suspects a magical motive for the crimes. The reassuring narrative pattern of *Charmed* is heavily dependent upon plot reiteration presented by non-magical policemen who are appropriately dumbfounded when their cases are resolved by the magical intervention of the sisters.

The subsequent scene is again in the Halliwell Manor and the plotline concerning tension between Prue and Phoebe is continued. Piper reveals that she has been in contact with Phoebe and has invited her to return to live in the manor. It is in this section that we discover that the manor is owned by all three sisters. The visual aspects of the inside of the Halliwell Manor are introduced and the two sisters' dialogue serves to indicate that this communal living space will serve as a defining visual for the subject of family relationships. The narrative pattern that this physical space represents for the entire series is defined in this early scene.

Phoebe finally arrives and the tension between Prue and Phoebe is delineated as having some financial basis. Prue is concerned about money and the possibility that Phoebe simply wants to sell the manor. One the other hand, Phoebe believes that Prue is angry because of some supposed romantic involvement between her and one of Prue's boyfriends. The narrative pattern is based upon the essentialist depiction of Prue as a woman concerned with practical matters and Phoebe's belief that love is the most important consideration. Piper's attempts to reconcile the tension by cooking a meal are consistent with her character as it develops in the series. It is interesting to note that although the supernatural has been hinted at in the opening plot element, it has not been introduced in conjunction with the sisters. In contrast, the tension between Prue and Phoebe that is introduced even before Phoebe arrives, remains as a primary plot motivator for the entire series until Doherty's departure.

The single-episode parallel plot of the witch's death is reintroduced in this segment through a news story playing on a television in Phoebe's room. This follows the pattern of television narrative; although episode segments tend to focus on a single plotline, they often include reminders of the parallel plot. This redundant information aids in maintaining audience interest in the multiple storylines. Therefore, it comes as no surprise that the subsequent scene again centres on the murder. Despite the fact that this segment is focused on the simple detective story elements of the episode, we are reminded of the overarching mystic theme through the introduction of another one of the visual leitmotivs for the series. Andy looks at a tattoo of the triquetra symbol on the shoulder of the corpse, then later in the scene after an expository discussion of witchcraft the symbol is revealed on the tag of the dead witch's cat. Whenever this symbol appears in *Charmed* the supernatural is introduced.

After introducing the leitmotiv of the triquetra, the action returns to the Halliwell Manor but continues to refer to the occult; the symbol has served as a visual equivalent of a transitional paragraph. Piper and Phoebe are playing with a 'spirit board'[14] which starts to move on its own, spelling out the word 'attic'. As the segment progresses, the longer narrative goal of the sisters developing and exercising their powers is presented. They go to the attic with Phoebe serving as the impetus for supernatural events while Prue is presented as reluctant. The series creators have seen fit to start with relationships before introducing magic and this is some indication of the real plot focus of the series. In the attic Phoebe first sees the Book of Shadows and a cinematographic cliché is used to signal the onset of the powers. When Phoebe recites the incantation from the Book of Shadows that initiates the sisters' powers, the scene cuts to a photograph in the downstairs hallway and the images of the three sisters in the photograph move closer together. Shots with tight groupings indicate intimacy. The attic and the Book of Shadows are introduced in this segment, and their close connection with the supernatural elements of the series are introduced. Phoebe's function as risk taker is also introduced in the context of magic.

The narrative is composed of a number of scenes that focus in turn on each of the major narrative goals set up in the expository section of the episode. During the course of the detective story we discover the murderer is actually a warlock named Jeremy, who has been dating Piper. By the end of the episode the sisters have discovered their nascent powers and have vanquished the warlock. Most of the primary narrative themes that dominate the repetitive structures of the series are presented in the first episode, moreover, many of the visual leitmotivs that serve to support the plot variants are also presented.

Conclusion

In this brief discussion of the importance of narrative and visual repetition in *Charmed* it is clear that the series may serve as an exemplar for a specific style of television that borrows structural elements from well-established formats, ranging from soap opera to sitcom. What is unique about *Charmed* is that it managed to balance this hotchpotch of paradigms successfully, enabling the series to run for a full eight seasons. This is no small feat in the cut-throat world of prime-time television series. The creators of *Charmed* were able to turn the potential death-blow of a major casting problem into an asset, coming back even stronger with a renewed plot structure after the departure of a primary cast-member. Building upon powerful character templates and narrative patterns developed from the very beginning of the series, *Charmed* not only pleased its audience through its reassuring use of narrative repetition, it presented them with a renewed form of feminist ideology. The four Charmed Ones, while not giving up the hard-earned independence of second-wave feminism, managed to invoke the more individualistic and less confrontational aspects of third-wave feminism.

It Really Isn't All Black and White

Colour Coding, Postfeminism and Charmed

JAMES R. KNECHT

' PECIAL EFFECTS HAVE always been a magical form'.[1] This statement, the opening line to Michele Pierson's 2002 text tracing the history and development of special effects in media, feels particularly apt for any discussion of the visual aesthetics of one of the WB's longest-running shows, *Charmed*. Over the course of eight seasons, this television series has undergone a number of diverse changes, from adding and replacing cast members to granting and withdrawing magical powers from specific characters. These changes, some dramatic, some minor, have helped keep a world of witches, warlocks, Whitelighters, angels, demons, gods and a whole host of other magical beings fresh year after year at a time when successful television shows come few and far between.

Nevertheless, certain constants within the show, such as the focus on three strong, intelligent, postfeminist lead characters operating in a magical world where wit and gumption work hand in hand with special-effect-generated magic, clearly have helped maintain the show's steadfast following. These same features have also made the series an intriguing area of study for both gender and art. In particular, the show's specific use of colour-coded (or colour-less) special effects and costuming as a means of conveying characters' magical abilities has worked throughout the many episodes as more than simply a device to advance plotlines. Though such effects are often employed as a mode of magical transportation to move the Halliwell sisters (and their friends or enemies) quickly from location to location (for instance, through Whitelighter 'orbing' or demon 'shimmering'), they also serve as an interesting exploration of particular gender roles (and role reversals) as they appear in this postfeminist television show.

This chapter examines the ways in which specific visual effects and costuming have developed and expanded over the course of the show, affecting how (and how quickly) characters are able to operate in (and move through) their magical universe. Specifically, it focuses on the special effects and clothing used in relation to the following character types: Whitelighters and Darklighters, demons (with a particular emphasis on the character, Cole) and two versions of Cupid who have appeared on the show during its eight-year run. This examination explores how certain colour choices (or colour exclusions) serve as an interesting commentary on contemporary gender issues within the narrative. As Tammy A. Kinsey points out in her examination of another fantasy-favourite of the WB, *Angel*: 'The ways in which meaning is ascribed to any visual representation (often without conscious thought) are not accidental. Filmmakers since the early days of the motion picture have been interested in the methods of engendering specific responses in their viewers to various works.'[2]

Kinsey's point concerning 'engendering specific responses' in viewers is key. A similar argument can be made about the 'magical' special effects of *Charmed*. In their presentation, these effects sometimes reinscribe and other times rework more 'traditional', stereotypical meanings behind particular colours. The true art of *Charmed* is the smart play that it takes (and makes) with its special effects in order to move meaning beyond the stereotypical and into the realm of postfeminism.

Lending a 'Hand': Whitelighters and Darklighters

In the world of *Charmed* the magical beings known as Whitelighters first appear in the Season One episode 'Secrets and Guys' (1.14) in the form of Leo Wyatt (Brian Krause). In the episode, Phoebe (Alyssa Milano) accidentally discovers that the Halliwell's handyman (hired to repair the inevitable damage done to the family manor by demons and other 'baddies') is actually a Whitelighter, a magical being sent down by the Elders to aid and oversee new witches as a sort of 'guardian angel', as Leo describes it. Leo has been assigned the Charmed Ones as his 'charges', a fact he is forced to reveal to Phoebe after she discovers him using his magical powers to change a light bulb in the chandelier. The confrontation between Phoebe and Leo sets the stage for many of the obvious colour connotations that the show quickly ties to Whitelighters through special effects. Initially, Phoebe catches Leo levitating himself in the air to change the bulb (a power that, interestingly, Whitelighters seem to lose over the course of the succeeding seasons), and, when he returns to the ground, he is still holding the light bulb. The white bulb is lit by his hand, clearly indicating Leo's 'magical' abilities, and it is a 'white light', confirming Leo's status as one of the show's 'good guys'. When it comes to Good versus Evil within *Charmed*, at least early on, the positioning of characters is very clear. In this case, one can indeed say that it is 'black and white'.

By the end of 'Secrets and Guys' Leo's other two primary Whitelighter powers are revealed, both of which are connotatively connected to his role as guardian angel for the sisters and visually require a colour-coded special effect to convey them. The first power, of course, is the Whitelighter ability to 'orb', or change into bluish-white orbs of light that magically allow the Whitelighter to travel anywhere almost instantaneously. Visually, the special effect is rendered (along with a musical sound effect) by having the character's image fade and reshape into a blue-white stream of light-orbs that quickly travel out of the scene. In terms of the narrative, a Whitelighter has this ability so that he can reach his charges and/or travel 'up' to see the Elders to gain information and guidance. Leo's ability to go up to talk with the Elders reinforces a correlation between Whitelighters and angels, playing off obvious connections to stereotypical representations of heaven (a stereotype reinforced when the Halliwell sisters, in the episode 'Blinded by the Whitelighter', 3.11, go 'up' themselves and discover a world of airy whiteness, with white pillars and white clouds inhabited by white-robed Whitelighters – their traditional, colour-appropriate garb).

Leo's second primary Whitelighter power, the ability to heal instantaneously through touch, is also displayed in 'Secrets and Guys' (1.14) as he heals the father of a young future witch suffering from a gunshot wound. The connection to Christian healing rituals such as the 'laying of hands' is obvious, yet it is made even more so by the fact that a sound effect and a visual effect accompany the touching. Golden light emanates from Leo's hands as the wound is healed and the surrounding blood disappears; this golden colour again visually suggests connections with heaven, angels, and other aspects of the side of 'Good'.

These more traditional connotations indicated by the special effects used for Whitelighter powers are but the tip of the iceberg in terms of the meaning attached to these characters through colour. Perhaps most interesting are the potential connections made in terms of gender and the ways in which this postfeminist show initially codes the Whitelighter and his abilities as masculine and then, later, in Season Four, recoups them for the feminine. For the first three seasons, Whitelighters are predominantly connected with masculinity, and not simply because the primary Whitelighter character, Leo, is male. In at least three other ways Whitelighters are coded in opposition to the feminine (and postfeminist) Charmed Ones. First there is the structuring of the Whitelighter role in the narrative. Leo is often 'called upon' by the Charmed Ones whenever they need assistance, and – as a guardian angel and 'handyman' who 'fixes' things in both a literal and a figurative sense – there are implications that the role of Whitelighters is much more 'active' than passive, despite their claims to the contrary.

Second, the special effects used with Whitelighters are colour-coded, and stereotypically so. Though a Whitelighter power, orbing as a visual effect is actually both white and *blue*, the colour, at least for recent American cultural stereotypes, attached to the male.[3] Also, it is interesting to note that while Leo's powers are visually colour-coded, the original Charmed Ones' powers are, in fact, distinctly not colour-coded. Prue's (Shannen Doherty) telekinesis and Piper's (Holly Marie Combs) freezing abilities have no colour attached to them, and Phoebe's visions are displayed on screen in black and white. What is more, both 'orbing' and healing are considered 'active' powers, an interesting fact both in terms of the traditional, stereotypical correlations made between active/passive and masculine/feminine and because the show itself often confronts Phoebe's desire to have an active power that she can call upon at will.

Third, the Whitelighters' connection to the colour blue reappears in their evil alter egos: Darklighters. First appearing in the Season One episode 'Love Hurts' (1.21), Darklighters are shown to be hunters of Whitelighters. Wearing all black and wielding crossbows, they try to tempt future Whitelighters and good witches to turn evil. They too have magical abilities similar to Whitelighters, only 'reversed'. When they travel they 'orb', though their special effect is colour-coded blue-black (rather than blue-white), and, rather than having the ability to heal with their hands, they have the ability to kill with them (in 'Love Hurts' the Darklighter kills by grabbing his victims by the throat, at which point his hands glow red, burning the victim – thus the Whitelighter golden colour effect is replaced by a demonic red). The masculine connection is thus made both through colour choices and by the limiting of the show's casting to (primarily) male Darklighters who actively hunt (a male-coded activity) 'good guys'. Guardian or hunter, the Whitelighters and Darklighters of *Charmed*'s first three seasons are primarily male.

In fact, it is not until the eleventh episode of Season Three that a significant Whitelighter role is given to a woman, and even then she is masculinized and killed off by the episode's end. In 'Blinded by the Whitelighter' the Charmed Ones face a warlock bent on stealing powers and destroying all Whitelighters. A second Whitelighter,

Natalie (Audrey Wasilewski), meets the Charmed Ones after one of her charges is killed by the warlock, and she eventually is assigned to work with the Charmed Ones because of rumours concerning Leo and Piper's relationship. Natalie's characterization is decidedly masculine: she is upset that Leo and the Charmed Ones do not work 'by the rules', and, when she helps prepare the sisters for their fight with the warlock, she runs the training as a drill sergeant. She also spends much of the episode wearing grey (initially, a grey trouser suit) in contrast to the more sexualized clothing of the sisters. She even baulks at their mostly black, 'braless, strapless . . . fearless' outfits as inappropriate for fighting demons (inappropriate for her character, yes, but highly appropriate for the postfeminist text that is *Charmed*, as the sisters not only 'kick ass' but do so while wearing feminine and sexy attire). Near the end of the episode Natalie is killed by the warlock, thus removing the only major female Whitelighter and returning it to a primarily male Whitelighter world.

Though the masculinization of the Whitelighter early in the series may be more readily tied to the simple fact that the role was first inhabited by a male character, it nevertheless stands out as a feature of the *Charmed* universe during the first three seasons, and it might have continued so had Shannon Doherty not left the show, resulting in Prue's 'death'. That event, however, brought a shift as another sister had to be found – leading to the introduction of the long-lost Halliwell half-sister, Paige Matthews (Rose McGowan). Paige supposedly had been given up for adoption because she was the result of a liaison between the sisters' mother and her Whitelighter, and such witch–Whitelighter relations were forbidden. Thus, Paige's magical powers, which were needed to replace Prue's, had to be both telekinetic and tied to Whitelighter abilities, resulting in her power to move objects through 'orbing'. Thus the blue-white 'orbing' special effect had to serve a new, female witch. With Paige thus functioning as a half-Whitelighter, all of the masculine structures tied to the Whitelighter are reworked and reappropriated as Paige comes to terms with her Whitelighter heritage. At the same time, Leo's character also transitions, as he loses his abilities, regains them, and gains even more by becoming first an Elder and then an Avatar. These events simply show *Charmed* at its postfeminist best: it reinvents and reinvigorates itself time and again for the postfeminist viewer.

Colour Me Bad: The Charmed Ones' (Outer) Demons

Opposing the Charmed Ones and the forces of Good are the show's 'bad guys': the demons, the forces of Evil who square off each week with the Halliwell sisters. Stereotypically, most of the show's demons are easily visually identifiable, often appearing on the show wearing dark colours (most often black), with equally dark powers. They use them, obviously, to threaten, kill and generally wreak havoc on the otherwise peaceful 'innocents' whom the Halliwell sisters strive to protect. Over eight years the number of varieties of demons that have appeared on the show seems never-ending; however, certain features consistently reappear within the visual representations that characterize the evil magical powers of these demons. Once again, the show utilizes several visual cues and special effects in order to convey these abilities on screen, and the ways these effects take shape sometimes reinforce and sometimes subvert traditional (colour) meanings and connotations.

Perhaps the most obvious special effects used in connection with the demons of the show are the ways in which they 'travel'. Like Whitelighters, demons have the ability to transport themselves from one location to another. Unlike Whitelighter orbing, however, most demons 'shimmer' – their image on screen wavers and eventually disappears. Shimmering, though, is but one means of magical travel, and not all demon-travel is visually coded in this manner on the show. For instance, some demons travel via black smoke, as is the case with the 'seeker demons' who track Cole (Julian McMahon), Phoebe's demon love interest (and eventual husband), in the Season Three episode 'Death Takes a Halliwell' (3.16). Unlike Cole, a half-human, half-demon character who primarily travels via shimmer, the seeker demons' special effect is visually marked. This marking may perhaps correspond to the fact that the seeker demons operate on a different 'level' within the organizational schema of Evil on the show. Their function within this episode's narrative is to track down another rogue demon (Cole) rather than to (simply) do bad as 'ordinary' demons do. Thus their mission earns them a colour-coded special effect: in this case, a stereotypical black along the lines of the 'white equals good, black equals bad' dichotomy that the show relies on quite heavily.

The hierarchy of the demonic world seems to play an important role in the overall visual coding of the special effects used in conjunction with the demonic characters. A rule of thumb for the show seems to be that, the more important and/or higher up a character is within the Underworld, the more elaborate the special effects. While such a correlation seems obvious – after all, the more dangerous the demon, the more spectacular its magic should be – this coding has special relevance, particularly in relation to two demons: Cole and the Source of All Evil, the two major villains of Season Four. Over the course of this season, the newly reconstituted Charmed Ones discover a leader of the Underworld bent on their destruction, the Source (Bennet Guillory), a being whose powers the sisters ultimately must vanquish not once but twice.

What is particularly interesting about the Source, in addition to his many powers and obvious demonic looks (his head is shaved, his skin is eerily white, his eyes are completely black, his face is deformed, and he goes about in black robes), is that his transportation effect is fire. Violent, realistic red, yellow, and orange flames rise up and engulf him when he decides to travel to another location. Given that the Source can be seen as a highly stylized version of the Devil in Christianity, such an effect is apt. However, in terms of the *Charmed* narrative, the choice indicates more. On one level it clearly establishes a major visual difference between the magical powers of other beings and the Charmed Ones, whose magical abilities and appearances, for the most part, lack significant colour coding.[4]

On a second level, however, the use of flames is interesting because it is an effect that has been used on the show many times before the arrival of the Source. It is the special effect often used when the Charmed Ones vanquish a demon. Thus the Source's travelling effect is, in the case of other demons, a sign of destruction. The connotations of destruction are, of course, obvious and work in both circumstances as the Source of All Evil is a figure of destruction. However, because he travels by means of a flame special effect, the special effect used with his eventual vanquishing must be more spectacular, and it is. In the Season Four episode 'Charmed and Dangerous' (4.13), when the Halliwell sisters vanquish him using a Power of Three spell, the Source explodes in what looks like a fiery nuclear blast.

The special effects used in conjunction with the Source also have significance in regards to Cole. Introduced in the opening episode of Season Three, 'The Honeymoon's Over' (3.1), Cole, a demon-human hybrid who takes two forms, the human Cole and the red-skinned demon Belthazor, quickly becomes a series regular as the first great but forbidden demonic love of Phoebe. Over Seasons Three and Four the two fall in love, though it obviously is only the Cole half that Phoebe loves, and Belthazor is pushed aside as Cole tries to renounce that demonic personality in favour of his love for Phoebe. Nevertheless, evil eventually wins out, and he turns Phoebe into his Dark Queen.

Yet still, even after Phoebe and Cole are together, Belthazor rarely emerges, probably because his more stereotypical, red devil appearance is inappropriate for Phoebe's romantic lead. In his case, his demonic appearance – his red 'colour' – is repressed, though none of Cole's other demonic abilities are, even after he gains the powers of the Source when he is vanquished in 'Charmed and Dangerous'. What is most remarkable for Cole's character, however, is that, even after he gains the Source's abilities, he nevertheless still uses his own, particularly his ability to 'shimmer'. For narrative reasons he must keep his new powers a secret from the Halliwell sisters, who believe him to still be good, and 'shimmering' is a much less obvious, less extravagant mode of transportation than travelling by fire. Still, one can read more into the situation. By having Cole continue to 'shimmer', a special effect that lacks colour coding (as it is a distortion of an image and not a colour replacement), he thus remains more closely connected to the Charmed Ones (and to Phoebe), who also have magical abilities *sans* colour coding. Nevertheless, though he tries to maintain the connection with the show's heroines, his demonic powers eventually are revealed (interestingly after rigorous suspicion on the part of Paige, whose magical abilities are most closely tied to colour), and the sisters are forced to vanquish him (and his colour-coded abilities) in another fiery explosion at the end of Season Four.

Postfeminist Colouring: Cupid and the Power of Pink

Though it may seem like the demons of the *Charmed* universe receive the most elaborate attention in terms of the colour special effects, ultimately the show is much more generous to a variety of characters, Good or Evil, with the apparent exception of the Charmed Ones themselves. For instance, most of the magical beings the sisters have come into contact with are accompanied by their own unique special effect, and a number of these effects follow stereotypical interpretations of colour-coding and imagery depending on the being in question. For example, in Season Five, in the episode 'Lucky Charmed' (5.17), the Halliwell sisters attempt to help a number of leprechauns who are being hunted by a demon. In this episode, leprechaun magic is put on display, and their magical means of transportation is via a rainbow special effect. Whenever a leprechaun wants to travel, he (or she, though, as with Whitelighters early on, this role seems coded masculine as the actors chosen are all men) uses his staff to call the end of a rainbow into which he steps. The rainbow effect, of course, plays with the mythology surrounding leprechauns, who are said to keep their gold at the ends of rainbows. This process is repeated for a number of other mythical, magical beings, yet one 'race' in particular is given a uniquely postmodern, postfeminist twist: that of Cupid.

Much Greek and Roman mythology is reinterpreted within *Charmed* (the sisters are even turned into Greek goddesses during Season Five), and the show plays with the mythology of Cupid in multiple episodes. The Halliwell sisters (and viewers) learn that a large number of Cupids work on the side of Good, slipping in and out of people's lives in order to foster (romantic) love. These Cupids, like Whitelighters, are human in form. Two specific incarnations stand out, and both of these Cupids focus their attention on Phoebe. It is the way the show represents their magical abilities, though, that provides particularly interesting examinations of colour meaning.

The first Cupid who sparks such interest appears during Season Two, in the episode 'Heartbreak City' (2.10). In that episode the Charmed Ones meet a Cupid (Michael Reilly Burke) who has been attacked by a demon of hate named Drazi (Clayton Rohner). The demon, rather than simply killing Cupid, instead steals his ring, the source of his magical power. The ring allows Cupid to slow down time and slip into people's lives, nudging them to be open to love and to take chances on the people they meet. The special effect used is a slow-motion effect coupled with a flash of red light from the ring, a stereotypical colour choice indicating love. Cupid's character in the episode also plays into this traditional colour-coding, as he is dressed in a red-and-white tracksuit top.

What makes the manifestation of Cupid in 'Heartbreak City' so notable in terms of colour, however, is what happens after Drazi steals his ring. The use of red light from the ring, appropriate for Cupid, changes to an emerald green when wielded by the demon. Such a change is remarkable, especially given that the show so often uses blacks, blues, reds, or flame effects to display demonic powers. Green, too, does not immediately connote feelings of hate (jealousy or envy, perhaps). Still, the choice stands out, and it does so even more because, like postfeminism, it reverses a more traditional meaning, in this case of the colours red and green: stop versus go. In this instance, the red light, put into effect by Cupid's magic, urges people to 'go for it', with the 'it' being love, while the green light stops love, severing connections and creating hate.

Yet this version of Cupid still sticks too close to more traditional uses of colour. The red light, for instance, is a dark red (as is his jacket), giving it a decidedly masculine feel along the same lines as when red is used in relation to demons. Nevertheless, *Charmed* does not let the contemporary, postfeminist viewer down, as it resurrected Cupid for Season Eight, this time as a serious love interest for Phoebe. 'Coop' (Victor Webster), as he asks to be called, is sent to Phoebe by the Elders as a reward to help her find love (throughout the show Phoebe is the only sister whose romantic life remains troublesome and unresolved – by Season Eight both of her sisters have found happiness in marriage). As the season progresses, however, Coop develops feelings for Phoebe even as he attempts to help her find love with others, and the end of the series reveals that the two will marry.

This version of Cupid stands in stark contrast to the Season Two version, both in terms of characterization and visual presentation. Coop's dress, for instance, forgoes the red-and-white, relaxed look of the earlier Cupid (who wore jeans with his tracksuit top) in favour of tailored suits with vibrantly coloured dress shirts. Coop is a smart, sexy Cupid. In a sense, he's a Cupid for the twenty-first century as his poised, manicured look is along the lines of the contemporary 'metrosexual' movement. He is a Cupid unafraid to look good, suavely dressed in dark blues, vivid purples and, perhaps most importantly, pink.

In addition to wearing pink, this Cupid's magical powers are visually conveyed using the same colour, albeit a darker, sexier version of it. When Coop uses his powers, whether to conjure a vision or to transport Phoebe on a magical journey through time to revisit her past romances (as in the episode 'Generation Hex', 8.17), the special effect used in each case is a dark pink light. Such colour coding is more than simply another reworking of a colour connected with Cupid mythology – it also brings with it the metrosexual connection and a connection to postfeminism as well. As Carol M. Dole points out in her work on postfeminism and the film *Legally Blonde* (2001), the colour pink has reemerged as an acceptable colour for (feminist) women. As she argues, 'at the outset of the new millennium, women were ready to reclaim pink . . . it was not until the new century that women's fashion once again embraced the colour that had long served as the American cultural sign for femininity'.[5] In the case of *Charmed*, however, pink is not only reclaimed by women but also by men. Coop's connection to the colour is not accidental nor is it simply because he is a manifestation of a mythical figure also connected to the colour. Instead he serves as an example of a 'Good' man – a postfeminist man worthy of the love of a Charmed One.

It's Been Charm-*ing*

In the end, *Charmed* is a powerful, diverse postfeminist text. Throughout its eight years on television, despite a vast number of changes, many of which might have ended other programmes, the adventures of Prue, Piper, Phoebe and Paige have consistently drawn in and 'charmed' viewers, ultimately becoming the longest-running show with multiple female leads on network television (surpassing *Laverne and Shirley*, which ran from 1976 to 1983). Through a variety of colourful outfits (from black leather to Whitelighter robes) and the many distinctive special effects used to showcase the 'magic' of the *Charmed* universe, the show has conveyed a myriad of meanings to its faithful, all while making the sisters 'look good'. Though at times stereotypical, these colour-coded or colour-less special effects and other colour choices nevertheless continually work both to entice readers and to relay the message that women and men can be strong, successful, and can kick some demon ass, all at the same time. It thus seems fitting that the show ended just before the network that spawned it (and a number of other important postmodern, postfeminist television shows, including *Buffy the Vampire Slayer*, *Angel*, and *Dawson's Creek*) ceased to be. The WB drew to a close during the summer of 2006, merging with the United Paramount Network (UPN) to create the CW. Their respective ends both point the way toward a new beginning – a beginning situated squarely in the realm of twenty-first-century postfeminism.

There's No Place Like Charmed

Domesticity, the Uncanny and the Utopian Potential of the City

MARKUS REISENLEITNER

> But the uncanny . . . was also born out of the rise of the great cities, their disturbingly heterogeneous crowds and newly scaled spaces.[1]

IN THE EPISODE 'Is There a Woogy in the House?' (1.15) of the television series *Charmed*, an earthquake awakens an evil demon in the basement of the Halliwell family home. The demon takes possession of the dwelling, and one of the sisters, Phoebe, is lured into the basement despite her childhood fears of this uncanny part of the house. During the unfolding events that lead to the inevitable vanquishing of evil by the Power of Three, the sisters (as usual torn between the demands of pursuing love interests, maintaining steady jobs and entertaining guests at a dinner party) learn that their abode is a 'point of incredible energy equidistant to the five basal elements' that derives its Wicca potential of being a source of either good or evil from its privileged location in the city at the centre of a pentagram. The sisters draw on this connection to cleanse the domestic – a space traditionally coded as premodern and female – of its uncanny potential (evil being imagined romantically as being interred in the basement) by drawing on the quasi-elemental force of the city, the sphere of male modernity.

This episode, significantly titled 'La mansión Halliwell' in the Spanish version, provides only one instance of what I will argue is a recurring, and structuring, element in the show: the mobilization, and reworking, of gendered spatial metaphors that presents the audience with a gender-specific interlocution and interrogation of San Francisco's multi-faceted urban imaginary. It is a re-signification that opens up the traditionally male-coded spaces of modern urbanity to forms of female agency via the series' trademark heady appropriation of neo-pagan metaphysics, Wicca belief and New Ageism, while ultimately remaining limited by the locality and a-historicity of the series' frame of reference.

Order in the House!

Television's genre conventions have traditionally privileged the familiar locale, the neighbourhood, the private sphere and the intimate interior, reflecting the medium's community-building function. Viewers have become used to locations established by recurring shots of the setting from the outside that frame the inside action. *Charmed* is no exception here. The fuchsia-coloured mansion (a Victorian-style property actually located in Los Angeles²) is an easily recognizable marker and frames the majority of the plot activities that take place on sets in its interior, whereas the sisters' respective workplaces are featured far less frequently (the only exception being the semi-private P3 club), and the forces of evil have a definite preference for bothering the Halliwells at home. The demonic threat is thus very clearly defined as an irruption into, and disturbance of, *domestic* space (generally accompanied by the demons making a mess that upsets Piper's homemaker-obsessive cleanliness). Consequently, the sisters' sources of power, despite their Wicca origins in 'nature', are predominantly defined in the context of the manor's domesticity: they are able to defeat demons and warlocks because they are in this space together, with their source of witchcraft, the Book of Shadows, which is located in the attic and cannot, under normal circumstances, be taken out of the house. Plots frequently revolve around the reassertion of domestic order, imagined as social order in which the, albeit untraditional, family overcomes interpersonal irritations and is (re)united emotionally and physically (and the house is cleaned up). Implied in the reassertion of spatial order in the home is the reassertion of the cosmic order in the holistic cosmology of the series' eclectic assimilation of an already eclectic neo-pagan belief system. (At the end of each season, the door of the mansion closes magically – implying that the demon threat has been averted successfully, at least for the summer break.) Many of the plot elements thus rely on the pivotal role of the family mansion in establishing a 'contrast between a secure and homely interior and the fearful invasion of an alien presence'³ that has been the leitmotiv of the Gothic genre since the Romantic era, introducing the pleasurable thrills of the uncanny:

By far the most popular topos of the nineteenth-century uncanny was the haunted house. A pervasive leitmotif of literary fantasy and architectural revival alike, its depiction in fairy tales, horror stories, and Gothic novels gave rise to a unique genre . . . The house provided an especially favoured site of uncanny disturbances: its apparent domesticity, its residue of family history and nostalgia, its role as the last and most intimate shelter of private comfort sharpened by contrast the terror of invasion by alien spirits.[4]

Charmed indeed seems to cull the motifs of its romantic genre basis systematically (in Gothic novels, fairy tales and horror stories) for its plots (which involve motifs such as split personas, Doppelgänger, the blocking of vision, evil eyes and stealing of eyes, disinterment, magic mirrors that do not reflect a person's image, shadows that become independent, etc.) and characters (leprechauns, dwarves, elves, etc.). The somewhat vague, but recognizably Victorian style of the manor supports these generic evocations of Romanticism. At times, demons and warlocks personify the fears of and threats to the sisters (often rooted in their personal pasts) and are thus *unheimlich* (uncanny), which implies, in Freud's oft-quoted insight, '*irgendwie eine Art von heimlich*' (a highly ambiguous phrase notoriously difficult to translate, as Freud himself was aware, and many commentators have noted as well):[5] 'the uncanny is a kind of/species of the hidden/home(l)y' (using the North American English meaning of the homely as being something quite ugly). Exorcising the forces of evil implies, in psychoanalytic terms, the necessity of coming to terms with those aspects of the domestic (excavated, sometimes literally, from the past) that form the menacing aspects of domestic space – precisely because it is the repository and material memory space of the family romance that leaves indelible traces in the personalities of the protagonists.[6]

Yet there are some significant differences between the Romantic tradition of imagining the uncanny qualities of the haunted house and the *Charmed* television series, which reworks the uncanny qualities of this space into a source of female agency and empowerment. The Charmed Ones' domestic space may be the site of witchcraft and supernatural events, but it is not truly haunted; while mayhem, disaster and demonic powers regularly threaten the integrity of the manor, most sources of these disturbances do not really emanate from the *Heim* (home) itself, and the Halliwell abode displays none of the claustrophobic qualities of the genre tradition that make the ghosts of the past so inescapable (which would be the lesson of a Freudian reading of the uncanny in terms of a formative family romance). Unlike the house of Poe's Roderick Usher, for example, whose decrepit state is a projection of its male protagonist's unhealthy incestuous associations, the Halliwells' home is cosy, done up in warm tones, and the kitchen, bedrooms and attic feature prominently. At the same time, this material space is imagined as a powerful repository of (female) knowledge that frequently assists the sisters in dealing with the menaces and terrors of the nether (and outer) world. By conjuring up – sometimes literally – ghosts of the past that can have a positive impact on the present, family wisdom that has been forgotten but not erased is preserved, remembered, and asserted in the home's material environment, including the possibility of bringing back to life the sisters' family (matri-)lineage, their ultra-feminist matriarch Grams in particular.

While in Romantic literature 'the very traces of life extinguished, of death stalking through the centre of life, of the "unhomeliness" of filled space contrasted with the former homeliness of lived space (to use the terminology of psychologist Eugène Minkowski) raised the spectre of demonic or magical forces, ... threatening all cherished ideas of domestic harmony',[7] in *Charmed* these traces perform precisely the opposite function: they are the guardians of domestic (and, correspondingly, cosmological) harmony, while evil spirits from the outside are sent back into oblivion. Although individual episodes' plots may be taken from popular Romantic genre conventions, the wider arc of the series resembles the linearity of a multi-generational *Bildungsroman* rather than the self-sustaining circularity of soap operas: as the series develops, the sisters' powers increase, they acquire new ones precisely by learning more about their past, and thus about the cosmology in which their agency is inscribed. While the sisters are initially only able to intuit, freeze and dislocate the dark forces – in other words, perceiving and displacing them, limited powers over time and place – the powers of 'orbing', exploding and levitating are ways of interacting much more actively with the environment, a far cry from the suffering females imprisoned in the claustrophobic spaces of Gothic romances; the location of the Book of Shadows is a nice touch in this respect. These new powers are then exponentially passed on via Piper and Leo's procreation to their young son, Wyatt. This arc of development reflects how the sisters deal with the history of their domestic space. While modernist architecture would suggest a 'house-machine' in Le Corbusier's sense – dedicated to the clean slate, the erasure of the past obliterating the pathologies spawned by it in the present – the Charmed Ones derive their power from domestic materiality, not from the dreams for an unrecoverable past that constitute nostalgia (the flip-side of the uncanny, signifying, for Freud, the impossible desire to return to the womb), but the 'real' history materially embodied in the manor's walls, available to be inherited just as the building itself is. For example, in Season One's 'That '70s Episode' (1.17), Phoebe goes back in time to come to terms with her mother's death by confronting her 'in the flesh'. Piper may endlessly clean up, but the house remains cluttered, it has to, since its female power asserts the necessity of dwelling over the Heideggerian or Adornian (male) sense of the uninhabitability of the modern world. While Leo the healing handyman's male, modernist, fix-it approach is generally rather ineffectual vis-à-vis the dark spirits that menace the house and the cosmic order – at least until he becomes an Elder in Season Five – the sisters' commitment to their home and their willingness (and ability) to encounter its horrors, to bring the demons home, as it were, as well as to learn from the histories its walls remember, are presented as sources of empowerment.

While this revisionist approach to modern forms of the uncanny is admittedly a quite conservative notion, privileging the domestic sphere over the public, this spatial dimension of domesticity in no way implies the return to traditional family values or a reproduction of patriarchal structures; on the contrary, family space, framed in a postfeminist way, seems to be almost exclusively gendered female, leaving – literally – little space for the nuclear family (and, anyway, most eligible men turn out to be demons or jerks). Moreover, the particular cosmology of the series does not confine this particular form of young, female empowerment to the home; rather, it situates the home in the centre of a wider sphere and thus strategically connects it to the outside world.

Chaos in the Streets

While the house is certainly the most prominent and arguably the most significant location in the show, it is not the only space that the Charmed Ones turn into a habitable place; their mission operates on a much larger scale. Just as the house is established by stock footage recurring in almost every episode, the city of San Francisco gives *Charmed*'s plot elements special significance and adds to the overall imaginary of female empowerment through their postfeminist unconventionality. The framing opening and closing shots of individual episodes present assuasive sequences featuring (usually aerial shots of) San Francisco's recognizable urban landmarks (the Golden Gate Bridge, the Embarcadero, night skylines, etc.). While this in itself is also not unusual for television's streamlined and economical modes of establishing locations shot on sound stages, the fact that the episodes' plots often revolve around threats to the very fabric of the city suggests that the smooth functioning of urban space, and the reassertion of it at the end, plays a significant role in the show, linking – via New Age cosmology – the domestic with the urban in its assertion of female empowerment by re-signifying masculine approaches to city space.

In doing so, the show draws as much on genre traditions as on a reworking of the domestic uncanny. Urban imaginaries in popular culture have a long tradition of regarding 'natural' forces as sources of threat and disaster to rationally planned and administrated urbanity,[8] and therefore it is a characteristic of the modern city *sui generis* to be constructed as a structure of visibility in which monstrous spaces are always present beneath the surface, threatening the fabric of rational order imposed by city planners, administrators, social reformers and engineers in their (male) modernist attempts to sanitize and subject to surveillance what were thought to be sites of unrest and social/moral corruption. In the popular imaginary, cities are constantly threatened by what lies beneath them, what exists (literally) beneath the official face of the city, in its sewers – complex symbols of corruption, containment and threat – and dark back alleys; these are exactly the public spaces in which demons materialise in *Charmed*. The spatial and cultural containment of the criminal/uncanny/demonic element, depicted as an always already established presence within the metropolis, a leitmotiv of popular culture, speaks to the specifically modern fear of the irruption of the uncanny into urban spaces that defy planning and policing. James Donald, in his discussion of city films, reminds us that

> the primitive city [. . .] is the product, or projection, of a symbolizing kernel that continues to be marked by its infantile origin. It returns as a force that defies all calculation, the archaic force that can suddenly shake a great city built according to all the rules of architecture. On the cusp of terror and absurdity, these films tell of conflict with the claims of authority and the bonds of community, and also of the unfixing or uncertainty of identity. They play on the fragile, shifty boundaries between human and technology, between human and nature, or between adult and infant. They remind us of that ineradicable unease about who we are and where we belong that also haunts the very way we walk the streets of the modern city.[9]

The demons that have the unfortunate tendency to materialize behind P3 or hide in the family plots of cemeteries could certainly be read in these terms, as urbanity's demonic underbelly whose irrationality, like the uncanny spaces of domestic basements, is a pervasive threat to rational urban life. But while the series draws liberally on this tradition, the constant feeling of unease Donald sees as a constitutive feature of the city of modernity is not what *Charmed* episodes leave us with; on the contrary, they present us with a city that feels like home (again) because we know it so well and are so familiar with its views, a city that often hardly notices the existential menaces the sisters and their supernatural helpers have averted. It is also a city whose inhabitants, particularly its female ones, habitually lead chaotic personal lives, are late for appointments, work in precarious jobs, and rely on the help of family and neighbours. This kind of disorderliness is rather the reassuring normality of urbanity than an aberrational threat to a well-oiled machine of living. Urban space in *Charmed* is not a city of strangers, segmented social relationships and mean streets, but rather a city of innocents living in neighbourhoods in which the sisters – unlike the solitary and traditionally male figure of the *noir* detective who remains an observer – actively participate and which they help to maintain as liveable space, neighbourhoods that constitute a city in which dwelling without alienation is possible. Reading *Charmed*'s plots in terms of the modern city dwellers' existential alienation and fears would, I suggest, miss the point of the (at times charmingly naive) *Charmed* universe; its demons are precisely *not* irrational forces generated by urban space. Instead they are perfectly logical explanations for what goes wrong in the city because they come to it from the outside, and these wrongs can be righted by female acts of solidarity and agency, rather than solipsistic male cynicism and alienation. Urban space remains inscribed into a holistic cosmology that demons threaten, rather than generating threat and confusion from within, thus harbouring a utopian potential for urban dwelling squarely based on female and familial solidarity and agency.

Charming San Francisco, City of ~~Angels~~ Witches

Given *Charmed*'s modes of re-signifying the modern urban imaginary, it is no coincidence that it is set in San Francisco. Like every major city, the City by the Bay does not evoke a single, homogeneous imaginary but rather forms a semiotic reservoir capable of conjuring up a number of different and potentially contradictory associations. With its irregular streets, hilly terrain, and counter-cultural traditions, San Francisco occupies a special place in North American, and global, urban imaginaries, a place constituted by a heady gumbo of memories including Hispanic-era missions, the Gold Rush boomtown, the earthquake of 1906, the Beat poets, Haight Ashbury and the Summer of Love, queer activism and, most recently, the dot-com boomers.

Contemporary San Francisco provides the series with its structuring framework. The sisters' precarious forms of employment in a casual labour market dominated by the creative, communication and entertainment industries are a strong nod towards imaginings of the West Coast lifestyle, its challenges and opportunities. Prue works in an auction house and then as a photographer, Piper starts out as a chef and later owns a club, Phoebe becomes an advice columnist, while Paige has a series of casual jobs and is often unemployed, and all of the sisters participate very visibly in the dynamism of street fashion. Again this type of employment seems to apply particularly to women; the more permanent men in the show often hold more traditional jobs: they are policemen, lawyers, or manual workers like Piper's second-season flame Dan or Leo the handyman, or the occasional computer millionaire, media tycoon or art dealer who show up at P3. Evocations of contemporary San Francisco in all its digital glamour help to keep a more *noir*ish image of the city at bay, distancing New Age female agency from *femme fatale* images in the *noir* tradition of Dashiell Hammett's hard-boiled stories,[10] Hitchcockian vertigo[11] and Verhoeven's *Basic Instinct* (1992).[12]

Yet, despite the occasional foray into the genre, most prominently in Season Seven's episode 'Charmed Noir' (7.8), the overall impression we get from *Charmed*'s San Francisco has neither a *noir* shade nor is it predominantly the image of a global city at the cusp of technology; we rarely get to see visible reminders of the state of technology around the turn of the millennium, with the exception of the occasional laptop and cell phones. After all, why would the Charmed Ones resort to such modern communication technologies when ancient female wisdom turns out to be much more powerful in the very fields that modern technology has been mobilized to cope with, allowing them to orb when mortals get stuck in traffic or are held up by airport security, or giving them the power to produce ethereal jingles when mortals curse the bad reception of their cell phones? Again, the series subtly, and sometimes not so subtly, hints at the superiority of the sisters' brand of female empowerment by juxtaposing it with the image of the digital city that has been coded male in the popular imaginary, re-casting female empowerment in a specific urban context with its own version of a hi-tech fantasy of instant communication and mobility, achieved by reference to alternative, non-expert, non-rational (and, consequently, non-male) knowledge.

San Francisco's showy digital image may have been built on the ruins of a rusting industrial infrastructure and middle-class populism, but *Charmed*'s urban imaginary chooses instead to rely on, and to mobilize productively, the city's nationally and internationally recognizable counter-culture heritage. It does this both in terms of hearkening back to its utopian potential of bonding and solidarity and its spawning of the flaky New Age culture that intersects with the Wicca traditions on which the show ostensibly (if somewhat irreverently) builds. In doing this the series obviously taps into a trend of culling middle-brow elements of New Age and esoteric thinking for popular culture, noticeable, for example, in the *Stargate* franchise's playful engagement with ascendancy, reincarnation, crystal power, numerology and ancient civilizations – Atlantis, Ancient Egypt and so on. There is no place in North America other than the former capital of the counter-culture, it is implied, where the frolicking of nymphs and satyrs in fountains does not stand out too much, despite the occasional harassment by media and the police (which legitimizes New Age paranoia). Cast in this light, the city can easily be assimilated into the holistic universe of the series' mythology; in other words, San Francisco can be domesticated because of specific aspects of its history, and become part of a larger scheme that seems to reflect a 'natural' order. The counter-culture's message of earth-care is absorbed into the coherence of the Wicca mythology that the series presents and into the special meaning attributed to the city's topography, as in the example of the pentagram in 'Is There a Woogy in the House?'. Not only does the *Charmed* mythology revolve around the city and the Halliwell Manor, it connects them historically: the house is said to have taken its present shape after the earthquake of 1906, probably the most significant event in the city's history.

Again, the series' trick of presenting female empowerment is to draw on a well-established imaginary and re-signify it in a gendered manner. If the 1950s Beat generation presented San Francisco as a city on the edge (in which hardly any women participated), in constant turmoil and overwhelmed by the irrational, the *Charmed* version reintegrates this imaginary into the alternative, naturalistic, holistic and pantheistic rationality of its own cosmology. It does away with the dichotomy between the urban and nature by assimilating the urban into an all-encompassing 'natural' order that young women are perfectly able to deal with and therefore have no reason to be afraid (as is generally their ascribed lot in urban drama and the horror genre). Apart from their esoteric Wicca knowledge, the qualities that empower them to domesticate the urban in this particular way draw on New Age rationality – 'a countercultural formation in an age of technocratic crisis';[13] ideas of personal growth, individualism, amateurism and self-help (most prominently featured in Phoebe's advice column) as well as 'alternative', pre-modern and 'Eastern' belief systems are juxtaposed with the male rationality of professionalism, which is presented as rather powerless in the face of the existential threats of the underworld. Selecting San Francisco as the crucible of the Wicca universe allows for the transfer of the New Age love–hate affair with rational science[14] to the rationality of the city, restoring the possibility of urban dwelling in the digital age through a utopia of young feminine bonds of solidarity and family. The harmony that is restored at the end of an episode is also a restoration of an urban sphere that can operate in as balanced a way as the natural sphere. This ties into the overall message of the show that community can be achieved within the city (*Gesellschaft* is brought back into *Gemeinschaft*). This is why Phoebe, at the end of the fifth season, cannot bring herself to leave San Francisco to join Jason in Hong Kong; a global, jet-setting lifestyle is presented in stark contrast to the comfort zone of their home and the city's sense of locality, to which the witches remain tied as they are all too cognizant that they derive their power from it. This is where *Charmed*'s imagining of San Francisco ultimately has to fall short in its utopian potential: in its desire to create community, it cannot do justice to the diversity of the 'real' city.

The Urban Domesticated

Letting young, reasonably independent women be crucial for a utopia of urban harmony and community worked very well for eight seasons, with a loyal, almost cult following springing up on the internet, which has come to serve as the standard forum for the community formation of television fans, to the point where personal histories are recollected through watching as part of the fan community formation.[15] In an interview with Brad Kern, the show's producer and major scriptwriter after the second season, it becomes obvious how the consistency of the show's cosmology is a crucial and intentional element in its community-building function, and thus consistently reflects the presupposition of the show that female agency makes possible the utopia of harmonious community in a domesticated urban sphere.

> *Andrea:* In our day and age of technology, the best measurement of a show's popularity is the internet. Compared to other TV shows, past and present, 'Charmed' has the most websites dedicated to the show. Are you surprised that 'Charmed' has such a huge cult following on the internet?
>
> *BK:* Yes and no. Yes, because, in television, we basically work in a vacuum, which means we're always surprised by *ANY* reaction. No, because we've tried very hard to honor our fans and build a relatively consistent mythology. That tends to draw a more loyal following than other shows.
>
> *Andrea:* ... I hear from so many fans around the world, even in places (ex. Russia, Bosnia & Herzegovina, Greece, Malta and

Pakistan, just to name a few) I'm shocked would air the show. Why do you think 'Charmed' has such a worldwide appeal?

BK: I've been asked that question a lot over the years and the short answer is, I don't know. My guess is that at the heart of our show, it's about family, sisters, which transcends international borders. It's also about magic, which also transcends borders and, I think, speaks to the fundamental hope that there's more to this world than meets the eye.[16]

What is remarkable about this interview is that it addresses an international dimension that is noticeably absent in the show itself. While international viewers might take their inspiration from the fact that the utopia of the *Charmed* universe is possible anywhere, references to a world outside San Francisco in the show are few and far between. This would, of course, not curb its international appeal – viewers can easily adapt fictional universes to their own contexts, and have done so with a diet of films and shows originating in a relatively small suburb of Los Angeles for a long time. In fact, diversity might actually disrupt this process. The juxtaposition of San Francisco, the city where a sense of locality provides a source of strength, with Hong Kong, the anonymously 'global' city where Jason goes and Phoebe does not follow, is very telling in this respect.

While both cities are global Pacific Rim players with a history of Asian-American encounters marked by uneven, shifting power relations, Hong Kong is firmly cast as domestic San Francisco's global other, while the Asian presence in San Francisco itself (generated by a history of neo-colonial injustice during which the city's connections to the Pacific were exploited to import a labour force that made it possible to connect it to the rest of America) is subsumed into the stock repertoire of the wisdom of all ages retained by the usual suspects (Egypt, India, China, the Roma) that disguises the barbaric history of the West's exploitative contacts with these cultures, contacts which have left traces in the city that remain invisible.[17] The stock footage of San Francisco, for example, seems deliberately to exclude more 'exotic' elements of the city's image, such as Chinatown. Rather than dealing with the presence of minorities in San Francisco as part of its imperialist history of connectivity to the world,[18] the few minorities that appear, while portrayed sympathetically, are not so much exoticized as domesticated. In both Season One's episode 'Dead Man Dating' (1.4) and Season Five's 'The Eyes Have It' (5.6) – among the few episodes that explicitly deal with minorities in the city – the main characters are depicted as representatives of a young Western technocratic elite (a Chinese American student of molecular biology at Stanford and a Roma doctor), who learn to embrace their ancestors' 'original' myths and end up returning to their families/communities. The only continuing representative of a visible minority in the show, policeman Darryl (an African American) starts out as a rational male sceptic, becomes increasingly co-opted as a family man as he learns the sisters' secrets and increasingly relies on their help.

The vision of a universe in harmony, which underpins New Age identity politics, clearly shows a propensity to deny and render invisible the (public) history of minority struggles. By the same token, the show's trajectory towards domesticity and family as forms of empowerment and utopia sets definite limits to how public/visible forms of empowerment for women and minorities can become. Ultimately, the visible topography of *Charmed*'s San Francisco seems to offer no place or solutions for minorities, queers or AIDS sufferers. While interrogating and subverting patriarchal values in very fundamental ways, the series cannot extend its politically subversive agendas beyond the confines, values and norms of the (inherently white-bred) domestic sphere. Recoding San Francisco in terms of feminine New Age domestic empowerment may challenge the male-gendered hegemony of modern urbanity, but it cannot fully mobilize the democratizing potential of public urban space or its diversity; it cannot embrace the particular globalized imaginary of San Francisco described above. Bringing the demons home keeps the sisters there, at home, the only place that can ultimately assert the wholeness of the cosmological order. As Andrew Ross states in his trenchant critique of New Age feminism: 'All too often, the result is to dream us back to the pre-scientific and to the alchemist's kitchen – which, for all their charms, are rather claustrophobic places for us to be'.[19]

Un(Real) Humour

The Roles of Comedy and Fantasy in the First Season of Charmed

PETER RANS

CHARMED IS A fantasy series in which the comedic elements play a vital role in plot and character development and enhance our appreciation of the social milieu. This exploration of the first season of *Charmed* will consider the different forms of comedy in the dialogue, in the character creation and in the visual gags that are the heart of the series. These various forms of comedy are contained within a framework of fantasy. While critics may not agree on a single definition of fantasy or the fantastic, we can certainly agree that there are multiple fantasy elements present in the first season. These elements include witches, warlocks, demons, monsters, the practice of magic and the casting of spells, time travel and a pursuit through a subterranean complex.

How these two components of fantasy and comedy work together within the narrative is elusive. Nevertheless, our psychological response to the episodes has been well described by Eric Rabkin:

> Fantastic stories offer psychic economy by compensation; neither the reader nor the author needs to be consciously aware of the roots of this compensatory function. Compensation is the technical term for the substitution of one experience, symbol or behaviour or what have you for another which is desired or repressed ... That an author or reader feels drawn to, entertained by, a narrative already indicates that the narrative in some way deals with a significant issue.[1]

From our perspective then, fantasy becomes a perfect vehicle for social commentary. In addition, the constant use of intertextuality throughout the series pulls us back, momentarily to the 'real' world, thereby providing a constant juxtaposition between fantasy and social observation.

When we enter the world of *Charmed*, we enter an unusual space. To have a television series in which three women in their twenties dominate the screen was a brave concept at the outset. The sisters, we learn, are part of a matrilineal line that goes back generations, a line that must be protected from a hostile (male) world. All of the men in the series are consigned to supporting roles. It certainly helps that all three women are beautiful and have an onscreen 'attitude'. The combination is irresistible: no ugly witches need apply.

Not content with this bravado, the producers and director went further and made all three characters witches, thus initiating one of the most successful fantasy-comedies in television history. Undoubtedly, the success of *Buffy the Vampire Slayer* paved the way for this decision, but the characters in *Charmed* are a little older. This maturity enabled the three sisters to act as advocates as well as idols for their generation, and to challenge the boundaries of comic discourse from the safety of the sisterhood. Fantasy may make palatable what realism does not; comedy ameliorates the message.

Humour and pain are juxtaposed throughout the series, but the pain is never allowed to prevail for more than an instant.

> I am the sun and the air
> I am human and I need to be loved
> Just like everybody else does.

The opening refrain of the series succinctly captures the dilemma of the Halliwell sisters, and it is this need that drives the comedy and accentuates the fantasy elements of each episode. Their dilemma is how do these witches live a normal life and 'be loved' in a place where fantasy and comedy collide? I will explore the different ways in which comedy and fantasy intermingle in the first season of the series. Before doing so, it is worth acknowledging that there is no single definition of comedy that encompasses what we see enacted in the first season.

Rather, the scriptwriters borrow freely from a number of comic traditions to produce the overall effect of the comedy. Perhaps we should follow their example and not look too closely at rigid definitions of comedy, believing like Samuel Johnson that: 'Comedy has been particularly unpropitious to definers; though perhaps they might properly have contented themselves with declaring it to be such a dramatic representation of human life, as may excite mirth'.[2] The exchanges between the Halliwell sisters certainly achieve the status of mirth, and they do so because they freely range from taboo subjects to the most mundane jibes.

The comic elements of *Charmed* are balanced within narratives that take as their domain fantasy, horror and even soap opera. Indeed, some of the early fascination with the series for some viewers undoubtedly comes from the spectacle of Shannen Doherty, of *Beverly Hills 90210* fame, playing the eldest sister. Intertextually, the widely reported activities of Shannen off-screen were the stuff of multiple webpages in the early 1990s. The attitudes generated by these previous representations of Shannen were clearly imported into some of the early dialogue of the first few episodes. Much irony could be wrung from Prue's less than kind treatment of Phoebe, and her assumptions that Phoebe is feckless and sexually irresponsible.

In this sense then, the series takes advantage of many postmodernist techniques, and in particular, the knowing relationship between viewer (reader) and the text (script). Viewers are expected to decode for themselves the distance between the words spoken, their context, the intonation of the characters and the conventions of fantasy. Chris Weedon states in her discussion of Derrida's observation, 'what it (the text) means at any particular moment depends on the discursive relations within which it is located, and it is open to constant rereading and reinterpretation'.[3]

Another key component of the series is the use and abuse of conventions drawn from the literary tradition of horror. While it is not my intention to explore these conventions here, it is important to distinguish the overall effect of this incongruous mix of fantasy, horror, comedy and soap opera. In *Buffy the Vampire Slayer*, we really believe that the horror opens up areas of huge existential doubt. This is not the case in *Charmed*. Viewers are never allowed to dwell a moment longer than necessary on the manifestations of evil. Instead, these manifestations are dispensed with in almost indecent haste, and the perky light-hearted banter shuts down rather than extends our experience of evil. Neither *Buffy* nor *Charmed* takes itself too seriously, but the viewers of *Buffy* clearly do.

Instead of concentrating on the manifestations of evil, the central focus of the Halliwell sisters' lives is the attempt to integrate themselves into a wider community. Since classical times, the urge to be accepted in the broader community has been one of the standard concerns of comedy. What separates the sisters, of course, is their collection of powers and the need to maintain a secret identity, another identity. This 'otherness' is a constant source of ironic commentary on the real world or the 'normal' world to which they all aspire. Indeed, in many episodes what at first appears to be normal frequently turns into another example of the fantastic or horrific, thus driving the sisters back on their company, their own family, as the only safe place where they can be themselves.

Comedy ensues from the need for each of the sisters to resolve unfinished business with each other. The sibling rivalry is never far from the surface and erupts as the sisters quarrel over boyfriends or over their opinions of each other. Each sister, at times, resents the dramatic role assigned to her and struggles to define herself as something more than the sum of assumptions held by the other two sisters. In 'Something Wicca This Way Comes' (1.1), the characters of the three sisters are created in a series of early exchanges.

Prue:	Well, maybe we should send it to Phoebe. That girl is so in the dark, maybe a little light will help.
Piper:	You're always so hard on her.
Prue:	Piper, the girl has no vision, no sense of the future.
	. . .
Piper:	She left New York. She's moving back in with us.
Prue:	You have got to be kidding.
Piper:	Well, I could hardly say no. It's her house too. Grams left it to all three of us.
Prue:	Yeah, months ago, and we haven't seen or spoken to her since.
Piper:	Well, you haven't spoken to her . . .
Phoebe:	So, can we talk about what's really bothering you?
Prue:	No. I'm still furious with you.
Phoebe:	So, you'd rather have a tense reunion filled with boring chitchat and unimportant small talk?
Prue:	No, but otherwise we won't have anything to talk about.
Phoebe:	I never touched Roger.
Prue:	Whoa.
Phoebe:	I know you think otherwise because that's what the Armani-wearing, Chardonnay-slugging trust funder told you . . .
Piper:	Hey, I have a great idea. Why don't I make a fabulous reunion dinner?

With great economy, we understand that Prue is the domineering one, that Piper is the peacemaker and that Phoebe is irreverent and likely to cause trouble. This dialogue neatly combines the comedy and fantasy elements in one stroke. In an early comic reversal in the narrative, we will soon know that Phoebe's power will be an ability to see the future (the vision thing), that Prue's power will enable her to push things around and that Piper will be able to mediate by freezing things in time. Such then are the early indications of character that will drive the narrative and open up multiple comic situations.

Furthermore, the title of the first episode is itself a homage to, or possibly a parody of, the film *Something Wicked this Way Comes* (Jack Clayton, 1983).[4] Many other episodes carry this kind of ambiguity within their titles, such as 'Dead Man Dating' (1.4), 'Dream Sorceror' (1.5), 'From Fear to Eternity' (1.13) and 'The Truth is Out There and it Hurts' (1.8). Sometimes, as in 'Dream Sorceror', the original series of films *Nightmare on Elm Street* is directly alluded to and becomes a source of comparison for both character and plot. In the case of the episode 'From Fear to Eternity' only the title has been parodied and no other substantive connection with the original remains. This leaves the postmodern reader uncertain as to the cause for the reference, except perhaps as a sly way of placing the series of *Charmed* in a long series of horror and fantasy products, and the Hollywood tradition in general.

If we understand that one of the central preoccupations of the Halliwells is to become accepted into normal society, we also understand that this normal society is highly elusive. With the exception of the occasional street scene in various episodes, the locations the sisters each return to over and over again in the first season are the Halliwell Manor, the restaurant Quake, the police station and Buckland, the auction house. We know from the opening scenes that we are in San Francisco (the Golden Gate Bridge) and that an old rambling house will dominate our experience of the city. The house becomes a character in its own right within the series; this particular plot arc is fulfilled in 'Is There a Woogy in the House?' (1.15). The manor contrasts with the young adult perspective that permeates the series. This paucity of locations begs the question of how any of the characters can find the integration with the normal society they are seeking. Each of the locations becomes a place where the Halliwell sisters unleash their spells, thereby moving the place into the realm of the fantastic.

Taking Quake as an example, at first sight it is presented as a high-end expensive restaurant where all of the beautiful people go to encounter each other. In his first appearance in the restaurant, Leo is clearly uncomfortable at the prices on the menu and will only sit down when 'treated' by Piper. Quake is expensive then, yet Piper is constantly exploited by a succession of chefs and owners who take advantage of her work ethic and good nature. The role that she wants at Quake is to be the chef; instead, she is constantly forced back into being the manager, and thereby denied fulfilment and forced to contend with the problems that emerge in this restaurant/bar. The comedy comes from Piper's constant attempts to live up to their unreasonable expectations and her frequent use of her 'powers' to simply survive this environment.

Within the comic tradition, feasting has been one of the ways by which a group demonstrates that it has come together and that it has resolved the conflicts that produced disunity. Piper is the Halliwell sister most tied to food and the comic unity it symbolizes. The characters around her – like Chef Moore, who fakes a French accent to add to the ambience of the place – are often pretentious and ruthless in the pursuit of their own interests. She, conversely, is a hardworking girl just trying to get a sufficient paycheque to support herself. Unlike any other girl, though, she can call upon her powers to even the score, thereby modelling the fantasy or wish fulfilment of any young woman.

Chef Moore: Your time is up. Let's see roast pork with gratin of fennel and penne with pork giblet sauce.
Piper: Chef Moore . . .
Chef Moore: What?
Piper: Uh, the pork . . .
Chef Moore: Yes, without the sauce it is nothing more than a salty marinara. A recipe from a woman's magazine. Puh!
Piper: I didn't have the time for . . .
Chef Moore: Ah-ah
Piper: But, but (She then freezes. Chef Moore pours port over the forkful of food, unfreezes him as he puts the food in his mouth).
Chef Moore: Mmm . . . this is very good. C'est magnifique.[5]

Time and again, Piper's power allows for a form of interrupted slapstick comedy where something is about to be smashed without her intervention. Quake is a location full of dishes and glasses waiting to be broken unless she takes control of the situation. At another level, though, feasting, like marriage, has always been one of the key ingredients of the comic tradition, and Quake is well placed to represent this tendency in a spatial way. Piper is the nurturing member of the Halliwell sisters. She is the one most clearly seeking a husband and also seeking harmony.

Nonetheless, all of the relationships that begin at Quake seem to end badly. Perhaps this is because the characters who congregate at Quake are both rich and shallow. In 'Dream Sorceror', two of the patrons hit on Phoebe as she enters.

Guy #1: Are your parents terrorists? 'Coz baby you're the bomb.
Guy #2: Jim, Jim, ask her if it hurt when she fell.
Phoebe: Uh, excuse me?

> *Guy #2:*   When you fell from heaven. Did it hurt, 'Coz I know an angel
> when I see one.
> *Phoebe:*   Hmmm, I'm no angel. I'm a witch. But don't tell my sisters I
> told you.

These kinds of exchanges, involving the hyperbole of the pick-up line on the one hand, and the honest statement of fact on the other, are the comedy of manners and the comedy of confusion. The two guys believe that Phoebe is playing along with their scenario while Phoebe is brushing them off with the literal truth, a truth that is understood by the viewer.

Women viewers, in identifying with Piper, undoubtedly see the struggles taking place at Quake as similar to their own struggles to obtain agency over their own workplaces. Nevertheless, the men and women who congregate at Quake are clearly the rich and famous that Piper, Prue and Phoebe would aspire to be were they independently wealthy or married to money. Quake is both a workplace and a place of display, and it is this dual function that makes it interesting within the plot. With this duality in mind, it should be no surprise that a number of the demons choose to make Quake their hunting ground for victims (Javna in 'I've Got You Under My Skin', 1.2, Whittaker Berman in 'Dream Sorceror'). They too are drawn to the 'beauty' and youth of the patrons, as well as to their connectedness to the implied world of fashion that exists as a backdrop to the series.

Much of the incidental comedy of the Halliwell sisters' lives derives from their obsession with clothing. Indeed, the visual aspect of the sisters' various outfits is one of the constants throughout the series. Clothing is one of the means by which each of the Halliwell sisters aspires to the 'other' life, the life of the rich and famous from which their powers appear to exclude them.

In *Buffy the Vampire Slayer*, many of the undead (monsters) distinguish themselves by their poor fashion sense, thus mixing the fantasy and comedy elements. They die with their old clothes on, and continue their undead life oblivious to the fashion faux pas they are committing. In *Charmed*, there is no room for such ignorance. When Piper and Phoebe encounter the demon Jade, and Mrs (Grace) Spencer, the following exchange occurs.

> *Piper:*   Mrs Spencer, it's so nice of you to see me (to Jade). Um, wow,
> your dress, it's beautiful. I'd recognize the style anywhere. It's
> a Shiro, isn't it?
> *Jade:*   Is it?
> *Grace:*   How are things in the kitchen?[6]

During this exchange, Piper is claiming a kind of common ground of shared knowledge, shared fashion with the Spencer family, not yet knowing that Jade is a demon. Jade is unaware of the significance of her dress and Grace steps into reassert the social distance, the appropriate social hierarchy in the situation. Grace wants nothing to do with Piper's egalitarian conversation and assigns her back to her proper place in the kitchen. This conversation is a wonderful example of the comedy of manners that occasionally surfaces throughout the series. As far as Piper and Phoebe are concerned, Jade is about to achieve their own fantasy, marrying into a rich family. The dress fitting also establishes Jade's demonic origin when the dressmaker accidentally pokes a pin through Jade's leg without her feeling a thing.

Phoebe's constant theft of Prue's wardrobe is one of the ways of established the ongoing sibling rivalry. Partly, Phoebe wishes to achieve the relative economic independence that her elder sister has managed, and partly she admires her sister's taste in clothing and wishes to emulate it. At a deeper level though, Phoebe dresses like Prue in an unconscious attempt to grow up faster and to take on her sister's personality. The repetition of this joke builds a bond between the sisters and also serves as a constant irritant, for in wearing Prue's dresses Phoebe is to an extent mimicking her. As viewers, we are left with the question of whether the Halliwell sisters are victims of fashion constructing themselves through consumerism.

Location is one of the keys to comedy in the series. A second major location for the first series is the Buckland auction house. Prue obtains employment in this place after first experiencing her own version of Piper's exploitation in her relationship with Roger at the Museum of Natural History.

Roger:	There's been a change of plans.
Prue:	Change of plans regarding the Beals' exhibition?
Roger:	The extra money that you helped raise through private donations has sparked significant corporate interest. The Beals' artefacts will now become part of our permanent collection.
Prue:	Well that's terrific.
Roger:	Which is why the board wants someone a little more qualified to handle the collection from now on. You look surprised.
Prue:	I don't know why; I'm furious . . .[7]

Prue refuses to mask her competency behind feminine mannerisms or in a servile relationship to her boss and ex-lover. This exchange leads to the first use of Prue's powers: she makes Roger's pen leak into his shirt pocket, and later, throttles him with his tie as her anger is unleashed. Viewers perceive this incident as a comic comeuppance for his manipulative chauvinism and personal preening; the tie is an obvious male phallic symbol. Roger, like so many other males, wants to take advantage of Prue's talents, and her recruitment to Buckland is meant to reverse such discrimination and economic exploitation. Yet, the apparent owners of Buckland turn out to be demons, once again undercutting Prue's search for respectability and ironically preventing her achievement of a normal life. Indeed, some of the artefacts that pass through the doors of Buckland are themselves sources of the quests to protect the innocent that employ the power of three. (The fertility symbol in 'The Wedding from Hell', 1.6; the locket in 'The Witch is Back', 1.9; the tiara in 'Wicca Envy', 1.10; and the urn in 'Feats of Clay', 1.11).

Buckland, then, is not a place where Prue can immerse herself in the 'normal' and create a normal life for herself, no more than Quake can provide such a refuge for Piper. Much of the comedy springs from their inability to separate their Wicca lives from the demands of the workplace. Prue comes perilously close to losing her employment as Claire becomes more and more exasperated by her sudden disappearances.

If these disappearances are hard to explain in the comic world of work, they are even harder to sustain in the world of romance. Much comic gender misunderstanding accrues from Prue's inability to explain to Andy why so many dates must be missed, and why his visits must be interrupted by sudden 'family' crises. Moreover, Andy's work as a detective constantly criss-crosses with the witches' work of dispensing with demons and eliminating warlocks. For all three women, the responsibilities of the Power of Three are playfully juxtaposed against their chance to have lasting relationships with men.

Prue:	I started to say, 'Yes'. then I stopped. I wondered if I could date. I mean, do witches date?
Piper:	Not only do they date, but they usually get the best guys.
Prue:	You two will not be laughing when this happens to you. Believe me everything will be different now.
Phoebe:	Well, at least our lives won't be boring.
Prue:	But they'll never be the same.
Phoebe:	And this is a bad thing?[8]

Each of the Halliwell sisters is absorbed with dating or trying to date throughout the series. The comedy is derived from the extra powers the witches bring to the dating game. No male is safe with them, and no male can get away with the usual ploys that work in the male/female comedy of misunderstanding. Prue's sustained on/off relationship with Andy is the most stable of these until the gradual growth of the Piper/Leo relationship. Andy's mounting frustration and, dare I say, impotence, as the Power of Three resolves all his murder investigations without them ever disappearing from his books, leaves them empowered and him powerless. Much as he wants to 'protect' Prue, she is usually far more capable of protecting herself and fighting her own battles. He inadvertently provides the element of bathos to their fantasy triumphs in his effort to get the paperwork straight.

Prue, Piper and Phoebe are not in the least prudish in their exchanges on the subject of sex, and their depiction of their various lovers is one of their shared confidences in which the viewer is uniquely included.

Piper:	Bad date?
Prue:	No. No. No. Not at all. It was great. You know, dinner, movie, sex.
Piper:	Excuse me? On your first date? You sleaze.
Prue:	It wasn't exactly our first date, Piper.
Piper:	High school doesn't count. That was last decade. Spill it. (Prue walks in the living room) Ooh, that bad, huh?
Prue:	No, actually that good . . .

The sisters often compare notes on their various dates and take a particular interest in pulling out the juicy details.

Phoebe:	. . . You, Leo, last night, dish.
Piper:	Um well, it was nice. It was . . . well wonderful. We just had a few problems.
Phoebe:	Problems?
Prue:	What problems?
Piper:	Well, it's been a while since, you know. I . . . I was a little nervous, and I kinda kept freezing him.
Prue:	Piper, you didn't?
Piper:	I didn't mean to . . . the first time.
Phoebe:	(making little noises) Ohhh!
Prue:	Okay, so um at what point exactly in the process did you freeze him?[9]

Viewers are meant to fill in the gaps and picture the freezing of Leo's genitalia. Here is a witch that can solve the problem of early ejaculation and prolong her pleasure when the world of fantasy and comedy intertwine.

Piper is not the only sister to use her powers in romantic situations to give her an advantage over the other sex. They all do, despite their apparent pledge only to use their abilities to protect the innocent. In Piper's case, the comedy comes from our recognition that all men have their moments of triumph and moments of embarrassment:

> In practicing the art of love, men endure their most terrible confusions, miseries and disasters. No matter how great and certain a man may have become in every other area of his life, in courtship (trying to convince a certain sweet someone that you are the sweetest someone ever produced by a certain other sex) all men are unsure, fumbling and feel rotten most of the time.[10]

Such knowing exchanges between the sisters, with their powers to fix the situation, transform the episodes into a deeper comedy of gender relations. In social situations, Phoebe appears to have the upper hand with her gift of predicting the future.

Phoebe:	Okay, see that poster boy to your left? (Piper looks at her) Just glance, don't be obvious.
Piper:	I approve. Who is he?
Phoebe:	His name is Alec and he is about to come over and ask if he could buy me a martini.
Piper:	How do you know?
Phoebe:	Let's just say I saw the age-old problem of who approaches who. I had a little premonition.
Piper:	What? Phoebe, you are not supposed to use your powers, we agreed.
Phoebe:	No, you and Prue agreed. I abstained.[11]

The ability to foresee the future has its own currency in the dating game. In another reversal of comic expectations the men become the objects, their intentions and their likely performance are already predicted in the world of fantasy; the sisters are shameless in exploiting their advantages.

Yet despite these apparent advantages, Phoebe falls for the charm of Stefan/demon Javna and his offer to make her a model. Lured by the prestige of his work as a photographer, she fails to appreciate the threat he represents. Indeed the initial attempts of Phoebe and Piper to find suitable men lead each to actual demons or warlocks, such as Jeremy in the first episode, or Rex in 'Wicca Envy'. At some level, of course, the joke is that all men are monsters, particularly after sex, and the transformation of many of their seeming men into demons is a normal experience for many women.

There is clearly a connection between this understanding and the frequent arrival of various warlocks intent on taking away the power of the Halliwell sisters, and in stealing the Book of Shadows. The powers themselves and the Book of Shadows represent a source of energy and resistance to male domination, their very independent existence is a threat to male hegemony. On this level, the fantasy takes a turn into social commentary, and is far from subtle in its condemnation of the suppression of women's perspectives and women's rights. As Rosemary Jackson comments:

> A literary fantasy is produced within, determined by its social context: ... The forms taken by any particular fantastic text are determined by a number of forces which intersect and interact in different ways in each individual work. Recognition of these forces involves placing authors in relation to historical, social, economic, political and sexual determinants, as well as to the literary tradition of fantasy.[12]

Some of the forces bearing down on the Halliwell sisters in the late 1990s are the questions of whether women have made and can sustain any real gains in their relative freedom from the dominance of the patriarchy. By mediating these questions through fantasy and comedy, it is hoped that women viewers will accept the legitimacy of the question, and indeed internalize the debate.

These questions come to a particular head when the sisters are forced to bring back the founder of their matriarchal line, Melinda Warren, to battle their mutual enemy, Matthew Tate. Matthew was imprisoned in a locket after leaving Melinda to burn at the hands of the Salem witch-finders, but released by the manipulation of Rex and Hannah. On a surface level, Melinda comments on the invention of the zip on her dress ('a wise witch made this') and on the improvements in a woman's lot.

> *Melinda:* So did it and did it take you long to make the dress?
> *Phoebe:* Make it. No, no. I bought it.
> *Melinda:* Oh you must be rich.
> *Prue:*   No, she's got credit cards.[13]

This humour cuts both ways. Have the women exchanged the slavery to men for the slavery to consumerism and the unseen mounting debt of the instruments of capitalism? Perhaps this is the naivety of Miranda in *The Tempest*, who likewise only sees the beauty and not the wider context 'O brave new world that has such people in't'.[14]

'The Witch is Back' episode is particularly poignant because it reminds the Halliwelll sisters of their shared responsibility to protect their power and their 'line' from the calculating and cruel depredations of men. Not coincidentally, it is also a low point in the relationship between Prue and Andy, as she traps him behind an airbag in his attempts to do his duty as a police officer. His parting comment is 'You don't know what you are doing', which of course she does, and he does not; one more ironic reversal in their string of failed attempts to communicate.

Melinda Warren is not the last of the family to be drawn to dangerous men. Even those who are not warlocks or demons can pose a threat to the Power of Three. In 'Feats of Clay', one of Phoebe's ex-lovers returns to challenge the solidarity of the sisters. For most of the episode, Phoebe believes that Prue is being her usual judgemental self in rejecting the possibility that Clay has reformed and returned out of a genuine desire to be with Phoebe. This scenario would fit comfortably on *The Young and the Restless*, were it not for the fact that Clay has brought a curse with him after the theft of an Egyptian urn. At the same time, the comic potential of Piper's decision to boost the lovesick Doug's confidence with a spell is developed in a subplot that explores the limits of fantasy intervention into the course of true love. For Piper and Phoebe, the contrast between the two love affairs offers an opportunity for them to reflect on the kind of men they want.

> *Piper:*   No, you see the good in people and that's never wrong. Besides, the wrong guys are usually the most interesting. Until you get your hopes up and let your guard down and they reveal their true selves.
> *Phoebe:* So true.
> *Piper:*   Look at Doug. Great guy, kind of boring on the surface, easy to overlook, but maybe in the long run, we're better off with his type.
> *Phoebe:* Maybe in the long run. I think I'm still looking for adventure.
> *Piper:*   Then you risk paying the price.[15]

What 1990s woman wants a boring man? But then, what is the social price of this decision? The alternative is often the 'Armani-wearing, Chardonnay-slugging trust funder!' that bedevils the lives of the Halliwell sisters. How representative are the Charmed Ones of their audience? Do the women listening to such exchanges nod in affirmation and thereby allow the fantasy relationships to intrude on their personal and cultural practices? Or does the comic distance allow a further reflection? Certainly, there are key messages about sex and relationships that recur in the Charmed Ones' discussions.

> *Phoebe:* Three dates, no sex. There could only be one talk he's talking about: safe sex, prior partners, standard dating protocol.
> *Piper:*   And sex equals relationship.

Prue:	And you're not sure whether you want to be a couple?
Piper:	Well, I thought Leo and I were a couple and then we coupled and he took off.
Prue:	Yeah well, men seem to have a different definition of coupling than women do.[16]

These messages, particularly the ones about safe sex, are clearly intended to be didactic, but emerge from the comic frustration of women attempting to understand the dating peculiarities of men.

Female/male relationships are the constant currency of the comic exchanges. When Leo confides in Phoebe about his love for Piper but his need to go away in 'Secrets and Guys' (1.14), we know this is too good an opportunity to let pass. In the world of postmodernism, where there is supposed to be a chain between the signifier and the signified, the chain breaks in the act of interpretation. Up to this point in the series, Piper has dated a demon, a ghost and only attracted 'normal' male interest after the casting of a love charm. She could be forgiven a certain amount of incredulity in believing, ever again, that men mean what they say.

Phoebe:	. . . We can go over your plan. You know. What you're gonna tell Piper.
Leo:	Oh, well. I thought that I'd tell her that, uh, as much as I love her and as much as I'd like to stay in San Francisco, I can't. A—and I don't know how long my work will keep me away.
Phoebe:	No. no. What you just said to her is as much as you'd like to stay and have sex with her, you've got a wife and kids in another part of the country. Try again.
Leo:	Uh, Piper, um, you know how much you mean to me, and more than anything, I wish things could work out, but they can't, and no one is more sorry than I am.
Phoebe:	Translation – I found someone I like even better.
Leo:	I'm completely confused.
Phoebe:	Uh, look Leo. It's not that complicated. OK. Um, just avoid the following. We can still hang out. I don't deserve you yet. I need more 'me time' before we can have 'we time'. And my personal favourite, 'It's not you. It's me'. And whatever you do, do not start with 'we need to talk'. Other than that, you'll do fine.[17]

Leo is left speechless and bewildered; when placed in the context of the collective experience of women his good intentions only appear to be clear evidence of insincerity. It is in these moments that we chuckle with the Charmed Ones. We can hear the 'yes' of recognition from thousands of female viewers. Like Andy, Leo is out of his depth, swimming against the rising tide of female consciousness.

We have considered slapstick comedy, the comedy of manners, the constant ironies and the playful disjunction between character and viewer assumptions. Moreover, we have noted that these various forms of comedy are frequently rooted in the misunderstandings that spring from gender. How will we ever forget the black humour of the pizza-carrying male stripper being devoured by demons at the bachelorette party in 'The Wedding from Hell'? The incongruity of the gender reversal, combined with the demons drawn from fantasy, subverts both comedy and fantasy conventions. Yet there is one more insight to be derived from another form of comedy employed in the first season of *Charmed*.

In his celebrated study on laughter, Henri Bergson identified one of the principal sources of an audience's appreciation of comedy:

> I mean our gestures can only be imitated in their mechanical conformity and therefore exactly in what is alien to our living personality. To imitate any one is to bring out the element of automatism he has allowed to creep into his person. And as this is the very essence of the ludicrous it is no wonder that imitation gives rise to laughter . . . The truth is that a really living life should never repeat itself. Wherever there is repetition or complete similarity, we always suspect some mechanism at work behind the living . . . This deflection of life towards the mechanical is here the real cause of laughter.[18]

One of the best episodes of the first season, 'Déjà Vu All Over Again' (1.22) employs this understanding in the final development of the character Rodriguez. Rodriguez is a demon given the opportunity to replay his failed attempts to kill the Halliwell sisters. Over and over again, his mentor, the demon Tempus, reverses time to enable Rodriguez to try and be successful in killing the Charmed Ones. Each time he fails, and in each rendition, his efforts to change the outcome become more ludicrous and comical. (Viewers will no doubt notice the similarity of this comic technique to the efforts of Bill Murray to win his dream woman in *Groundhog Day*). Many of the demons and warlocks become 'mechanical' in their efforts to defeat the Charmed Ones, thus converting potential horror into comedy.

At the end of the first season, we are left with an image, an image of the Power of Three. This is a world that is uncluttered or unfettered by the demands of men. Andy dies so that the power may be preserved. The death of Andy is necessary in the sense that he is a 'blocking character' as described by Northrop Frye in his essay, 'The Mythos of Spring: Comedy': 'Comedy usually moves toward a happy ending, and the normal response of the audience to a happy ending is "this should be", which sounds like a moral judgment. So it is, except that it is not moral in the restricted sense, but social.'[19] A sisterhood based in blood that transcends the complexities of the outside world and beats back the monsters survives. The sisterhood, the family of three sisters, is the social unit that must endure. This is fantasy triumphant and comedy confirmed; we are beguiled.

Episode Guide

Suzann Martin and Stephanie Morgan

Season One: First Aired 1998–9

1.1   Something Wicca This Way Comes
Writer: Constance M. Burge
Director: John T. Kretchmer
Phoebe moves back home to live with her two sisters, finds a book in the attic of their grandmother's house and recites an incantation that gives the sisters strange powers.

1.2   I've Got You Under My Skin
Writer: Brad Kern
Director: John T. Kretchmer
Piper fears that she will be unable to enter a church because she is a witch. Phoebe is almost killed by a photographer who steals youth from women.

1.3   Thank You for Not Morphing
Writers: Zack Estrin, Chris Levinson
Director: Ellen S. Pressman
The sisters' father returns, attempts to steal the Book of Shadows and teams up with their 'shapeshifter' neighbours, who are also trying to steal the book.

1.4   Dead Man Dating
Writer: Javier Grillo-Marxuach
Director: Richard Compton
Phoebe works as a psychic to make money for Prue's birthday gift, and the ghost of a recently deceased man asks her for help. Piper falls for the ghost as she attempts to find his body.

1.5   Dream Sorcerer
Writer: Constance M. Burge
Director: Nick Marck
Prue is stalked in her dreams by a man who wants to kill her. Piper and

Phoebe attempt a spell to attract men and are overcome by their many admirers.

1.6   The Wedding from Hell
Writers: Greg Elliot, Michael Perricone
Director: Richard Ginty

Piper's restaurant caters a wedding where the bride has been supplanted by demon named Hecate, who is trying to conceive a child through a mortal man.

1.7   The Fourth Sister
Writer: Edithe Swensen
Director: Gilbert Adler

The sisters' cat goes missing and Aviva, a girl who has been granted powers by a demon named Kali, brings the cat back. Aviva is possessed by Kali, and the sisters must save her.

1.8   The Truth is Out There and it Hurts
Writers: Zack Estrin, Chris Levinson
Director: James A. Cotner

The sisters follow Phoebe's premonitions to stop a killer from the future. Prue casts a truth spell to find out how Andy will react to knowing she is a witch.

1.9   The Witch is Back
Writer: Sheryl J. Anderson
Director: Richard Denault

The sisters bring back their ancestor, Melinda Warren, to fight a warlock from the past that Prue accidentally releases from a locket.

1.10   Wicca Envy
Writers: Brad Kern, Sheryl J. Anderson
Director: Mel Damski

The auction house serves as the site of a 'theft' since Rex, Prue's boss, has framed her. Rex's identity as a warlock is revealed.

1.11   Feats of Clay
Writers: Michael Perricone, Greg Elliot, Chris Levinson, Zack Estrin
Director: Kevin Inch

Phoebe's ex-boyfriend, Clay, brings a stolen cursed urn to her for Prue to sell.

1.12 The Wendigo
Writer: Edithe Swensen
Director: James L. Conway
Piper is attacked and scratched by a wendigo, which causes her to slowly turn into a wendigo. Prue gets Phoebe a job at the auction house.

1.13 From Fear to Eternity
Writers: Tony Blake, Paul Jackson
Director: Les Sheldon
The sisters are forced to contend with Barbas, a demon of fear, as he attempts to kill Phoebe on Friday the 13th.

1.14 Secrets and Guys
Writers: Constance M. Burge, Sheryl J. Anderson
Director: James A. Cotner
Phoebe discovers that Leo is a Whitelighter, and Piper breaks up with him. Prue is sent messages from a kidnapped child.

1.15 Is There a Woogy in the House?
Writers: Zack Estrin, Chris Levinson
Director: John T. Kretchmer
An earthquake unleashes a shadow demon, and Phoebe, controlled by the Woogyman, attempts to kill Prue and Piper.

1.16 Which Prue is it Anyway?
Writer: Javier Grillo-Marxuach
Director: John Behring
Prue casts a spell to add to her strength, but the spell ends up creating replicas. Phoebe has a premonition of a warrior named Gabriel attempting to kill the eldest Halliwell sister.

1.17 That '70s Episode
Writer: Sheryl J. Anderson
Director: Richard Denault
The sisters go back to the 1970s when their mother was still alive to prevent a pact between their mother and a warlock that would cost the sisters their powers.

1.18 When Bad Warlocks Turn Good
Writer: Edithe Swensen
Director: Kevin Inch
Prue attempts to help a warlock who is escaping his fate to become a priest. Phoebe urges Piper to start dating again.

1.19   Out of Sight
Writers: Tony Blake, Paul Jackson
Director: Craig Zisk
Prue uses her powers to attempt to stop a kidnapping, but a reporter sees her abilities. Andy finds out about Prue's powers.

1.20   The Power of Two
Writer: Brad Kern
Director: Elodie Keene
Phoebe sees a ghost take over the body of a guard at Alcatraz while she takes a tour. She then has to stop the ghost from escaping.

1.21   Love Hurts
Writers: Chris Levinson, Zack Estrin, Javier Grillo-Marxuach
Director: James Whitmore Jr.
Leo is attacked by a Darklighter, and the sisters have to protect the witch he has been protecting; Piper accidentally switches Phoebe and Prue's powers.

1.22   Déjà Vu All Over Again
Writers: Constance M. Burge, Brad Kern
Director: Les Sheldon
A demon named Tempus, who controls time, attempts to kill the sisters, turning time back repeatedly.

Season Two: First Aired 1999–2000

2.1   Witch Trial
Writer: Brad Kern
Director: Craig Zisk
When a demon steals the Book of Shadows on their one-year anniversary as witches, the Halliwell sisters must retrieve the book or lose their powers permanently.

2.2   Morality Bites
Writers: Chris Levinson, Zack Estrin
Director: John Behring
Phoebe's premonition of her own death leads this sister to cast a spell that thrusts all three sisters ten years into the future – a future of failed relationships, murder and a modern witch hunt.

2.3   The Painted World
Writer: Constance M. Burge
Director: Kevin Inch
Phoebe must undo a spell that has Prue and Piper trapped in a painting before the original inhabitant burns the painting.

2.4   The Devil's Music

Writer: David Simkins
Director: Richard Compton

Piper books Dishwalla to play at her club, which leads to the disappearance of female fans. The Charmed Ones discover the band's manager has made a pact with a demon: an exchange of innocents for fame and fortune.

2.5   She's a Man, Baby, a Man

Writer: Javier Grillo-Marxuach
Director: Martha Mitchell

Phoebe dreams that she has been killing her lovers and fears that she may be a succubus. Prue casts a spell to determine if Phoebe is right but accidentally turns herself into a man. Prue finds herself the man-hating demon's next target.

2.6   That Old Black Magic

Writers: Vivian Mayhew, Valerie Mayhew
Director: James L. Conway

Prue locates a magic sceptre that a recently released evil witch is hunting for while Leo, Piper and Phoebe try to locate the Chosen One who can wield the sceptre to defeat her.

2.7   They're Everywhere

Writer: Sheryl J. Anderson
Director: Mel Damski

The Halliwell sisters save a young man from the collectors, who seek the knowledge he has amassed from ancient tablets that are supposed to detail history, including the future.

2.8   P3 H20

Writers: Chris Levinson, Zack Estrin
Director: John Behring

Visiting the place where their mother drowned, the Charmed Ones meet Sam, their mother's Whitelighter. Piper must reevaluate her relationship with Leo and Prue must face her deepest fear to defeat the demon that killed their mother.

2.9   Ms. Hellfire

Writers: Sheryl J. Anderson, Constance M. Burge
Director: Craig Zisk

After the sisters are attacked, Prue assumes the dead assassin's identity to discover who hired her while Piper and Phoebe race to find the next victim.

2.10   Heartbreak City

Writer: David Simkins
Director: Michael Zinberg

Unsuspecting lovers and the Halliwell sisters find themselves the targets of a demon of hate after it steals Cupid's ring and seeks to shatter the relationships that Cupid has forged.

2.11   Reckless Abandon

Writer: Javier Grillo-Marxuach
Director: Craig Zisk

The Charmed Ones experience motherhood as they protect an abandoned baby boy from a vengeful spirit who has been killing men in his family line.

2.12   Awakened

Writers: Vivian Mayhew, Valerie Mayhew
Director: Anson Williams

When Piper comes down with a mysterious and potentially fatal illness, Prue and Phoebe ignore the rule that says a witch cannot use a spell for personal gain, which results in the further spread of the disease.

2.13   Animal Pragmatism

Writers: Chris Levinson, Zack Estrin
Director: Don Kurt

Phoebe's college friends dabble with magic, turning three animals into men for Valentine's Day. When Phoebe attempts to intervene, she accidentally turns the patrons of P3 into animals too.

2.14   Pardon My Past

Writer: Michael Gleason
Director: John Paré

Phoebe's past life puts her present in jeopardy as she learns that in the 1920s she was seduced by a warlock and cursed by her 'cousins', Prue and Piper.

2.15   Give Me a Sign

Writer: Sheryl J. Anderson
Director: James A. Cotner

Prue is kidnapped by Bane Jessup and forced to use her powers to save him from a powerful demon while Phoebe tries to help Piper with her complicated love life.

2.16 Murphy's Luck

Writer: David Simkins
Director: John Behring

After saving a mentally tormented woman from committing suicide, Prue finds herself the Darklighter's next target as his curse throws her into a deep depression.

2.17 How to Make a Quilt Out of Americans

Writers: Javier Grillo-Marxuach, Robert Masello
Director: Kevin Itch

A family friend asks the Charmed Ones to stop a demon that steals skins from corpses, only to find out that the old woman is using them to obtain eternal youth and beauty. Piper speculates whether she wants the return of her powers.

2.18 Chick Flick

Writers: Zack Estrin, Chris Levinson
Director: Michael Schultz

A demon of illusion brings horror film characters to life and sends his creations to kill the Halliwell sisters, who find their powers have no effect on the crazed characters.

2.19 Ex Libris

Writer: Peter Chomsky
Director: Brad Kern

A student publishing a thesis proving the existence of evil is killed. Phoebe attempts to help the ghost while Prue helps a man find justice for his murdered daughter. Piper confronts part of Leo's past.

2.20 Astral Monkey

Writers: David Simkins, Constance M. Burge
Director: Craig Zisk

During a blood transfusion, Piper's former doctor acquires the powers of the three Halliwell sisters and begins to harvest organs, originally to save his dying sister. However, having the Power of Three eventually drives him mad.

2.21 Apocalypse Not

Writers: Sanford Golden, Sheryl J. Anderson
Director: Michael Zinberg

Prue is trapped with one of the Four Horsemen of the Apocalypse in a vortex after trying to vanquish the quartet; Phoebe and Piper decide to sacrifice Prue to save earth from the end of the world.

2.22   Be Careful What You Witch For

Writers: Chris Levinson, Zack Estrin, Brad Kern
Director: Shannen Doherty

A genie, attempting to gain mortality and under the direction of an infernal council, will grant each of the Halliwell sisters a wish: Prue becomes seventeen, Phoebe flies and Dan, Piper's friend, grows very old.

Season Three: First Aired 2000–1

3.1   The Honeymoon's Over

Writer: Brad Kern
Director: James L. Conway

With Piper and Leo away, Phoebe and Prue have to deal with a slew of guardians, and must testify in court. Phoebe falls for district attorney Cole Turner.

3.2   Magic Hour

Writers: Zack Estrin, Chris Levinson
Director: John Behring

The sisters break a curse that causes a woman to turn into a wolf at night and her boyfriend into an owl during the day. Prue discovers how to allow Piper and Leo to wed without anyone finding out.

3.3   Once Upon a Time

Writer: Krista Vernoff
Director: Joel J. Feigenbaum

The sisters save a fairy princess and a little girl from trolls, and Piper's preoccupation with Leo's absence causes her to make a spell backfire and places the girl in danger.

3.4   All Halliwell's Eve

Writer: Sheryl J. Anderson
Director: Anson Williams

Pulled back in time to the seventeenth century, the sisters must save a pregnant witch and her unborn child from the hands of an evil witch that wants the child.

3.5   Sight Unseen

Writer: William Schmidt
Director: Perry Lang

Prue becomes paranoid about attacks from Belthazor and the Triad, which forces her to construe a simple house robbing by a mortal as a demonic attack.

3.6 Primrose Empath
Writer: Daniel Cerone
Director: Mel Damski
Prue gains empathic powers from a demon and soon loses control of them; Cole breaks up with Phoebe.

3.7 Power Outage
Writers: Monica Breen, Alison Schapker
Director: Craig Zisk
Cole enlists the anger demon Andras into helping him and the Triad attack the sisters, while the three sisters fight and lose their powers after using them against each other.

3.8 Sleuthing With the Enemy
Writer: Peter Hume
Director: Noel Nosseck
Cole's identity as Belthazor is revealed, and Phoebe fights with the decision to vanquish her boyfriend.

3.9 Coyote Piper
Writer: Krista Vernoff
Director: Chris Long
Piper is possessed by an evil life essence at her high-school reunion, and Prue and Phoebe try to oust the essence known as Terra.

3.10 We All Scream for Ice Cream
Writer: Zack Estrin, Chris Levinson
Director: Allan Kroeker
Victor comes to visit, and the sisters investigate an ice cream van that is abducting children. Trying to defeat the Nothing forces the sisters to ask for help from their father.

3.11 Blinded by the Whitelighter
Writer: Nell Scovell
Director: David Straiton
An ancient warlock, Eames, is stealing powers from witches by killing them as he attempts to kill all Whitelighters in the world.

3.12 Wrestling with Demons
Writer: Joel J. Feigenbaum
Director: Sheryl J. Anderson
Prue finds out her old college boyfriend is being turned into a demon, and the sisters attempt to save him by entering a wrestling competition to save his soul.

3.13 Bride and Gloom

Writer: William Schmidt
Director: Chris Long

A shape-shifting demon tricks Prue into marrying him so he can turn the witches evil and get the Book of Shadows.

3.14 The Good, the Bad, and the Cursed

Writers: Monica Breen, Alison Schapker
Director: Shannen Doherty

Phoebe sees an injured ghost in a deserted town and is inexplicably tied to the ghost. Prue is forced to go back to the nineteenth century to save the man from local thugs to free Phoebe.

3.15 Just Harried

Writer: Daniel Cerone
Director: Mel Damski

On the day of Leo and Piper's wedding, Prue's astral self develops its own wild personality that threatens the wedding, and she is accused of murder.

3.16 Death Takes a Halliwell

Writer: Krista Vernoff
Director: Jon Paré

Prue fights the Angel of Death, and is forced to turn her back on a dying soul, making her come to grips with the death of her mother. Cole is attacked by seeker demons who are attempting to kill him.

3.17 Pre-Witched

Writers: Zack Estrin, Chris Levinson
Director: David Straiton

Piper and Leo decide to move out, causing the sisters to think about the last time one of them moved out of the manor. The three fight a warlock who grows stronger each time it is vanquished.

3.18 Sin Francisco

Writer: Nell Scovell
Director: Joel J. Feigenbaum

The sisters are cursed after they contend with a demon named Lucas who has the ability to curse people with one of the seven deadly sins.

3.19 The Demon who Came in from the Cold

Writer: Sheryl J. Anderson
Director: Anson Williams

Cole attempts to sneak into the Brotherhood of Demons as Belthazor to find out information about an internet organization that is attempting to control the world's information. The sisters must vanquish the head of the organization without the Brotherhood finding out about Cole's involvement.

3.20   Exit Strategy
Writers: Daniel Cerone, Peter Hume
Director: Joel J. Feigenbaum
The Brotherhood attempts to sabotage Cole and Phoebe's relationship in an attempt to return him to evil. Piper's powers go out of control, and she ends up blowing things up accidentally.

3.21   Look Who's Barking
Writers: Monica Breen, Curtis Kheel, Alison Schapker
Director: John Behring
The sisters cast a spell, and it backfires, turning Prue into a dog. Prue is killed by a car, and Phoebe turns into a banshee after her remorse allows the banshee they were tracking to attack her.

3.22   All Hell Breaks Loose
Writer: Brad Kern
Director: Shannen Doherty
The sisters have their identity as witches revealed on national television and make a deal with the Source to have time reversed to repair the damages. The demon Shax continues to follow the sisters.

Season Four: First Aired 2001–2

4.1   Charmed Again
Writer: Brad Kern
Director: Michael Shultz
Dealing with the death of Prue, Piper and Phoebe discover their half-sister, a Whitelighter named Paige Matthews, who can complete their trio for the Power of Three, if Prue's killer lets her live that long.

4.2   Charmed Again II
Writer: Brad Kern
Director: Mel Damski
Paige is tempted by the Source to turn evil and forever destroy the Power of Three. Piper and Phoebe are faced with a suspicious inspector who believes the pair are responsible for Prue's death.

4.3   Hell Hath No Fury
Writer: Krista Vernoff
Director: Chris Long
Due to her inability to deal with Prue's recent death and the inexperience that Paige displays, Piper begins to turn into a Fury, a mystical vigilante.

4.4   Enter the Demon

Writer: Daniel Cerone
Director: Joel J. Feigenbaum

After Paige accidentally mixes potions that switch their bodies, she and Phoebe learn how to control each other's powers.

4.5   Size Matters

Writer: Nell Scovell
Director: Noel Nosseck

Phoebe is shrunk to five inches tall as bait to lure her sisters into a demonic trap.

4.6   A Knight to Remember

Writers: Alison Schapker, Monica Breen
Director: David Straiton

Phoebe and Piper become stuck in the past when Paige summons a medieval prince, discovering that one of her past lives was that of an evil enchantress.

4.7   Brain Drain

Writer: Curtis Kheel
Director: John Behring

The Source twists Phoebe's sense of reality by entering her brain. Piper and Paige must stop Phoebe from abandoning her powers.

4.8   Black as Cole

Writers: Brad Kern, Nell Scovell
Director: Les Landau

While helping a woman seek revenge on the demon that killed her fiancé, Phoebe is faced with the reality of Cole's demonic past.

4.9   Muse to My Ears

Writer: Krista Vernoff
Director: Joel J. Feigenbaum

The Charmed Ones must free the Muses, who have been kidnapped by warlocks seeking a way of turning the Muses' inspirational abilities to evil.

4.10   A Paige from the Past

Writer: Daniel Cerone
Director: James L. Conway

Paige must deal with a ghost from her past while Piper must prevent the marriage of Phoebe and Cole, who have been possessed by ghosts.

4.11 Trial by Magic
Writer: Michael Gleason
Director: Chip Scott Laughlin
Phoebe must persuade her fellow jurors that magic does exist and that the defendant is innocent, while Piper, Paige and Leo rush to find the real killer.

4.12 Lost and Bound
Writer: Nell Scovell
Director: Noel Nosseck
Cole gives Phoebe her grandmother's wedding ring, which turns her into the perfect 1950s housewife. Piper and Leo locate a firestarter before he can be given to the Source.

4.13 Charmed and Dangerous
Writers: Monica Breen, Alison Schapker
Director: Jon Paré
The Source steals the Hollow, a mist that can absorb the powers of the Charmed Ones, in an attempt to weaken the sisters. Phoebe lets Cole intervene despite her premonition that he might die.

4.14 The Three Faces of Phoebe
Writer: Curtis Kheel
Director: Joel J. Feigenbaum
Phoebe, worried about her forthcoming nuptials, casts a spell that brings a young Phoebe and an old Phoebe to the manor to help her gain some perspective on her life. Cole continues to be overcome by the Source.

4.15 Marry-Go-Round
Writer: Daniel Cerone
Director: Chris Long
As her wedding day approaches, Phoebe argues with her sisters while Cole is consumed by the Source. The Source plans a dark wedding in a bid to obtain more power.

4.16 The Fifth Halliwell
Writer: Krista Vernoff
Director: David Straiton
Paige, feeling left out by her married siblings, suspects Cole is still a demon. The Source plots to sire his evil spawn with Phoebe.

4.17 Saving Private Leo
Writer: Daniel Cerone
Director: John Behring
Paige and Phoebe face the possibility of losing another sister when two

ghosts from Leo's past seek retribution. Cole attempts to separate Phoebe from her sisters by insisting they need a place of their own.

4.18   Bite Me
Writer: Curtis Kheel
Director: John T. Kretchmer
Paige is turned into a vampire in a vampire queen's bid to oust Cole from his position in the underworld.

4.19   We're Off to See the Wizard
Writers: Alison Schapker, Monica Breen
Director: Timothy Lonsdale
Still ignorant that Cole is the head of the Underworld, and that the newly pregnant Phoebe is his queen, Piper and Paige collaborate with a wizard to stop the coronation of the new Source.

4.20   Long Live the Queen
Writer: Krista Vernoff
Director: Jon Paré
Phoebe must kill Piper and Paige to avoid a bloody uprising in the Underworld after she has them help her save an innocent.

4.21   Womb Raider
Writer: Daniel Cerone
Director: Mel Damski
The Seer schemes to abduct Phoebe's unborn child when it begins to show signs of gaining its supernatural powers.

4.22   Witch Way Now?
Writer: Brad Kern
Director: Brad Kern
After vanquishing the Source of All Evil, the Charmed Ones are offered the reward of normal lives. However, their decision is placed on hold as they have many responsibilities left to tend to.

Season Five: First Aired 2002–3

5.1   A Witch's Tail Part 1
Writer: Daniel Cerone
Director: James L. Conway
A mermaid, Mylie, threatened with losing her immortality from a pact she made with a sea hag, implores the sisters for their help. Phoebe attempts to divorce Cole, and Piper deals with her fear of her unborn baby dying because of the water demon.

5.2 A Witch's Tail Part 2

Writers: Monica Breen, Alison Schapker
Director: Mel Damski

The sisters and Leo ask Phoebe, who has suddenly turned into a mermaid, to come back to her duties as a Charmed One. Piper suppresses her fears with a spell and endangers herself and the baby.

5.3 Happily Ever After

Writer: Curtis Kheel
Director: John T. Kretchmer

The sisters are trapped in fairy tales by an evil witch. Piper plays a role in the tale of Little Red Riding Hood, Phoebe is turned into Cinderella and Paige eats a poisoned apple.

5.4 Siren Song

Writer: Krista Vernoff
Director: Joel J. Feigenbaum

Cole and Phoebe are placed under the spell of a siren, who attempts to kill both of them. Piper's unborn child switches Piper's and Leo's powers.

5.5 Witches in Tights

Writer: Mark Wilding
Director: David Straiton

A boy's drawing turns a demon into a supervillain, and the Charmed Ones are forced to ask the boy to turn them into superheroes to combat the evil.

5.6 The Eyes Have It

Writer: Laurie Parres
Director: James Marshall

Phoebe loses her powers of premonition and discovers a demon is stealing the eyes of gypsies. Piper goes against Leo's wishes and attempts to visit a doctor regarding her pregnancy.

5.7 Sympathy for the Demon

Writer: Henry Alonso Myers
Director: Stuart Gillard

Paige is tricked into giving Barbas, a demon of fear, Cole's powers. Barbas attacks the sisters by plaguing them with their greatest fears.

5.8 A Witch in Time

Writer: Daniel Cerone
Director: John Behring

Phoebe accidentally opens a tunnel in time by saving the life of her new boyfriend multiple times, thus allowing a warlock to kill her and Paige. Piper must decide whether or not to let the boyfriend die.

5.9   Sam I Am

Writers: Alison Schapker, Monica Breen
Director: Joel J. Feigenbaum

Cole attacks the sisters, hoping that they will destroy him so he cannot kill them. Paige meets her father, Sam, in her first act as a Whitelighter.

5.10   Y Tu Mummy Tambien

Writer: Curtis Kheel
Director: Chris Long

Phoebe is mummified so that Jeric, a demon attempting to find the perfect body, can resurrect his dead lover Isis.

5.11   The Importance of Being Phoebe

Writer: Krista Vernoff
Director: Derek Johansen

Cole kidnaps Phoebe and sends a shapeshifter to replace her and trick the sisters into giving him control of the house. Cole also gets Paige arrested and fails Piper's club's health inspection.

5.12   Centennial Charmed

Writer: Brad Kern
Director: Jim Conway

Cole casts a spell, hoping to gain Phoebe's love again; the spell alters reality, and the two eldest sisters forget their relation to Paige.

5.13   House Call

Writer: Henry Alonso Myers
Director: Jon Paré

The sisters summon a witch doctor to remove evil from the house.

5.14   San Francisco Dreamin'

Writers: Alison Schapker, Monica Breen
Director: John T. Kretchmer

The sister's nightmares come to life after a demon attacks them with dream dust; the sisters destroy the demon by figuring out the symbolic meaning of the images.

5.15   The Day the Magic Died

Writer: Daniel Cerone
Director: Stuart Gillard

The sisters go to a summit meeting with evil leaders and discover that all magic has suddenly stopped. These leaders steal Piper's unborn child to make him evil.

5.16   Baby's First Demon
Writer: Krista Vernoff
Director: John T. Kretchmer

Demonic kidnappers target Piper's child, and they try to use Paige as a tool to attack Leo and the baby.

5.17   Lucky Charmed
Writer: Curtis Kheel
Director: Roxann Dawson

The sisters gain magical luck from a leprechaun when they attempt to vanquish a demon who has been targeting leprechauns.

5.18   Cat House
Writer: Brad Kern
Director: Jim Conway

Piper sends her sisters and, inadvertently, a warlock back in time with a spell to allow her and Leo to work out their marital issues. The warlock attempts to change the future by killing their cat.

5.19   Nymphs Just Want to Have Fun
Writers: Andrea Stevens, Doug E. Jones
Director: Mel Damski

After a demon kills one of three nymphs that protect a spring, the sisters are forced to help the remaining two nymphs. The creatures force Paige to become one of them.

5.20   Sense and Sense Ability
Writers: Daniel Cerone, Krista Vernoff
Directors: Jim Conway, Joel J. Feigenbaum

The sisters have their senses (hearing, speech, sight) stolen by an old crone attempting to steal Wyatt.

5.21   Necromancing the Stone
Writers: Monica Breen, Henry Alonso Myers, Alison Schapker
Director: Jon Paré

A Wiccan ceremony celebrating Wyatt's birth brings Grams to the house. Grams remembers a former lover who tries to kill the Charmed Ones so that their love can be reunited.

5.22   Oh My Goddess Part 1
Writers: Chris Kheel, Krista Vernoff
Director: Jonathan West

Titans manage to kill all the Elders, and Leo is forced to take over. Leo grants the sisters the power of Greek goddesses to kill the Titans.

5.23   Oh My Goddess Part 2

Writer: Daniel Cerone
Director: Joel J. Feigenbaum

The sisters must fight the distractions that accompany their new powers and focus on their fight with the Titans. Leo must choose to become an Elder permanently or stay with Piper and Wyatt.

Season Six: First Aired 2003–4

6.1   Valhalley of the Dolls Part I

Writer: Brad Kern
Director: James L. Conway

After Paige accidentally wipes Piper's memory, she and Phoebe try to get Leo's help, only to find that he has been taken to the island of Valhalla. Chris turns out to be responsible.

6.2   Valhalley of the Dolls Part II

Writer: Brad Kern
Director: James L. Conway

After Piper's arrival on the island, her memories are restored. The Valkyries that inhabit the island follow Paige and Phoebe when they return to San Francisco, while Phoebe attempts to comprehend her new power of empathy.

6.3   Forget Me Not

Writer: Henry Alonso Myers
Director: John T. Kretchmer

Wyatt makes the mistake of conjuring a dragon, and the cleaners erase Wyatt's existence. The sisters experience the day that Wyatt is taken for a second time. Phoebe has trouble with her empathy and Paige deals with sexual harassment.

6.4   The Power of Three Blondes

Writer: Daniel Cerone
Director: John Behring

The Charmed Ones have their identity stolen by three evil sisters and they have to persuade Chris that they are the originals. Piper tells Leo that he should spend more time with his son.

6.5   Love's a Witch

Writer: Jeanine Renshaw
Director: Stuart Gillard

Paige falls in love with Richard Montana and becomes possessed by his late lover. This brings about the sisters' involvement in a grudge between two magical families. Chris journeys to the Underworld for a potion, and Leo questions Chris' activities.

6.6   My Three Witches

> *Writers: Scott Lipsey, Whip Lipsey*
> *Director: Joel J. Feigenbaum*

In an attempt to educate the Charmed ones, Chris arranges to have the sisters running from magical realities where their wishes come true. Leo demands that Chris' Whitelighter abilities be removed.

6.7   Soul Survivor

> *Writer: Curtis Kheel*
> *Director: Mel Damski*

To reclaim her boss' soul, Paige attempts to bargain with a demon. Piper learns that Wyatt has been sabotaging her dating attempts, and Chris and Leo are bumped back in time.

6.8   Sword and the City

> *Writer: David Simkins*
> *Producer: Derek Johansen*

Magical beings congregate at the manor, attempting to wrest Excalibur from a stone after the Lady of the Lake entrusts the Charmed Ones with the sword.

6.9   Little Monsters

> *Writer: Julie Hess*
> *Director: James L. Conway*

The Charmed Ones become foster parents to a half-Manticore baby after vanquishing the parent, disregarding Chris' recommendation to vanquish it.

6.10   Chris-Crossed

> *Writer: Cameron Litvack*
> *Director: Joel J. Feigenbaum*

Chris' past is revealed when a woman named Bianca arrives from the future; Leo ascertains that she is part of a coven of assassin witches.

6.11   Witchstock

> *Writer: Daniel Cerone*
> *Director: James A. Contner*

Putting on a pair of Grams' go-go boots throws Paige back into the 1960s, where Grams is a hippie. In order to get her back, Piper and Phoebe consult a summoned version of Grams.

6.12   Prince Charmed

> *Writer: Henry Alonso Myers*
> *Director: David Jackson*

Piper decides to swear off men after vanquishing a demon found in

Wyatt's room. Paige and Phoebe attempt to create the perfect man for Piper's birthday. Demons twist Wyatt's sense of ethics.

6.13   Used Karma
Writer: Jeannine Renshaw
Director: John T. Kretchmer
Jason rejects Phoebe when he discovers that she is a witch, and Richard accidentally transfers someone else's karma into her while attempting to rid himself of his family's negative karma.

6.14   The Legend of Sleepy Halliwell
Writer: Cameron Litvack
Director: Jon Paré
Leo's mentor, Gideon, asks the Charmed Ones to find out who cast a spell that summoned the headless horseman to a magic school.

6.15   I Dream of Phoebe
Writer: Curtis Kheel
Director: John T. Kretchmer
After Phoebe is tricked into becoming a genie, Chris uses her to wish Piper and Leo back together so he can be born. Richard uses Phoebe to wish Paige back into his life.

6.16   The Courtship of Wyatt's Father
Writer: Brad Kern
Director: Joel J. Feigenbaum
Gideon plots with a Darklighter, who instead of killing Leo, sends Leo and Piper to another plane; Paige and Phoebe believe the pair dead.

6.17   Hyde School Reunion
Writer: David Simkins
Director: Jonathan West
Phoebe's teenage personality dominates during a high-school reunion, and her magic is misused.

6.18   Spin City
Writers: Andy Reaser, Doug E. Jones
Director: Mel Damski
Chris turns into a spider after being bitten, and Piper is kidnapped when a spider demon emerges from its 100-year hibernation.

6.19   Crimes and Witch Demeanors
Writer: Henry Alonso Myers
Director: John T. Kretchmer
The Charmed Ones are brought to trial after they are filmed using their powers.

6.20 A Wrong Day's Journey into Right
Writer: Cameron Litvack
Director: Derek Johnson
Overworked, Paige tries to re-conjure Piper's Mr Right, but instead creates Mr Wrong, who tricks her into believing that bad is the way to go.

6.21 Witch Wars
Writer: Krista Vernoff
Director: David Jackson
Gideon schemes to have the sisters participate in a reality television show where the challengers are demons who hunt down the Charmed Ones to acquire their powers.

6.22 It's a Bad, Bad, Bad, Bad World Part I
Writer: Jeannine Renshaw
Director: Jon Paré
Gideon sends Chris and Leo to a parallel universe where evil is triumphant. Phoebe and Paige travel there to save them but find themselves unable to vanquish their evil counterparts.

6.23 It's a Bad, Bad, Bad, Bad World Part II
Writer: Jeannine Renshaw
Director: Jon Paré
Returning home, the sisters find their world is so good that minor offences are major crimes. Piper's memory has been erased, and Leo and Chris are left to stop Gideon when he tricks Piper into altering Phoebe's and Paige's memories too.

Season Seven: First Aired 2004–5

7.1 A Call to Arms
Writer: Brad Kern
Director: James L. Conway
Piper and Leo attend a Hindu wedding and accidentally gain the powers of Hindu gods. Barbas continues to try to get Wyatt.

7.2 The Bare Witch Project
Writer: Jeannine Renshaw
Director: John Kretchner
A student of magic brings Lady Godiva and Lord Dyson to the magic school accidentally, and the sisters have to stop Lord Dyson from killing Lady Godiva before she can complete her historic ride.

7.3   Cheaper by the Coven
Writer: Mark Wilding
Director: Derek Johansen

Grams casts a spell on Piper's boys, hoping to stop them from fighting, but the spell instead causes the sisters to turn into squabbling teenagers.

7.4   Charrrmed
Writer: Cameron Litvack
Director: Mel Damski

Captain Black Jack Cutting, an eighteenth-century pirate with a death curse who is on a quest to find the fountain of youth, meets Paige and forces her to deal with his curse.

7.5   Styx Feet Under
Writer: Henry Alonso Myers
Director: Christopher Leitch

Paige casts a spell, hoping to stop a demon from killing his human kin. The spell inadvertently stops death everywhere, and the sisters are forced to fix the problem.

7.6   Once in a Blue Moon
Writer: Debra J. Fisher, Erica Messer
Director: John T. Kretchmer

The Elders assign the sisters a new Whitelighter after becoming suspicious of Leo. After this Whitelighter dies, the Elders blame Leo.

7.7   Someone to Witch Over Me
Writer: Robin Wright
Director: Jon Paré

Sarpedon, a demon, has been stealing guardian angels to protect himself. Brody convinces Paige to help him deal with the problem.

7.8   Charmed Noir
Writer: Curtis Kheel
Director: Michael Grossman

Paige and Brody are pulled into an unfinished novel written by two students from the school, and must run away from gangsters who are after the Burmese falcon. Friends of the sisters try to write a new ending for the story.

7.9   There's Something About Leo
Writer: Natalie Antoci, Scott Lipsey
Director: Derek Johansen

Leo confides in Piper that he is an Avatar, despite the fact that other Avatars have cautioned him against this.

7.10   Witchness Protection
Writer: Jeannine Renshaw
Director: David Jackson
The other Avatars force Leo to protect the Seer and the information she possesses on how to stop demons.

7.11   Ordinary Witches
Writer: Mark Wilding
Director: Jonathan West
Phoebe has a vision of a possible utopian world and agrees to trade powers with Piper so she can see the vision; a demon intercedes, and both their powers are granted to normal people.

7.12   Extreme Makeover: World Edition
Writer: Cameron Litvack
Director: LeVar Burton
Zankou kidnaps Brody and casts a paranoia spell on the sisters. The Avatars attempt to create their utopia.

7.13   Charmageddon
Writer: Henry Alonso Myers
Director: John T. Kretchmer
Leo discovers that the utopian world the Avatars created is controlled by fixing every person's destiny and joins with Zankou to reverse the change.

7.14   Carpe Demon
Writer: Curtis Kheel
Director: Stuart Gillard
Paige's attempts to find a new professor for the school brings out Drake, an ex-demon with a human appearance.

7.15   Show Ghouls
Writer: Debra J. Fisher, Erica Messer, Rob Wright
Director: Mel Damski
A fire leaves hundreds of people dead, and one of these spirits of the dead possesses a human. Phoebe and Drake go back in time to 1899 and cannot return to their own time without help from the other sisters.

7.16   The Seven Year Witch
Writer: Jeannine Renshaw
Director: Michael Grossman
Piper ends up in a coma after a demon attack; Phoebe and Paige attempt to find Leo after his memories are wiped when the Elders give him a choice between remaining an Elder or becoming mortal.

7.17 Scry Hard
Writer: Doug E. James, Andy Reaser
Director: Derek Johansen
Zankou attempts to gain access to the Nexus; Wyatt shrinks his parents to protect them by placing them in a doll house.

7.18 Little Box of Horrors
Writer: Cameron Litvack
Director: Jon Paré
Pandora's box falls into the hands of a demon who attempts to let the evil loose; Paige begins to hear calls from the Elders.

7.19 Freaky Phoebe
Writer: Mark Wilding
Director: Michael Grossman
A sorceress changes places with Phoebe, and she is trapped in the Underworld until the others can save her.

7.20 Imaginary Friends
Writer: Henry Alonso Myers
Director: Jonathan West
Wyatt's new invisible 'friend' turns out to be Vicus, a demon who is attempting to turn the baby evil. Piper casts a spell to understand Wyatt and accidentally calls his future self to the present.

7.21 Death Becomes Them
Writer: Curtis Kheel
Director: John D. Kretchmer
Zankou steals the Book of Shadows when Phoebe begins to doubt herself when a person killed in front of her blames her for the death. Paige deals with a charge who has no idea about magic.

7.22 Something Wicca This Way Goes
Writer: Brad Kern
Director: James L. Conway
Zankou attempts to steal the sisters' powers to gain access to the Nexus, and they are forced to decide whether to keep their powers or their lives.

Season Eight: First Aired 2005–6

8.1 Still Charmed and Kicking
Writer: Brad Kern
Director: James L. Conway
The Charmed Ones fake their own death, and are held under a spell that alters their appearances. They attempt to lead normal lives despite the

actions of demons who seek possession of the manor and a mysterious new charge for Paige.

8.2 Malice in Wonderland
Writer: Brad Kern
Director: Mel Damski

Hoping to lure the Charmed Ones out of hiding, demons prey on the innocent, using the Alice in Wonderland story. These activities interfere with their attempt at normality.

8.3 Run Piper, Run
Writer: Cameron Litvack
Director: Derek Johansen

Piper gets arrested when she finds out that the appearance she has adopted is wanted for murder. The sisters work together to find the real killer. Phoebe continues her relationship with Dex.

8.4 Desperate Housewitches
Writer: Jeannine Renshaw
Director: Jon Paré

Piper's competitive nature is awoken when a 'perfect mother' attacks Piper's parenting ability. Actually a demon, she plots to revive the Source using Wyatt as the catalyst. Paige attempts to stop Phoebe from pursuing Dex.

8.5 Rewitched
Writer: Rob Wright
Director: John D. Kretchmer

Billie tips off Homeland Security Agent Murphy, who suspects that the sisters are not dead, by using her powers and uses magic to help Phoebe with Dex, thus complicating their relationship.

8.6 Kill Billie Vol. 1
Writer: Elizabeth Hunter
Director: Michael Grossman

Having returned to their old identities, the sisters garner unwanted media attention. Billie has difficulty vanquishing the Dogan, a demon who evokes Billie's painful childhood memories.

8.7 The Lost Picture Show
Writers: Andy Reaser, Doug E. Jones
Director: Jonathan West

When Sam, Paige's father, suddenly appears, Paige has to help him and discontinue her plans of going back to the profession of social work.

Piper and Leo seek marriage counselling and Phoebe visits a sperm bank.

8.8   Battle of the Hexes
Writer: Jeannine Renshaw
Director: LeVar Burton
On their first assignment for Homeland Security, Billie puts on a belt that gives her superpowers and a certain hatred of men. Piper has problems with P3 and Paige receives a Whitelighter charge.

8.9   Hulkus Pocus
Writer: Liz Sagal
Director: Joel J. Feigenbaum
Agent Murphy sends the sisters after an escaped demon who is infected with a virus that makes magical beings possess hulk-like power. However, the virus proves to be fatal and the Charmed Ones have to save Billie before she succumbs.

8.10   Vaya Con Leos
Writer: Cameron Litvack
Director: Janice Cooke. Leonard
When the Angel of Death comes for Leo, Piper calls upon higher beings for a reason. Billie continues to uncover information about her sister's disappearance.

8.11   Mr. and Mrs. Witch
Writer: Rob Wright
Director: James L. Conway
While Piper adjusts to life without Leo, Billie's parents come to dinner and she unintentionally turns them into assassins. Paige continues to pursue Henry.

8.12   Payback's a Witch
Writer: Brad Kern
Director: Mel Damski
Phoebe and Piper deal with Wyatt turning his toys into real people during his birthday party; Paige is involved in a hostage situation with Henry when his parolee robs a bank.

8.13   Repo Manor
Writer: Doug E. Jones
Director: Derek Johansen
While Paige plans how to tell Henry she is a witch, Piper worries when Phoebe signs the lease to her own apartment. A trio of demons seeking to capture the Charmed Ones' power shrinks the sisters.

8.14   12 Angry Zen
Writer: Cameron Litvack
Director: Jon Paré
When Piper searches for news about Leo she is called to protect Buddha's magical staff. Phoebe's housewarming party goes awry and a monk tutors Billie in the use of her power of projection.

8.15   The Last Temptation of Christy
Writer: Liz Sagal
Director: John D. Kretchmer
Paige feels confused as two men vie for her affections: Henry and a magical suitor. Having finally found her sister, Billie tries to help the traumatized Christy. An old flame sparks Piper's interest.

8.16   Engaged and Confused
Writer: Jeannine Renshaw
Director: Stuart Gillard
Paige and Henry rethink the timing of their marriage while Piper throws them an engagement party; Cupid begins to follow Phoebe, and Christy is kidnapped.

8.17   Generation Hex
Writer: Rob Wright
Director: Michael Grossman
Piper is told that demons Leo had imprisoned in the school's dungeons have escaped and are seeking revenge, Cupid tries to help Phoebe find love again by visiting the past, and Christy has difficulty facing her parents.

8.18   The Torn Identity
Writer: Andy Reaser
Director: LeVar Burton
Having convinced Christy that she needs to lure Billie away from the Charmed Ones, demons seek to unleash the pair's evil destinies. Cupid falls for Phoebe but believes her destiny is to be with a mortal.

8.19   The Jung and the Restless
Writer: Cameron Litvack
Director: Derek Johansen
The Charmed Ones fight over what to do about Billie, who is being manipulated by Christy. Paige receives a new charge who is being chased by Darklighters.

8.20   Gone with the Witches
Writer: Jeannine Renshaw
Director: Jonathan West
The good standing of the sisters in the magical community is ruined when Christy tries to persuade Billie that the sisters are too self-involved.

8.21   Kill Billie Vol. 2
Writer: Brad Kern
Director: Jon Paré
Life is topsy-turvy: the Charmed Ones are in the Underworld and Billie and Christy control the manor. Billie and Christy seek the Hollow to vanquish the Charmed Ones. The ultimate battle is fought.

8.22   Forever Charmed
Writer: Brad Kern
Director: James L. Conway
After the death of their sisters, Piper and Billie each travel through time, determined to restore their families and create a better possible future.

Notes

Introduction

1 Jennifer Baumgardner and Amy Richards, *Manifesta: Young Women, Feminism and the Future* (New York: Farrar, Strauss and Giroux, 2000): 134.

Part One

'Something Wicca This Way Comes'

1 Michael P. Lucas, 'The Real Stories Behind a Trio of "Charmed" Lives: Television Witch Siblings on the WB Sitcom Have Mortal Touchstones in the Show's Writer and her Two Sisters', *Los Angeles Times*, 4 August 1999: F7.
2 Raymond Buckland, *Buckland's Complete Book of Witchcraft* (St Paul, MN: Llewellyn Publications, 2000): 1–12.
3 Scott Cunningham, *Wicca: A Guide for the Solitary Practitioner* (St Paul, MN: Llewellyn Publications, 1998): 3–20.
4 Michael Leff, 'Things Made by Words: Reflections on Textual Criticism', *Quarterly Journal of Speech*, 78 (1992): 223.
5 The data collected for this study was approved by the Institutional Research Board at Ohio University. All questions posted to the internet sites contained a self-informed disclosure statement: 'By responding, you agree to have your remarks quoted in my research and do not hold Ohio University and/or its employees liable for your participation'.
6 Janet Farrar and Stewart Farrar, *A Witches' Bible: The Complete Witches' Handbook* (Custer, WA: Phoenix Publishing, 1996): 105–55.
7 Starhawk, *The Spiral Dance: A Rebirth of the Ancient Religion of the Great Goddess* (San Francisco: HarperCollins, 1989): 39.
8 Cunningham, *Wicca*: 73–7.
9 Farrar and Farrar, *A Witches' Bible*: 117.
10 'Ms. Hellfire' (2.9).
11 'All Halliwell's Eve' (3.4).
12 'The Honeymoon's Over' (3.1).
13 'Chick Flick' (2.18).

14　'Awakened' (2.12).
15　'Magic Hour' (3.2).
16　Farrar and Farrar, *A Witches' Bible*: 107.
17　Scott Cunningham, *Living Wicca: A Further Guide for the Solitary Practitioner* (St Paul, MN: Llewellyn Publications, 1997).
18　'Sight Unseen' (3.5).
19　'Astral Monkey' (2.20).
20　'Pardon My Past' (2.14).
21　'When Bad Warlocks Turn Good' (1.18).
22　Buckland, *Buckland's Complete Book of Witchcraft*: 17–18.
23　Starhawk, *The Spiral Dance*: 112–13.
24　Kenneth Burke, *Philosophy of Literary Form* (rev edn) (Berkeley, CA: University of California, 1967): 293–304.
25　Michael McGee, 'Text, Context, and the Fragmentation of Contemporary Culture', *Western Journal of Speech Communication*, 54 (1990): 274–89.
26　Bradley C. Courtenay, Sharan B. Merriam and Lisa M. Baumgartner, 'Witches' Ways of Knowing: Integrative Learning in Joining a Marginalized Group', *International Journal of Lifelong Education*, 22 (2003): 111–31.
27　Charlotte Allen, 'The Scholars and the Goddess', *Atlantic Monthly*, 287, 1 (2001): 18.
28　A. McKee, 'Images of Gay Men in the Media and the Development of Self Esteem', *Australian Journal of Communication*, 27 (2000): 81–98.
29　Michaela Meyer, 'The Process of Developmental Empowerment in *Charmed*: Representations of Feminism, Empowerment and Disempowerment in Television Narrative', *Carolinas Communication Annual*, 21 (2005): 15–29.
30　Michaela Meyer, '"It's Me. I'm It": Defining Adolescent Sexual Identity Through Relational Dialectics in *Dawson's Creek*', *Communication Quarterly*, 51 (2003): 262–76.
31　See, for example, A. Carlson, 'Creative Casuistry and Feminist Consciousness: A Rhetoric of Moral Reform', *Quarterly Journal of Speech*, 78 (1992): 16–32 as well as, Bonnie Dow, 'Performance of Feminine Discourse in *Designing Women*', *Text and Performance Quarterly*, 12 (1992): 125–45.
32　Joshua Meyrowitz, 'Images of Media: Hidden Ferment – and Harmony – in the Field', *Journal of Communication*, 43, 3 (1993): 556. For more on this topic, see Joshua Meyrowitz, *No Sense of Place: The Impact of Electronic Media on Social Behavior* (New York: Oxford University Press, 1985).
33　Stuart Hall, 'Encoding/Decoding', in Stuart Hall, Dorothy Hobson, Andrew Lowe and Paul Willis (eds) *Culture, Media, Language* (London: Hutchinson, 1980): 128–38.

Reclaiming Women's Power for Power and Agency

1 'After Eight Super, Supernatural Years, the Cast and Crew of *Charmed* Say Goodbye to Magic', *Science Fiction Weekly*, 17 May 2006, at http://www.scifi.com/sfw/interviews/sfw12717.html

2 Melissa Levine, 'Charmed and Dangerous: The So-Called Power of Celluloid Witches', *Bitch*, 31 August 2006: 58ff.

3 Victoria Ann Newsome, 'Girl Power Enacted: A Popular Artifact as Metaphor for Contained Power', paper presented at Popular Communication Division, International Communication Association, New York, May 2005.

4 Starhawk, *The Spiral Dance: A Rebirth of the Ancient Religion of the Great Goddess* (San Francisco: HarperCollins, 1994): 225.

5 Alicia Ostriker, 'The Thieves of Language: Women Poets and Revisionist Mythmaking', in Elaine Showalter (ed.), *The New Feminist Criticism: Essays on Women, Literature, and Theory* (New York: Pantheon, 1985): 317.

6 Michelle Osherow, 'The Dawn of a New Lillith: Revisionary Mythmaking in Women's Science Fiction', *NWSA Journal*, 12, 1 (2000): 68ff.

7 Marion Zimmer Bradley, *The Mists of Avalon* (New York: Del Ray, 1987).

8 Holy Bible, King James Version, Exodus 22:18, at Electronic Text Center, University of Virginia Library, http://etext.virginia.edu, accessed 13 August 2006.

9 Sandra M. Gilbert and Susan Gubar, 'Infection in the Sentence: The Woman Writer and the "Anxiety of Influence"', in Robyn R. Warhol and Diane Price Herndl (eds), *Feminisms: An Anthology of Literary Theory and Criticism*, 2nd edn (New Brunswick, NJ: Rutgers University Press, 1997): 293.

10 William Covino, *Magic, Rhetoric, and Literacy: An Eccentric History of the Composing Imagination* (Albany, NY: State University of New York Press, 1994): 1.

11 Jacqueline de Romilly, *Magic and Rhetoric in Ancient Greece* (Cambridge, MA: Harvard University Press, 1973): 27–40.

12 Covino, *Magic, Rhetoric, and Literacy*: 2.

13 Ibid.: 9.

14 Starhawk, *The Spiral Dance*: 13.

15 Phyllis Curott, *Book of Shadows: A Modern Woman's Journey into the Wisdom of Witchcraft and the Magic of the Goddess* (New York: Broadway, 1998): 227.

16 Covino, *Magic, Rhetoric, and Literacy*: 3.

17 Cheryl Glenn, *Unspoken: A Rhetoric of Silence* (Carbondale, IL: Southern Illinois University Press, 2004): 1.

18 Starhawk, *The Spiral Dance*: 42.

19 Covino, *Magic, Rhetoric, and Literacy*: 18.

20 Ibid.: 19.

21 Ibid.: 142.
22 Ibid.: 9.
23 Starhawk, *The Spiral Dance*: 22.
24 Ibid.: 78.
25 Silver RavenWolf, *To Stir a Magic Cauldron: A Witch's Guide to Casting and Conjuring* (St Paul, MN: Llewellyn, 1997): 260.
26 Lise Shapiro Sanders, 'Feminists Love a Utopia: Collaboration, Conflict, and the Futures of Feminism', in Stacy Gillis, Gillian Howe and Rebecca Munford (eds), *Third Wave Feminism: A Critical Exploration* (Houndmills: Palgrave Macmillan, 2004): 52.
27 Gillian Howie and Ashley Tauchert, 'Feminist Dissonance: The Logic of Late Feminism', in Gillis, Howe and Munford, *Third Wave Feminism*: 45.
28 Starhawk, *The Spiral Dance*: 150.
29 Judith Butler, *Gender Trouble: Feminism and the Subversion of Identity* (New York: Routledge, 1999): 143.
30 Starhawk, *The Spiral Dance*: 223.
31 Valerie R. Renegar and Stacey K. Sowards, 'Liberal Irony, Rhetoric, and Feminist Thought: A Unifying Third Wave Feminist Theory', *Philosophy and Rhetoric*, 36, 4 (2003): 339.
32 Ibid.: 339.

The Power of Three

1 Speech act theory examines linguistics or spoken utterances in a linguistic context, see J.L. Austin, *How to do Things with Words* (Oxford: Clarendon Press, 1962) or John R. Searle, *Speech Acts: An Essay in the Philosophy of Languages* (Cambridge: Cambridge University Press, 1969).
2 Tanya Krzywinska, 'Hubble-Bubble, Herbs and Grimoires: Magic, Manichaeanism, and Witchcraft in *Buffy*', in Rhonda V. Wilcox and David Lavery (eds), *Fighting the Forces: What's at Stake in Buffy the Slayer* (Lanham, MD: Rowman & Littlefield, 2002): 178–94.
3 As a character, Cole is perhaps the most ambiguous in his status as demon. At several points throughout the show his love for Phoebe pulls him towards the side of 'good', but he is continually drawn to evil all the same, to the end that the sisters vanquish him.
4 The episode has much in common with 'Bewitched, Bothered and Bewildered' (2.16) in *Buffy the Vampire Slayer*, where Xander casts a similar spell to attract Cordelia's affections but instead is inundated with the attention of every other female in Sunnydale.
5 There is no definitive Book of Shadows; it is a magic book or diary personally written by a Wiccan witch.
6 Modern Wicca is often linked to Gerald Gardner (1884–1964), who wrote on his involvement with Wicca and his interest in magic, folklore and myth. Gardner became interested and involved with Wicca in the earlier part of the 1900s, and he is often linked with other

magical practitioners such as Aleister Crowley. It is often considered that Gardner's writings on Wicca brought this religion to the public eye, or were a major factor in doing so.

7   Cole is Phoebe's lover and then husband early on in the show; he is part-demon and part-human, see note 3 above.

8   Caroline Ruddell, '"I Am the Law" "I Am the Magics": Speech, Power and the Split Identity of Willow in *Buffy the Vampire Slayer'*, *Slayage: The Online International Journal of Buffy Studies*, 20 (2006), at http://www.slayageonline.com/essays/slayage20/Ruddell.htm.

9   Within the diegetic world of the show, witches have a 'Whitelighter', who is a being sent to assist them and watch over them; in essence to protect them from harm. Leo is the sisters' Whitelighter and he is able to heal injury and orb them away from danger if necessary. He also lends a hand in planning the vanquishing of demons.

10 Gerald Gardner, *The Meaning of Witchcraft* (York Beach: Samuel Weisner; Enfield: Airlift, 2004), first published 1959: 84.

11 Kevin Saunders, *Wiccan Spirituality: A System of Wiccan Spirituality and Magic for the 21st Century* (London: Green Magic, 2002): 103.

12 In structuralist thought, systems of communication allow individuals to take meaning from sign systems, codes and conventions etc. While the signs at work in systems of meaning are arbitrary, without them there would be no way of communicating with each other and we are all part of the same system. *Charmed*, however, along with other similar shows that feature witchcraft, makes use of pre-structuralist understandings of language where words may have actual power and where there may be a difference in meaning when different persons say the same thing; where words cannot be relied upon to communicate their intent successfully. Pre-structuralist understandings of language allow for the idea that words may have 'real' power, depending upon who says them. See Jeanne Favret-Saada, *Deadly Words: Witchcraft in the Bocage*, trans. Catherine Cullen (Cambridge: Cambridge University Press, 1980); James Frazer, *The Golden Bough: A Study in Magic and Religion* (Ware: Wordsworth, 1993); and Geoffrey Hughes, *Swearing: A Social History of Foul Language, Oaths and Profanity in English* (London: Penguin, 1998) for more on magical discourse in this sense.

13 Frazer, *The Golden Bough*. See Ruddell, '"I Am the Law"' for further discussion of this and Geoffrey Hughes' discussion in *Swearing* of 'taboo' words. Jeanne Favret-Saada also discusses the use of words in her book *Deadly Words*, where she argues that it is through words that magic has power.

'We Are Witches, Dear. We Can Do Anything'

1   The term 'ritual theories' was first used in the late 1970s by Ronald L. Grimes to describe the multitude of mutually complementing or mutually excluding approaches to rituals and ritualistic

behaviour beyond exclusively theological thought patterns since the groundbreaking works of Emile Durkheim at the beginning of the twentieth century. The interdisciplinary project 'Dynamics of Ritual' at the University of Heidelberg (Germany), the world's largest research centre on ritual (with more than twenty subprojects) thus attempts to gain some insight into the workings of ritual in modern societies (see their homepage: http://www.ritualdynamik.uni-hd.de/en/index.htm, accessed 19 April 2007). A good introduction to the advantages and pitfalls of modern ritual theories can be found in the critical works of Catherine Bell: *Ritual Theory, Ritual Practice* (New York: Oxford University Press, 1992) and *Ritual: Perspectives and Dimensions* (New York: Oxford University Press, 1997).

2   For the terminology used above see Michael Oppitz, 'Montageplan von Ritualen', in C. Caduff and J. Pfaff-Czarnecka (eds), *Rituale heute: Theorien – Kontroversen – Entwürfe* (Berlin: Reimer, 1999): 73–95.

3   As with the symbolic aspect behind the altar decorations, it is not important to decipher what or who 'Auger de gomay' might be or stand for, only that it stands for something. However, the most obvious interpretation stems from the Latin word 'augur, augures'. During the Roman Republic the 'augures' were an integral part of governmental decision making. Their number varied over the centuries between three and seventeen. In order to find out if a planned endeavour would be successful, the Romans interpreted a certain number of signs, or auspices. The most frequently employed method in the city of Rome was to observe the flight of the birds. During military campaigns the eating habits of the camp chickens signalled the possible outcome of a battle.

4   Twenty-seven of the 178 episodes of the show have the words 'Wicca' or 'witch' in their titles but there never is an indepth discussion of the Wiccan religion, the Wiccan Church. This might stem from the fact that, as far as I could find out, Wicca defies the confinement of easy definition as every group of practioners, every coven, though adhering to a set of ground-rules, follows its own rules and traditions. As an introduction to the origins and principles of modern 'witchcraft', see among others Ronald Hutton, 'Modern Pagan Witchcraft', in B. Ankarloo and S. Clark (eds), *Witchcraft and Magic in Europe. The Twentieth Century* (Philadelphia: University of Pennsylvania Press, 1999): 1–79; and Faye Ringel, 'New England Neo-Pagans: Medievalism, Fantasy, Religion', *Journal of American Culture*, 17, 3 (1994): 65–8.

5   Phoebe not only has visions of the past and future, she also develops into an Empath and learns how to levitate. Piper complements her ability to freeze time by blowing things up. Paige develops into the perfect blend of witch and Whitelighter. Prue moves objects, first with her eyes and then with her hands, and masters astral projection; there's no telling what she would have been able to do, had she not been killed at the end of the third season.

6 'You can't keep wolfsbane and holy thistle on the same shelf. Their harmonics are in complete opposition. I mean I don't want to second guess a sister witch but this is all wrong. I don't see how you can cast a spell that's worth a darn' ('Ms. Hellfire', 2.9).

7 So Piper ends up delivering her great great ... great grandmother – another example of the mind-boggling temporal mechanics in the show.

8 The same principle is acted on in Season Eight when the sisters repeatedly hold Billie back from demon hunting in favour of learning.

9 'Something Wicca This Way Comes' (1.1).

10 'Pre-Witched' (3.17).

11 'If we were ever going to do this, now, midnight on a full moon – is the most powerful time. – "This"? Do what "this"? – Receive our powers' ('Something Wicca This Way Comes', 1.1).

12 See 'Something Wicca This Way Comes' (1.1). According to 'The Witch is Back' (1.9), Melinda is killed during the Salem witch trials of 1692. When the sisters call her from the realm of the dead to help them defeat the warlock Matthew Tate, she is pleasantly surprised that 'it's gotten so thick', indicating that the book already existed in her lifetime. The first page of the book, however, has the year 1693 on it, one year after Melinda's death. Unfortunately this inconsistency – as well a number of other continuity oversights – is never explained in further episodes.

13 See 'Something Wicca This Way Comes' (1.1). Jeremy's first demise occurs in this episode.

14 In Christian tradition the number 13 is seen as a portent of evil and a sign of bad luck. The Judaic tradition in contrast sees 13 as positive. In this case the thirteen repetitions indicate a potential openness about which direction the Charmed Ones will take in their future development.

15 Arnold van Gennep, *Les Rites de passage. Étude systématique des rites de la porte et du seuil, de l'hospitalité, de l'adoption, de la grossesse et de l'accouchement, de la naissance, de la puberté, de l'initiation, de l'ordination, du couronnement, des finançailles et du marriage, des funérailles, des saisons etc.* (Paris: Erny, 1909). His theories were too radically modern to be widely accepted by his contemporaries, but gained notoriety especially through the equally ground breaking works of Victor Turner; see among others Victor Turner, *The Ritual Process: Structure and Anti-Structure* (London: Routledge and Kegan Paul, 1969); and Volker Barth, 'Gesellschaft als dialektischer Prozess – Victor Turner zwischen Ndembu und Bob Dylan. Rezensionsaufsatz zu: Victor Turner (2000): Das Ritual. Struktur und Anti-Struktur', *Forum Qualitative Sozialforschung / Forum: Qualitative Social Research*, 3, 2 (2002), 25 paragraphs, online journal available at http://www.qualitative-research.net/fqs-texte/2-02/2-02review-barth-d.htm, accessed 19 April 2007.

16   The most obvious sign of their changed awareness is the fact that from now on they actively write Power of Three spells.

17   The 'happy end' in the last episode of Season Eight ('Forever Charmed', 8.22) is only made possible with their active support.

18   She continues: 'The next generation has been born into our family, our legacy. We pledge to be with this child, this beautiful boy, always. Apart, but never separate, free, but never alone. He is one of us and because of that, we will bless him with all the goodness that we are. [. . .] Blessed be' ('Necromancing the Stone', 5.21).

19   'That's right, Phoebe. It's my responsibility, isn't it? The oldest sister, always supposed to be able to figure things out. Well, if that's the case, then how come I couldn't save Andy? If I'm supposed to be so powerful, how come I couldn't save him? I mean, my God, don't you understand? Andy died because of me, it doesn't matter what he said, it was my fault. How could it be good to be witches if all it does is get the people we love killed?' ('Witch Trial', 2.1).

20   For example, when Aunt Gail separates the sisters from their powers in 'How to Make a Quilt Out of Americans' (2.17), Piper is more than reluctant to regain them because she sees being a witch as the cause of her problems: 'Because not wanting to be a witch isn't a symptom of something else like it is for you, Prue. For me it's the problem. It's the cause, it's the problem of everything. I just, I want a life that hasn't got a lot of death in it. I don't think that's too much to ask.'

21   A spell cast by her sisters gets her out of her coma, but they have to reverse it to protect innocents and ultimately only the unauthorized intervention of a Whitelighter (Leo) can save her life.

22   'Well, simply put, Dr Williamson is cosmically screwed. He's got your powers in his mortal body. It took generations to prepare you for that, you can handle it, he can't. [. . .] See, your magic is meant for doing good but in the wrong person, somebody not ready for it, that need to do good things . . . – Could go bad? – Real bad' ('Astral Monkey', 2.20).

23   And their fight with him is played out on a purely power-based level. Their attempt to defeat him with a potion is not more than half-hearted and they don't even try to use or invent a ritual to strip him of these dangerous powers.

24   Leo has to ally with Zankou to make them see the error of their ways and to undo this 'extreme makeover', while Paige's boyfriend Kyle Brody even has to pay with his life ('Charmageddon', 7.13). After their experience in 'It's a Bad, Bad, Bad, Bad World' (6.22 and 6.23), they should have known better.

25   With the introduction of the Elders, the Cleaners, and especially the Tribunal, the show leaves no doubt that there are powers superior to the 'Powerful Three'. One may only think of the at best uneasy relationship of the Elders and the sisters, or their fight for their friend Darryl and against the Cleaners in 'Crimes and Witch-Demeanors' (6.19). For this episode see Julie D. O'Reilly, 'The Wonder Woman

Precedent: Female (Super) Heroism on Trial', *Journal of American Culture*, 28, 3 (2005): 273–83, especially 275–6 and 280–2.
26 'Power Outage' (3.7) and 'Bride and Gloom' (3.13).
27 Piper freezing Leo during sexual intercourse comes to mind ('Wicca Envy', 1.10).

The Power of Three as Communitas

1 John Fiske, *Power Plays, Power Works* (London and New York: Verso, 1993): 68–9.
2 Michel Foucault, *Discipline and Punish: The Birth of the Prison*, 2nd edn (New York: Vintage Books, 1995): 169–70.
3 Crystal Kile, 'Endless Love Will Keep Us Together: The Myth of Romantic Love and Contemporary Popular Movie Love Themes', in Jack Nachbar and Kevin Lause (eds) *Popular Culture: An Introductory Text* (Bowling Green: Bowling Green State University Popular Press, 1992).
4 Shulamith Firestone, *The Dialectic of Sex: The Case for Feminist Revolution* (Toronto: Bantam Books, 1970).
5 There are numerous episodes where statements like this are uttered. These specific quotes come from 'She's a Man, Baby, a Man' (2.5) and 'Secrets and Guys' (1.14).
6 'Witch Way Now?' (4.22).
7 Fiske, *Power Plays, Power Works*: 12.
8 'Something Wicca This Way Comes' (1.1).
9 'Pre-Witched' (3.17).
10 Prue's quote from 'Something Wicca This Way Comes' (1.1). Outsider-within concept from Patricia Hill Collins, *Fighting Words: Black Women and the Search for Justice* (Minneapolis: University of Minnesota, 1998).
11 Gwyn Kirk and Margo Okazawa-Rey, *Women's Lives: Multicultural Perspectives* (New York: McGraw Hill, 2003): 62.
12 Fiske, *Power Plays, Power Works*: 69.
13 'Something Wicca This Way Comes' (1.1).
14 'Something Wicca This Way Comes' (1.1).
15 'Power Outage' (3.7).
16 This may seem no different to any other teamwork focus of even the most disciplinary, mainstream organization; however, *communitas* is defensive because the marginalized are voluntarily together as a group and it is as a group where they have the strongest ability to resist disciplinary power.
17 There are various works that examine the conflicts between different types of feminist philosophies. See for example Sarah Gamble (ed.), *The Routledge Companion to Feminism and Post-Feminism* (London: Routledge, 2001).
18 This is Superman's motto and one that is focused on abstract principles rather the more concrete care ethics.

19   Carol Gilligan, *In a Different Voice: Psychological Theory and Women's Development* (Cambridge, MA: Harvard University Press, 1982).
20   Ibid.
21   Both of these phrases are in numerous episodes. See for example, 'Morality Bites' (2.2).
22   'Ex Libris' (2.19).
23   'Charmed and Dangerous' (4.13).
24   Fiske, *Power Plays, Power Works*: 182.
25   'Apocalypse Not' (2.21).
26   'Chick Flick' (2.18).
27   'Sin Francisco' (3.18).
28   Fiske, *Power Plays, Power Works*: 182.
29   'Thank You for Not Morphing' (1.3).
30   'Necromancing the Stone' (5.21).
31   Three other main character males are important in the sisters' lives but are not part of the *communitas*. Cole as Phoebe's boyfriend/husband is only tied to Phoebe. Dan, Piper's boyfriend, is so upset by magic that Piper has a genie make him forget the magic he has seen and their relationship. Finally, Darryll is tied emotionally to all the sisters; however, he does not really join the *communitas* because he never really accepts the magical secrets. On several occasions he states that he 'doesn't want to know' what is really going on. In the end, Daryll abandons the sisters.
32   'Awakened' (2.12).
33   'Murphy's Luck' (2.16).

Part Two: Feminist Power

'I Just Want to Be Normal Again'

1   Jennifer Pendleton: 'A Place for Spunky Gals', *Television Week*, 22, 45 (10 November 2003): 26.
2   Diana G. Gallagher and Paul Ruditis, *The Book of Three – The Official Companion to the Hit Show* (London: Simon & Schuster, 2004): xiii.
3   Fantasy in this context is not used with any implication of a psycho-analytic reading, but rather in the sense of a particular genre.
4   Letter to *Birmingham Evening Mail*, 6 March 2003.
5   Michel Foucault, *Power/Knowledge* (Brighton: Harvester Press, 1980): 90.
6   Michel Foucault, *The Will to Knowledge: History of Sexuality Volume 1* (London: Penguin Books, 1998): 93.
7   A term from linguistic analysis developed by Michel Foucault to mean ways of thinking, talking, representing, doing and acting which actively shape our understanding of reality.
8   Angela McRobbie: 'Post-Feminism and Popular Culture', *Feminist Media Studies*, 4, 3 (2004): 262.

9 Such as 'Morality Bites' (2.2) or 'Witchstock' (6.11) or, of course, the presence throughout Season Six of Chris, Piper's son from the future, and regular appearances from the girls' dead mother and grandmother.

10 The majority of their foes are demons.

11 See Season Five.

12 See 'The Bare Witch Project' (7.2).

13 See 'Lucky Charmed' (5.17).

14 See 'Once Upon a Time' (3.3).

15 Foucault, *The Will to Knowledge*: 93.

16 Ibid.: 99.

17 See 'Awakened' (2.12).

18 See Season Six recurring.

19 See Season Eight recurring.

20 Foucault, *Power/Knowledge*: 97.

21 Ibid.: 98.

22 See 'Oh My Goddess Part 1' (5.22).

23 Hans Biedermann, *Dictionary of Symbolism* (New York: Facts on File, 1992): 386.

24 Arthur Cotterell, *A Dictionary of World Mythology*. (Leicester: Windward, 1979): 162.

25 See 'The Witch is Back' (1.9).

26 Many terms such as 'second-wave' or 'postfeminist' are highly contested terms. I have attempted to make it clear in which sense I am employing them, but there is no widespread agreement. For further discussion see Sarah Gamble (ed.), *The Routledge Companion to Feminism and Postfeminism* (London: Routledge, 2001): 293; and Amanda D. Lotz, 'Postfeminist Television Criticism: Rehabilitating Critical Terms and Identifying Postfeminist Attributes', *Feminist Media Studies*, 1, 1 (2001): 105–21 is also useful in this context.

27 Mary Daly, *Gyn/Ecology: The Metaethics of Radical Feminism* (New York: Anchor Press, 1979): 180.

28 Ibid.: 186.

29 Ibid.: 193.

30 See Foucault, *Power/Knowledge*: 81.

31 See for example Diane Purkiss: *The Witch in History: Early Modern and Twentieth Century Representations* (London: Routledge, 1996); or Helen Berger, *A Community of Witches: Contemporary Neopaganism and Witchcraft in the United States* (Columbia, SC: University of South Carolina Press, 1999).

32 For more on this see Rachel Moseley 'Glamorous Witchcraft: Gender and Magic in Teen Film and Television', *Screen*, 43, 4 (Winter 2002): 403–22.

33 Ibid.: 422.

34 Ibid.: 422.

35 Ann Braithwaite, 'The Personal, The Political, Third-Wave And Postfeminisms', *Feminist Theory*, 3, 3 (2002): 338.

36 Ibid.: 338.
37 Piper in 'I've Got You Under My Skin' (1.2).
38 Piper in 'I've Got You Under My Skin' (1.2).
39 Foucault, *Power/Knowledge*: 86.
40 Gamble, *The Routledge Companion to Feminism and Postfeminism*: 293.
41 These figures are drawn from a close reading of all eight seasons of the show. Season Six is the one exception, where only 58% of attacks were from male creatures, and 28% from female creatures. By far the majority of attacks, however, still come from masculine sources.
42 Such as the water demon in 'P3 H2O' (2.8).
43 Such as 'Once in a Blue Moon' (7.6).
44 See 'Crimes and Witch Demeanors' (6.19).
45 See 'Desperate Housewitches' (8.4).
46 Moseley, 'Glamorous Witchcraft': 416.
47 There are some attempts to introduce other female figures of power, such as Sandra (Elizabeth Dennehy), an Elder, and Avatar Beta (Patrice Fisher) in Season Seven, but they are relatively minor characters.
48 *Cult Times*, 127 (April 2006): 36.
49 See 'Morality Bites' (2.2).
50 See 'Rewitched' (8.5).
51 See 'Awakened' (2.12).
52 Gallagher and Ruditis, *The Book of Three*: 6.
53 Grams in 'Magic Hour' (3.2).
54 'The Wendigo' (1.12).
55 'Siren Song' (5.4).
56 'Love's a Witch' (6.5).
57 Foucault, *Power/Knowledge*: 106.
58 For more on this see Catherine Johnson, *Telefantasy* (London: BFI, 2005).
59 It is worth noting that as of September 2006, Warner Brothers Network (TimeWarner) and UPN (CBS Corporation part of Paramount/ Viacom) have joined forces to create the CW Television Network, thus maximizing access to the teen and young adult demographic that they had previously competed for.
60 See http://www2.warnerbros.com (accessed 24 April 2007).
61 For instance in 'The Truth is Out There and it Hurts' (1.8) Prue is clearly seen wearing a Bulgari watch and there are long stretches of pop music featured in every episode.
62 Piper in 'Apocalypse Not' (2.21).
63 The question remains, however, to what extent this undermines any empowering effect the show might have – is feminism in the eye of the beholder?
64 The religious cult of modern witchcraft referred to in the show as the kind of magic the Charmed Ones practise (see also Michaela D.E. Meyer, 'Something Wicca This Way Comes', in this volume).

65 See Ronald Hutton, 'Paganism and Polemic: The Debate over the Origins of Modern Pagan Witchcraft', *Folklore*, 111, 1 (April 2000), for a useful summary of the arguments.

66 Douglas Ezzy, 'White Witches and Black Magic: Ethics and Consumerism in Contemporary Witchcraft', *Journal of Contemporary Religion*, 21, 1 (2006): 15. See also Adam Possamai, 'Alternative Spiritualities and the Cultural Logic of Late Capitalism', *Culture and Religion*, 4, 1 (2003): 31–45.

67 Douglas Ezzy, 'New Age Witchcraft? Popular Spell Books and the Re-Enchantment of Everyday Life', *Culture and Religion*, 4, 1 (2003): 62.

68 To foretell the future (or find lost objects) using a medium such as a crystal.

69 Gallagher and Ruditis, *The Book of Three*: 63.

70 Janet Farrar and Stewart Farrar, *The Witches' Way* (London: Book Club Associates, 1984): 207–9.

71 Daly, *Gyn/Ecology*: xv.

72 Foucault, *The Will to Knowledge*: 101.

The Power of Two – Plus One

1 See http://www.visimag.com/culttimes/c78_feat01.htm

2 Elizabeth Lenhard, *Charmed Again* (New York: Simon & Schuster, 2002): 9–10.

3 See http://www.themediadrome.com/content/articles/tv_articles/doherty_spelling.htm

4 Lenhard, *Charmed Again*: 179.

5 Ibid.: 35.

6 See http://www.empowerment4women.org/entertainment/reviews/television/charmed_season4.php

Charming the Elders

1 *The L-Word* (Showtime, 2004–), set in contemporary Los Angeles, is the first television series to focus primarily on the lives and relationships of a group of lesbians. With multiple plot lines and ensemble acting, the series treats a wide range of issues important to lesbians and bisexual women.

2 Astrid Henry, *Not My Mother's Sister: Generational Conflict and Third-Wave Feminism* (Bloomington: Indiana University Press, 2004): 41.

3 The Triple Goddess became familiar to many readers through Robert Graves' *The White Goddess: A Historical Grammar of Poetic Myth* (New York: Farrar, Straus, and Cudahy, 1948), but the Triple Goddess is treated as an archetype earlier in C. G. Jung and C. Kerenyi, *Essays on a Science of Mythology* (Princeton, NJ: Bolligen/Princeton University Press, 1967), and archaeologist Marija Gimbutas traces the Goddess' origins back more than 7,000 years in *The Gods and Goddesses of Old Europe* (London: Thames and Hudson, 1974).

4   'Necromancing the Stone' (5.21).

Old Myths, New Powers

1   Catherine Johnson uses the term telefantasy 'to describe a wide range of fantasy, science-fiction and horror television programmes' (Catherine Johnson, *Telefantasy* (London: BFI, 2005): 2).
2   Debbie Viguié, 'Charmed: A Modern Fairy Tale', in Jennifer Crusie (ed.), *Totally Charmed: Demons, Whitelighters and the Power of Three* (Dallas: BenBella Books, 2005): 43.
3   Most of the episodes discussed in this chapter belong to Season Four and beyond and thus, include Piper, Phoebe and Paige as the Charmed Ones. Prue, the oldest sister in the first part of the series, died at the end of Season Three, but is mentioned in a relevant way in 'Hell Hath No Fury' (4.3).
4   The two terms are often used interchangeably. Third wave feminism 'is often labeled "postfeminism"' (Leslie Heywood and Jennifer Drake, 'Introduction', in Leslie Heywood and Jennifer Drake (eds), *Third Wave Agenda: Being Feminist, Doing Feminism* (Minneapolis and London: University of Minnesota Press, 1997): 1). Some critics have argued that the term postfeminist has more problematic associations with a movement away from feminist ideals – see the discussion of this issue and the distinction between the two terms in the introduction to this book.
5   The Furies in 'Hell Hath No Fury' are identified with an ancient force, but they do not appear to be chronologically older in appearance than the Charmed Ones since they are 'modern knockoffs'.
6   See Pauline Bartel's *Spellcasters: Witches and Witchcraft in History, Folklore, and Popular Culture* (Dallas: Taylor Publishing, 2000) and Mary Daly's *Gyn/Ecology: The Metaethics of Radical Feminism* (New York: Anchor Press, 1979).
7   Heywood and Drake, 'Introduction': 14.
8   Ibid.: 4.
9   Astrid Henry, *Not My Mother's Sister: Generational Conflict and Third Wave Feminism* (Bloomington: Indiana University Press, 2004): 3.
10   Kathy Bail, cited in ibid.: 111.
11   Ibid.: 110.
12   Ana Marie Cox et al., 'Masculinity Without Men: Women Reconciling Feminism and Male Identification', in Heywood and Drake, *Third-Wave Agenda*: 198.
13   Lee Parpart, '"Action, Chicks, Everything": On-Line Interviews with Male Fans of *Buffy the Vampire Slayer*', in Frances Early and Kathleen Kennedy (eds), *Athena's Daughters: Television's New Women Warriors* (Syracuse, NY: Syracuse University Press, 2003): 78.
14   The ghostly presence of Patty (mother) and Penny (Grams) suggests the suppression of earlier generations in the series so that the 'third-wave' Charmed Ones can express themselves. Piper's embracing

of the domestic realm and her role as 'Übermom' may be read as a third-wave feminist reclaiming of women in the domestic sphere. Second wave feminists sometimes devalued women's roles in the home in their determination to work for women's privileges in the workforce.

15 Daly, *Gyn/Ecology*: 180.
16 This combination of the beautiful and the ugly is evident in fairy tales, myths, or medieval romances where the crone and the beautiful woman occur within the same narrative (e.g. the old woman and the beautiful young woman in *Sir Gawain and the Green Knight*).
17 Henry, *Not My Mother's Sister*: 111.
18 Phoebe's killing of the hag clearly indicates the younger generation's displacement of an older order; however, it is worth noting that even though Phoebe destroys the hag, she does not remain a mermaid. Her eventual return to her sisters may reflect a desire to find a third-waver's space between the world of the hag and that of the mermaid. It is telling that she also accepts her role as a mediator between Piper and her new sister Paige, a role previously held by Piper. This repositioning and adaptation suggest the kind of 'hybrid thinking' (Heywood and Drake, 'Introduction': 17) attributed to third-wave feminists.
19 See Jennifer Purvis, 'Grrrls and Women Together in the Third Wave: Embracing the Challenges of Intergenerational Feminism(s)', *NWSA Journal*, 16, 3 (2004): 93–123.
20 See ibid.
21 Heywood and Drake, 'Introduction': 3.
22 Irene Karras discusses Buffy's relationship with her mother 'as a metaphor for the tenuous relationship between second and third wave feminists', thus illustrating how television series in the early 2000s can present this kind of generational tension: 'just as second wave feminists accuse the third wave of perceived apathy for not embracing their politics, Joyce [Buffy's mother] was often exasperated by what she perceived to be Buffy's lack of motivation in the areas she considered to be the most important', Irene Karras, 'The Third Wave's Final Girl: *Buffy the Vampire Slayer*', *thirdspace*, 1, 2 (2002) 21 pars, at http://www.thirdspace.ca/articles/karras.htm
23 The scene in 'Witchstock' shows how Penny (Grams) is affiliated with second-wave feminism and the 1960s. However, this episode also demonstrates how she is actually influenced by the present-day 'kick ass' feminism espoused by third-wave feminist heroes like the Charmed Ones and Buffy. Penny says, 'Snuff this warlock, his days are done, but make him good for the ecosystem.' The warlock explodes into a bunch of daisies, and Piper responds, 'Now that's what you call flower power.' The flower power reference may suggest second-wave feminism, but the destruction of the warlock mimics the actions of the third-wave Charmed Ones in their typical way of disbanding 'evil'. Penny, a member of an older feminist generation

has apparently learned something from the younger generation of feminists.

24 'Siren Song' (5.4).
25 While the siren destroys couples and not just men, her initial target is men, and in this sense she preserves the characteristics of her 'ancient' mythological depiction.
26 Henry, *Not My Mother's Sister*: 3.
27 Ibid.: 90, 88.
28 Ibid.: 90, 111.
29 Arthur Cotterell and Rachel Storm, *The Ultimate Encyclopedia of Mythology* (London: Hermes House, 1999): 44.
30 'Hell Hath No Fury' (4.3).
31 The methods used by Cole and Paige to vanquish the Furies reveal two different approaches to dealing with a feminine force. Cole uses a fireball to kill two of the Furies, but Paige uses her intuition to vanquish the 'Fury' within Piper.
32 The strategy of using the Furies to represent an ancient regime is not limited to contemporary television. In Aeschylus' tragedy, *The Oresteia*, Orestes is hounded by the Furies because he killed his mother Clytemnaestra. They are spirits who avenge the death of a family member, juxtaposed with younger gods like Apollo and Athena, they say: 'You, you younger gods! – you have ridden down / the ancient laws' (Aeschylus, *The Oresteia*, ll. 792–3).

Postfeminism Without Limits?

1 Linda Badley, 'Scully Hits the Glass Ceiling: Postmodernism, Postfeminism, Posthumanism, and *The X-Files*', in Elyce Rae Helford (ed.), *Fantasy Girls: Gender in the New Universe of Science Fiction and Fantasy Television* (Oxford: Rowman and Littlefield Publishers, 2000): 69.
2 Ibid.: 69.
3 Angela McRobbie, 'Post-feminism and Popular Culture', *Feminist Media Studies*, 4, 3 (2004): 255.
4 Ibid.: 256.
5 Sarah Projansky and Leah R. Vande Berg, 'Sabrina, The Teenage . . .?: Girls, Witches, Mortals, and the Limitations of Prime-Time Feminism', in Helford (ed.), *Fantasy Girls*: 16.
6 Ibid.: 32.
7 Ibid.: 27.
8 Dee Amy-Chinn, ''Tis Pity She's a Whore: Postfeminist Prostitution in Joss Whedon's *Firefly*?', *Feminist Media Studies*, 6, 2 (2006): 177.
9 Ibid.: 180.
10 Rachel Moseley, 'Glamorous Witchcraft: Gender and Magic in Teen Film and Television', *Screen*, 43, 4 (2002): 413.

11 Jane Gaines, 'Costume and Narrative: How Dress Tells the Woman's Story', in Jane Gaines and Charlotte Herzog (eds) *Fabrications: Costume and the Female Body* (London: Routledge, 1990): 181.

12 For an enlightening study on the representation of the woman in horror film, see Barbara Creed, *The Monstrous-Feminine: Film, Feminism, Psychoanalysis* (London: Routledge, 1993).

13 Gaines, 'Costume and Narrative': 188.

14 Creed, *The Monstrous-Feminine*: 61.

15 Joanne Hollows, 'Feeling Like a Domestic Goddess: Postfeminism and Cooking', *European Journal of Cultural Studies*, 6, 2 (2003): 179–202. See also Charlotte Brunsdon, 'Feminism, Postfeminism, Martha, Martha, and Nigella', *Cinema Journal*, 44, 2 (2005): 110–16.

16 Julia Kristeva, *Powers of Horror: An Essay on Abjection* (New York: Columbia University Press, 1982): 102.

17 Matt Hills and Rebecca Williams, '*Angel*'s Monstrous Mothers and Vampires with Souls: Investigating the Abject in "Television Horror"', in Stacey Abbott (ed.), *Reading Angel: The TV Spin-Off with a Soul* (London: I.B.Tauris, 2005): 204.

18 Ibid.: 207, italics theirs.

19 Linda Williams, 'Film Bodies: Gender, Genre, and Excess', in Robert Stam and Toby Miller (eds), *Film and Theory: An Anthology* (Oxford: Blackwell, 2000), first published 1991: 210.

20 Creed, *The Monstrous-Feminine*: 82.

21 Ibid.: 70.

22 Eric Freedman, 'Television, Horror and Everyday Life in *Buffy the Vampire Slayer*', in Michael Hammond and Lucy Mazdon (eds), *The Contemporary Television Series* (Edinburgh: Edinburgh University Press, 2005): 174.

23 Tanya Krzywinska, *Sex and the Cinema* (London: Wallflower Press, 2006): 166.

24 Andrea Weiss, *Vampires and Violets: Lesbians in the Cinema* (London: Cape, 1992): 103.

25 Moseley, 'Glamorous Witchcraft': 404.

26 Carol Clover, *Men, Women and Chainsaws: Gender in the Modern Horror Film* (London: BFI, 1992): 102.

27 Creed, *The Monstrous-Feminine*: 31.

28 Moseley, 'Glamorous Witchcraft': 409.

29 Freedman, 'Television, Horror and Everyday Life': 171.

30 Tanya Krzywinska, 'Hubble-Bubble, Herbs, and Grimoires: Magic, Manichaeanism, and Witchcraft in *Buffy*', in Rhonda V. Wilcox and David Lavery (eds), *Fighting the Forces: What's at Stake in Buffy the Vampire Slayer* (Oxford: Rowman and Littlefield Publishers, 2002): 185.

31 Ibid.: 185.

Part Three: Visual Power, Place and Genre

There is Nothing New in the Underworld

1 Umberto Eco, *The Limits of Interpretation* (Bloomington and Indianapolis: Indiana University Press, 1990): 84.

2 Ibid.: 97. It is interesting to note that *Charmed* plots often develop around characters and stories from popular mythology. For example, fairytale characters, Norse and Greek mythology and legendary figures such as mermaids figure prominently. This use of the familiar as a basis for the narrative excursions of *Charmed* is surprisingly similar to the Baroque use of familiar tunes in elaborate musical compositions.

3 To continue the metaphor, Piper is the tonic and Phoebe the subdominant.

4 Michael Z. Newman summarizes this as follows: '. . . each serial episode resolves some questions but leaves many others dangling; serials tend to focus on ensembles, with each episode interweaving several strands of narrative in alternation scene by scene . . .', 'From Beats to Arcs: Toward a Poetic of Television Narrative', *Velvet Light Trap*, 58 (Fall 2006): 16.

5 Ibid.: 18.

6 'Chris-Crossed' (6.10).

7 Jane Feuer, *Seeing Through the Eighties: Television and Reaganism* (Durham, NC and London: Duke University Press, 1995).

8 Ibid.: 127–8.

9 Michael Porter, Deborah L. Larson, Allison Harthcock and Kelly Berg Nellis, 'Redefining Narrative Events: Examining Television Narrative Structure', *Journal of Popular Film and Television* (Spring 2003): 23.

10 Jason Mittell, 'Narrative Complexity in Contemporary American Television', *Velvet Light Trap*, 58 (Fall 2006): 36.

11 There is some discussion as to the first use of the technique, but there is general agreement that Wagner certainly popularized the term and the technique.

12 Catherine Johnson, *Telefantasy* (London: BFI, 2005): 11.

13 See Johnson, *Telefantasy*, for a comprehensive discussion of the importance of the visual in this genre.

14 This is usually called a Ouija board, but in the context of *Charmed* it is always referred to as a spirit board.

It Really Isn't All Black and White

1 Michele Pierson, *Special Effects: Still in Search of Wonder*, Film and Culture Series (New York: Columbia University Press, 2002): 11.

2 Tammy A. Kinsey, 'Transitions and Time: The Cinematic Language of *Angel*', in Stacey Abbott (ed.), *Reading Angel: The TV Spin-Off with a Soul* (London: I.B.Tauris, 2005): 45.

3 As Joanne Entwistle notes in her text, *The Fashioned Body: Fashion, Dress and Modern Social Theory* (Cambridge: Polity Press, 2000): 140, colour choices, particularly for infants' clothing, are both culturally historically situated. As she notes: 'babies, whose sex cannot usually be established at first glance, are very often dressed in colors, fabrics, and styles of clothing which differentiate them and announce their sex to the world. Such practices are culturally and historically specific: the common association, pink for a girl, blue for a boy is a recent historical invention: "in the early years of the twentieth century, before World War I, boys wore pink ('a stronger, more decided color' according to the promotional literature of the time) while girls wore blue (understood to be 'delicate and dainty')".'
   Entwistle's position is further supported in a number of works, see Andrée Pomerleau, Daniel Bolduc, Gérard Malcuit and Louise Cossette, 'Pink or Blue: Environmental Gender Stereotypes in the First Two Year's of Life', *Sex Roles*, 22 (1990): 359–67; and Martha Picariello, Danna N. Greenberg and David B. Pillemer, 'Children's Sex-Related Stereotyping of Colours', *Child Development*, 61 (1990): 1453–60. On page 1459 Picariello et al. note how colour stereotypes are established at a very young age, with 'clothing color [acting] as one of several defining attributes of sex' that children are aware of 'even before they are knowledgeable about the biological differences between the sexes'. Thus it seems clear that stereotypical meanings, connections and connotations concerning colour exist, though they must be seen through the lens of history. What one must remember is that a 'stereotypical' interpretation of a particular colour today (and/ or for *Charmed*) may not mean the same in another period of time.
4 The major exception, of course, consists of the special effects used for Paige's Whitelighter abilities, which contain the colours of blue and gold. The colour coding of the special effects used with these abilities, however, pre-date Paige's character within the *Charmed* universe and thus can be explained more by the show's need to explain the appearance of a new half-sister after Shannen Doherty's exit. A similar argument also might be made concerning the sisters' clothing. Though over eight seasons they wear a variety of outfits and colours, there nevertheless seems to be a preponderance of black and white, perhaps indicating the delicate balance between Good and Evil that the sisters maintain.
5 Carol M. Dole '*Legally Blonde*, Third-Wave Feminism and the Case of the Playboy Bunny', paper presented at the Popular Culture Association/American Culture Association Conference, Atlanta, GA, 14 April 2006: 1.

There's No Place Like Charmed

1 Anthony Vidler, *The Architectural Uncanny: Essays in the Modern Unhomely* (Cambridge, MA: MIT Press, 1992): 4.

2   Located at 1329 Carroll Ave in the Echo Park Section of Los Angeles ('List of locations in Charmed', Wikipedia, The Free Encyclopedia, at http://en.wikipedia.org/w/index.php?title=List_of_locations_in_ Charmed&oldid=68287241, accessed 24 April 2007).

3   Vidler, *The Architectural Uncanny*: 3.

4   Ibid.: 17.

5   David R. Ellison, *Ethics and Aesthetics In European Modernist Literature: From the Sublime to the Uncanny* (Cambridge and New York: Cambridge University Press, 2001): 52.

6   The way this psychoanalytic tenet structures many episodes is a clear indication of how psychoanalysis has made inroads, particularly into New Age-inspired popular culture.

7   Vidler, *The Architectural Uncanny*: 146.

8   Mike Davis, *Ecology of Fear: Los Angeles and the Imagination of Disaster* (New York: Vintage, 1999).

9   James Donald, *Imagining the Modern City* (Minneapolis: University of Minnesota Press, 1999): 89.

10   Most memorably translated to the screen in John Huston's *The Maltese Falcon* (1941).

11   For example *Final Analysis* (Phil Joanou, 1992).

12   See also Nathaniel Rich, *San Francisco Noir: The City in Film Noir from 1940 to the Present* (New York: The Little Bookroom, 2005).

13   Andrew Ross, *Strange Weather: Culture, Science, and Technology In the Age of Limits* (London and New York: Verso, 1991): 21.

14   Ibid.: 19.

15   See, for example, http://www.thecharmedones.com/reflections.htm (accessed 24 April 2007).

16   At http://www.thecharmedones.com/brad_interview2.htm (accessed 24 April 2007).

17   See Norman M. Klein, *The History of Forgetting: Los Angeles and the Erasure of Memory* (London and New York: Verso, 1998).

18   See Gray Brechin, *Imperial San Francisco: Urban Power, Earthly Ruin* (Berkeley: University of San Francisco Press, 1999); and James Brook, Chris Carlsson and Nancy Peters (eds), *Reclaiming San Francisco: History, Politics, Culture* (San Francisco: City Lights Books, 1998).

19   Ross, *Strange Weather*: 30.

(Un)Real Humour

1   Eric S. Rabkin (ed.), *Fantastic Worlds: Myths, Tales and Stories* (New York: Oxford University Press, 1979): 33.

2   Samuel Johnson in *The Rambler*, 125 (1751), cited in Paul Lauter (ed.), *Theories of Comedy* (New York: Doubleday, 1966): 254.

3   Chris Weedon, *Feminist Practice and Post Structuralist Theory* (New York: Basil Blackwell, 1987): 25.

4   The screen version of the 1962 novel by Ray Bradbury.

5   'Something Wicca This Way Comes' (1.1).

6 'The Wedding from Hell' (1.6).
7 'Something Wicca This Way Comes' (1.1).
8 'Something Wicca This Way Comes' (1.1).
9 'Secrets and Guys' (1.14).
10 Al Copp, 'The Comedy of Chaplin', in Robert Corrigan (ed.), *Comedy Meaning and Form* (San Francisco: Chandler, 1965): 226.
11 'I've Got You Under My Skin' (1.2).
12 Rosemary Jackson, *Fantasy: The Literature of Subversion* (London: Methuen, 1981), 'Introduction': 3.
13 'The Witch is Back' (1.9).
14 William Shakespeare, *The Tempest*, V.i, line 183.
15 'Feats of Clay' (1.11).
16 'Out of Sight' (1.19).
17 'Secrets and Guys' (1.14).
18 Henri Bergson, 'Laughter', in Wylie Sypher (ed.), *Comedy* (New York: Doubleday, 1956): 81–2.
19 Northrop Frye, 'The Mythos of Spring: Comedy' in Corrigan, *Comedy Meaning and Form*: 145.

Further Reading

Books and Articles

Aeschylus, *The Oresteia*, trans. Robert Fagles (New York: Viking Press, 1975).

'After Eight Super, Supernatural Years, the Cast and Crew of *Charmed* Say Goodbye to Magic', *Science Fiction Weekly*, 17 May 2006, at http://www.scifi.com/sfw/interviews/sfw12717.html

Amy-Chinn, Dee, '"Tis Pity She's a Whore: Postfeminist Prostitution in Joss Whedon's *Firefly*?', *Feminist Media Studies*, 6, 2 (2006): 175–89.

Austin, J.L., *How to Do Things with Words* (Oxford: Clarendon Press, 1962).

Badley, Linda, 'Scully Hits the Glass Ceiling: Postmodernism, Postfeminism, Posthumanism, and *The X-Files*', in Elyce Rae Helford (ed.), *Fantasy Girls: Gender in the New Universe of Science Fiction and Fantasy Television* (Oxford: Rowman and Littlefield Publishers, 2000): 61–90.

Bail, Kathy (ed.), *DIY Feminism*, in Henry, *Not My Mother's Sister*: 111.

Bartel, Pauline, *Spellcasters: Witches and Witchcraft in History, Folklore, and Popular Culture* (Dallas: Taylor Publishing, 2000).

Bell, Catherine, *Ritual Theory, Ritual Practice* (New York: Oxford University Press, 1992).

——, *Ritual: Perspectives and Dimensions* (New York: Oxford University Press, 1997).

Berger, Helen, *A Community of Witches: Contemporary Neopaganism and Witchcraft in the United States* (Columbia, SC: University of South Carolina Press, 1999).

Bradley, Marion Zimmer, *The Mists of Avalon* (New York: Del Rey, 1987).

Braithwaite, Ann, 'The Personal, the Political, Third-Wave and Post-feminisms', *Feminist Theory*, 3, 3 (2002): 335–44.

Brechin, Gray, *Imperial San Francisco: Urban Power, Earthly Ruin* (Berkeley: University of California Press, 1999).

Brook, James, Chris Carlsson and Nancy Peters (eds), *Reclaiming San Francisco: History, Politics, Culture* (San Francisco: City Lights Books, 1998).

Brunsdon, Charlotte, 'Feminism, Postfeminism, Martha, Martha, and Nigella', *Cinema Journal*, 44, 2 (2005): 110–16.

Buckland, Raymond, *Buckland's Complete Book of Witchcraft* (St Paul, MN: Llewellyn Publications, 2000).

Butler, Judith, *Gender Trouble: Feminism and the Subversion of Identity* (New York: Routledge, 1999).

Carlson, A., 'Creative Casuistry and Feminist Consciousness: A Rhetoric of Moral Reform', *Quarterly Journal of Speech*, 78 (1992): 16–32.

Clover, Carol, *Men, Women and Chainsaws: Gender in the Modern Horror Film* (London: BFI, 1992).

Collins, Patricia Hill. *Fighting Words: Black Women and the Search for Justice* (Minneapolis: University of Minnesota, 1998).

Courtenay, Bradley C., Sharan B. Merriam and Lisa M. Baumgartner, 'Witches' Ways of Knowing: Integrative Learning in Joining a Marginalized Group', *International Journal of Lifelong Education*, 22 (2003): 111–31.

Covino, William, *Magic, Rhetoric, and Literacy: An Eccentric History of the Composing Imagination* (Albany, NY: State University of New York Press, 1994).

Cox, Ana Marie, Freya Johnson, Annalee Newitz and Jillian Sandell, 'Masculinity Without Men: Women Reconciling Feminism and Male-Identification', in Leslie Heywood and Jennifer Drake (eds), *Third Wave Agenda: Being Feminist, Doing Feminism* (Minneapolis and London: University of Minnesota Press, 1997): 178–99.

Creed, Barbara, *The Monstrous-Feminine: Film, Feminism, Psychoanalysis* (London: Routledge, 1993).

Crowley, Aleister, *Magical and Philosophical Commentaries on the Book of the Law* (Montreal: 93 Publishing, 1974).

Cunningham, Scott, *Wicca: A Guide for the Solitary Practitioner* (St Paul, MN: Llewellyn Publications, 1998): 3–20.

Currott, Phyllis, *Book of Shadows: A Modern Woman's Journey into the Wisdom of Witchcraft and the Magic of the Goddess* (New York: Broadway, 1998).

Daly, Mary, *Gyn/Ecology: The Metaethics of Radical Feminism* (New York: Anchor Press, 1979).

Davis, Elizabeth Gould, *The First Sex* (New York: G.P. Putnam's Sons, 1971).

Davis, Mike, *Ecology of Fear: Los Angeles and the Imagination of Disaster* (New York: Vintage Books, 1999).

De Romilly, Jacqueline, *Magic and Rhetoric in Ancient Greece* (Cambridge, MA: Harvard University Press, 1973).

Dicker, Rory, and Alison Piepmeier, *Catching a Wave: Reclaiming Feminism for the 21st Century* (Boston, MA: Northeastern University Press, 2003).

Dole, Carol M., '*Legally Blonde*, Third-wave Feminism, and the Case of the Playboy Bunny', paper presented at the Popular Culture Association/American Culture Association Conference, Atlanta GA, 14 April 2006.

Dow, Bonnie, 'Performance of Feminine Discourse in *Designing Women*', *Text and Performance Quarterly*, 12 (1992): 125–45.

Donald, James, *Imagining the Modern City* (Minneapolis: University of Minnesota Press, 1999).

Eco, Umberto, *The Limits of Interpretation* (Bloomington and Indianapolis: Indiana University Press, 1990).

Ellison, David R., *Ethics and Aesthetics in European Modernist Literature: From the Sublime to the Uncanny* (Cambridge and New York: Cambridge University Press, 2001).

Entwistle, Joanne, *The Fashioned Body: Fashion, Dress and Modern Social Theory* (Cambridge: Polity Press, 2000).

Ezzy, Douglas, 'White Witches and Black Magic: Ethics and Consumerism in Contemporary Witchcraft', *Journal of Contemporary Religion*, 21, 1 (2006): 15–31.

——, 'New Age Witchcraft? Popular Spell Books and the Re-Enchantment of Everyday Life', *Culture and Religion*, 4, 1 (2003): 47–65.

Farrar, Janet, and Stewart Farrar, *The Witches' Way* (London: Book Club Associates, 1984): 207–9.

Favret-Saada, Jeanne, *Deadly Words: Witchcraft in the Bocage*, trans. Catherine Cullen (Cambridge: Cambridge University Press, 1980).

Feuer, Jane, *Seeing Through the Eighties: Television and Reaganism* (Durham, NC, and London: Duke University Press, 1995).

Fiske, John, *Power Plays, Power Works* (London and New York: Verso, 1993): 68–9.

Foucault, Michel. *Power/Knowledge* (Brighton: Harvester Press, 1980).

——, *The Will to Knowledge: History of Sexuality Volume 1* (London: Penguin Books, 1998).

——, *Discipline and Punish: The Birth of the Prison*, 2nd edn (New York: Vintage Books, 1995).

Frazer, James, *The Golden Bough: A Study in Magic and Religion* (Ware: Wordsworth, 1993).

Friedan, Betty, *The Feminine Mystique* (New York: W.W. Norton, 1963).

——, *The Second Stage* (New York: Simon & Schuster, 1981).

Gaines, Jane, 'Costume and Narrative: How Dress Tells the Woman's Story', in Jane Gaines and Charlotte Herzog (eds), *Fabrications: Costume and the Female Body* (London: Routledge, 1990): 180–212.

Gallagher, Diana G., and Paul Ruditis, *The Book of Three – The Official Companion to the Hit Show* (London: Simon & Schuster, 2004).

Gamble, Sarah (ed.), *The Routledge Companion to Feminism and Postfeminism* (London: Routledge, 2001).

Gardner, Gerald, *The Meaning of Witchcraft* (York Beach and Enfield: Samuel Weisner and Airlift, 2004, first published 1959).

Gilbert, Sandra M., and Susan Gubar, 'Infection in the Sentence: The Woman Writer and the Anxiety of Authorship', in Robyn R. Warhol and Diane Price Herndl (eds), *Feminisms: An Anthology of Literary Theory and Criticism*, 2nd edn (New Brunswick, NJ: Rutgers University Press, 1997): 21–32.

Gilligan, Carol, *In a Different Voice: Psychological Theory and Women's Development* (Cambridge, MA: Harvard University Press, 1982).

Gillis, Stacy, Gillian Howe and Rebecca Munford (eds), *Third Wave Feminism: A Critical Exploration* (Houndmills: Palgrave Macmillan, 2004).

Glenn, Cheryl, *Unspoken: A Rhetoric of Silence* (Carbondale: Southern Illinois University Press, 2004).

Graves, Robert, *The White Goddess: A Historical Grammar of Poetic Myth* (New York: Farrar, Straus, and Cudahy, 1948).

Hall, Stuart, 'Encoding/Decoding', in Stuart Hall, Dorothy Hobson, Andrew Lowe and Paul Willis (eds), *Culture, Media, Language* (London: Hutchinson, 1980): 128–38.

Henry, Astrid, *Not My Mother's Sister: Generational Conflict and Third-Wave Feminism* (Bloomington: Indiana University Press, 2004).

Heywood, Leslie, and Jennifer Drake, 'Introduction', in Leslie Heywood and Jennifer Drake (eds), *Third Wave Agenda: Being Feminist, Doing Feminism* (Minneapolis and London: University of Minnesota Press, 1997): 1–20.

Hills, Matt, and Rebecca Williams, '*Angel*'s Monstrous Mothers and Vampires with Souls: Investigating the Abject in "Television Horror"', in Stacey Abbott (ed.), *Reading Angel: The TV Spin-Off with a Soul* (London: I.B.Tauris, 2005): 203–17.

Hollows, Joanne, 'Feeling Like a Domestic Goddess: Postfeminism and Cooking', *European Journal of Cultural Studies*, 6, 2 (2003): 179–202.

Howie, Gillian, and Ashley Tauchert, 'Feminist Dissonance: The Logic of Late Feminism', in Gillis, Howe and Munford, *Third Wave Feminism*: 37–48.

Hughes, Geoffrey, *Swearing: A Social History of Foul Language, Oaths and Profanity in English* (London: Penguin Books, 1998).

Hutton, Ronald, 'Modern Pagan Witchcraft', in B. Ankarloo and S. Clark (eds), *Witchcraft and Magic in Europe. The Twentieth Century* (Philadelphia, University of Pennsylvania Press, 1999): 1–79.

——, 'Paganism and Polemic: The Debate over the Origins of Modern Pagan Witchcraft', *Folklore*, 111, 1 (April 2000): 103–17.

Jackson, Rosemary, *Fantasy: The Literature of Subversion* (London: Methuen, 1981).

Johnson, Catherine, *Telefantasy* (London: BFI, 2005).

Jung, C. G., and C. Kerenyi, *Essays on a Science of Mythology* (Princeton, NJ: Bolligen/Princeton University Press, 1967).

Karras, Irene, 'The Third Wave's Final Girl: *Buffy the Vampire Slayer*', *thirdspace*, 1, 2 (March 2002), at http://www.thirdspace.ca/articles/karras.htm.

Kile, Crystal, 'Endless Love Will Keep us Together: The Myth of Romantic Love and Contemporary Popular Movie Love Themes', in Jack Nachbar and Kevin Lause (eds), *Popular Culture: An Introductory Text*, (Bowling Green: Bowling Green State University Popular Press, 1992): 149–59.

Kinsey, Tammy A., 'Transitions and Time: The Cinematic Language of *Angel*', in Stacey Abbott (ed.), *Reading Angel: The TV Spin-Off with a Soul* (London: I.B.Tauris, 2005): 44–56.

Klein, Norman M., *The History of Forgetting: Los Angeles and the Erasure of Memory* (London and New York: Verso, 1998).

Kristeva, Julia, *Powers of Horror: An Essay on Abjection* (New York: Columbia University Press, 1982).

Krzywinska, Tanya, 'Hubble-Bubble, Herbs, and Grimoires: Magic, Manichaeanism, and Witchcraft in *Buffy*', in Rhonda V. Wilcox and David Lavery (eds), *Fighting the Forces: What's at Stake in Buffy the Slayer* (Lanham, MD: Rowman and Littlefield, 2002): 178–94.

——, *Sex and the Cinema* (London: Wallflower Press, 2006).

Leff, Michael, 'Things Made by Words: Reflections on Textual Criticism', *Quarterly Journal of Speech*, 78 (1992): 223–31.

Lenhard, Elizabeth, *Charmed Again* (New York: Simon & Schuster, 2002): 9–10.

Lorde, Audre, 'Uses of the Erotic: The Erotic as Power', in Audre Lorde, *Sister Outsider: Essays and Speeches* (Freedom, CA: Crossing Press, 1984): 53–9.

Lotz, Amanda D., 'Postfeminist Television Criticism: Rehabilitating Critical Terms and Identifying Postfeminist Attributes', *Feminist Media Studies*, 1, 1 (2001): 105–21.

McGee, Michael, 'Text, Context, and the Fragmentation of Contemporary Culture', *Western Journal of Speech Communication*, 54 (1990): 274–89.

McKee, A., 'Images of Gay Men in the Media and the Development of Self Esteem', *Australian Journal of Communication*, 27 (2000): 81–98.

McRobbie, Angela, 'Post-Feminism and Popular Culture', *Feminist Media Studies*, 4, 3 (2004): 255–64.

Meyer, Michaela, 'The Process of Developmental Empowerment in *Charmed*: Representations of Feminism, Empowerment and Disempowerment in Television Narrative', *Carolinas Communication Annual*, 21 (2005): 15–29.

——, '"It's Me. I'm It": Defining Adolescent Sexual Identity Through Relational Dialectics in *Dawson's Creek*', *Communication Quarterly*, 51 (2003): 262–76.

Meyrowitz, Joshua, 'Images of Media: Hidden Ferment – and Harmony – in the Field', *Journal of Communication*, 43, 3 (1993): 55–66.

——, *No Sense of Place: The Impact of Electronic Media on Social Behavior* (New York: Oxford University Press, 1985).

Mittell, Jason, 'Narrative Complexity in Contemporary American Television', *Velvet Light Trap*, 58 (Fall 2006): 29–40.

Moseley Rachel, 'Glamorous Witchcraft: Gender and Magic in Teen Film and Television', *Screen*, 43, 4 (Winter 2002): 403–22.

Newman, Michael Z., 'From Beats to Arcs: Toward a Poetic of Television Narrative', *Velvet Light Trap*, 58 (Fall 2006): 16–28.

Newsome, Victoria Ann, 'Girl Power Enacted: A Popular Artifact as Metaphor for Contained Power', paper presented at the Popular Communication Division of the International Communication Association, New York, May 2005.

O'Reilly, Julie D., 'The Wonder Woman Precedent: Female (Super) Heroism on Trial', *Journal of American Culture*, 28, 3 (2005): 273–83.

Osherow, Michele, 'The Dawn of a New Lilith: Revisionary Mythmaking in Women's Science Fiction', *NWSA Journal*, 12, 1 (2000): 68–83.

Ostriker, Alicia, 'The Thieves of Language: Women Poets and Revisionist Mythmaking', in Elaine Showalter (ed.), *The New Feminist Criticism:*

Essays on Women, Literature, and Theory (New York: Pantheon, 1985): 314–38.

Parpart, Lee, '"Action, Chicks, Everything": On-Line Interviews with Male Fans of *Buffy the Vampire Slayer'*, in Frances Early and Kathleen Kennedy (eds), *Athena's Daughters: Television's New Women Warriors* (Syracuse, NY: Syracuse University Press, 2003): 78–91.

Picariello, Martha, Danna N. Greenberg and David B. Pillemer, 'Children's Sex-Related Stereotyping of Colors', *Child Development*, 61 (1990): 1453–60.

Piepmeier, Alison, 'Postfeminism vs. the Third Wave', at http://www. electronicbookreview.com/thread/writingpostfeminism/reconfig-uredrip2.

Pierson, Michele, *Special Effects: Still in Search of Wonder*, Film and Culture Series (New York: Columbia University Press, 2002).

Pomerleau, Andrée, Daniel Boldue, Gérard Malcuit and Louise Cossette, 'Pink or Blue: Environmental Gender Stereotypes in the First Two Years of Life', *Sex Roles*, 22 (1990): 359–67.

Porter, Michael J., Deborah L. Larson, Allison Harthcock and Kelly Berg Nellis, 'Redefining Narrative Events: Examining Television Narrative Structure', *Journal of Popular Film and Television*, 30 (Spring, 2002): 23–30.

Projansky, Sarah, and Leah R. Vande Berg, 'Sabrina, The Teenage . . .?: Girls, Witches, Mortals, and the Limitations of Prime-Time Feminism', in Elyce Rae Helford (ed.), *Fantasy Girls: Gender in the New Universe of Science Fiction and Fantasy* (Oxford: Rowman and Littlefield, 2000): 13–40.

Purkiss, Diane, *The Witch in History: Early Modern and Twentieth Century Representations* (London: Routledge, 1996).

Purvis, Jennifer, 'Grrrls and Women Together in the Third Wave: Embracing the Challenges of Intergenerational Feminism(s)', *NWSA Journal*, 16, 3 (2004): 93–123.

Rabkin, Eric S. (ed.), *Fantastic Worlds: Myths, Tales and Stories* (New York: Oxford University Press, 1979).

RavenWolf, Silver, *To Stir a Magic Cauldron: A Witch's Guide to Casting and Conjuring* (St Paul: Llewellyn, 1997).

Reed, Evelyn, *Women's Evolution: From Matriarchal Clan to Patriarchal Family* (New York: Pathfinder Press, 1975).

Renegar, Valerie R., and Stacey K. Sowards, 'Liberal Irony, Rhetoric, and Feminist Thought: A Unifying Third Wave Feminist Theory', *Philosophy and Rhetoric*, 36, 4 (2003): 330–52.

Rich, Adrienne, 'Compulsory Heterosexuality and the Lesbian Continuum', in Adrienne Rich, *Blood, Bread, and Poetry: Selected Prose, 1979–1985* (New York: Norton, 1986): 23–75.

Rich, Nathaniel, *San Francisco Noir: The City in Film Noir from 1940 to the Present* (New York: The Little Bookroom, 2005).

Ringel, Faye, 'New England Neo-Pagans: Medievalism, Fantasy, Religion', *Journal of American Culture*, 17, 3 (1994): 65–8.

Ross, Andrew, *Strange Weather: Culture, Science, and Technology in the Age of Limits* (London and New York: Verso, 1991).

Ruddell, Caroline, '"I am the Law" "I am the Magics": Speech, Power and the Split Identity of Willow in *Buffy the Vampire Slayer'*, *Slayage: The Online International Journal of Buffy Studies*, 20 (2006), at http://www.slayageonline.com/essays/slayage20/Ruddell.htm.

Sanders, Lise Shapiro, 'Feminists Love a Utopia: Collaboration, Conflict, and the Future of Feminism', in Gillis, Howe and Munford, *Third Wave Feminism*: 49–59.

Saunders, Kevin, *Wiccan Spirituality: A System of Wiccan Spirituality and Magic for the 21st Century* (London: Green Magic, 2002).

Schwartz, Larry, 'Billie Jean Won for All Women', *ESPN.com*, 29 August 2000, at http://sports.espn.go.com/espn/print?id=710273&type=story.

Searle, John R., *Speech Acts: An Essay in the Philosophy of Language* (Cambridge: Cambridge University Press, 1969).

Showalter, Elaine (ed.), *The New Feminist Criticism: Essays on Women, Literature, and Theory* (New York: Pantheon, 1985).

Starhawk, *The Spiral Dance: A Rebirth of the Ancient Religion of the Great Goddess*, 20th Anniversary edn (San Francisco: Harper, 1999).

Stone, Merlin, *When God Was a Woman* (New York and London: Harcourt Brace Jovanovich, 1976).

Turner, Victor, *The Ritual Process: Structure and Anti-Structure* (London: Routledge and Kegan Paul, 1969).

Viguié, Debbie, 'Charmed: A Modern Fairy Tale', in Jennifer Crusie (ed.), *Totally Charmed: Demons, Whitelighters and the Power of Three* (Dallas: BenBella Books, 2005): 43–7.

Vidler, Anthony, *The Architectural Uncanny : Essays in the Modern Unhomely* (Cambridge, MA: MIT Press, 1992).

Vidler, Anthony, *Warped Space: Art, Architecture, and Anxiety in Modern Culture* (Cambridge, MA: MIT Press, 2000).

Walker, Rebecca, 'Becoming the Third Wave', *Ms.*, 39 (January/February 1992): 39–41.

Weedon, Chris, *Feminist Practice and Post Structuralist Theory* (New York: Basil Blackwell, 1987).

Weiss, Andrea, *Vampires and Violets: Lesbians in the Cinema* (London: Cape, 1992).

Williams, Linda, 'Film Bodies: Gender, Genre, and Excess', in Robert Stam and Toby Miller (eds), *Film and Theory: An Anthology* (Oxford: Blackwell, 2000, first published 1991): 207–21.

Index